REBUILDING THE CITY

REBUILDING THE CITY

Property-led urban regeneration

Edited by

Patsy Healey
Simin Davoudi
Solmaz Tavsanoglu
University of Newcastle upon Tyne

Mo O'Toole
School of Advanced Urban Studies
Bristol

David Usher
Durham County Council

E & FN SPON
An Imprint of Chapman & Hall
London · Glasgow · New York · Tokyo · Melbourne · Madras

Published by
E & FN Spon, an imprint of Chapman & Hall, 2–6 Boundary Row,
London SE1 8HN

Chapman & Hall, 2–6 Boundary Row, London SE1 8HN, UK

Blackie Academic & Professional, Wester Cleddens Road, Bishopbriggs, Glasgow G64 2NZ, UK

Van Nostrand Reinhold Inc., 115 5th Avenue, New York NY10003, USA

Chapman & Hall Japan, Thomson Publishing Japan, Hirakawacho Nemoto Building, 6F, 1-7-11 Hirakawa-cho, Chiyoda-ku, Tokyo 102, Japan

Chapman & Hall Australia, Thomas Nelson Australia, 102 Dodds Street, South Melbourne, Victoria 3205, Australia

Chapman & Hall India, R. Seshadri, 32 Second Main Road, CIT East, Madras 600 035, India

First edition 1992

© 1992 Patsy Healey, Simin Davoudi, Mo O'Toole, Solmaz Tavsanoglu, David Usher

Typeset in 10/12 pt Garamond by Graphicraft Typesetters Ltd, Hong Kong
Printed in Great Britain by St Edmundsbury Press, Bury St Edmunds, Suffolk

ISBN 0 419 17280 7   0 442 31635 6 (USA)

A catalogue record for this book is available from the British Library

Library of Congress Cataloging-in-Publication data
Rebuilding the city : property-led urban regeneration / edited by
   Patsy Healey . . . [et al.].
        p.   cm.
   Includes bibliographical references and index.
   ISBN 0-442-31635-6
      1. Urban renewal—Great Britain—Case studies.   2. Urban renewal—
   Economic aspects—Great Britain—Case studies.   3. Real estate
   development—Great Britain—Case studies.   I. Healey, Patsy.
   HT178.G7R43   1992
   307.3′416′0941—dc20   92-20324
                                                              CIP

CONTENTS

LIST OF CONTRIBUTORS

Franco BIANCHINI
  Liverpool University
James CORNFORD
Christopher COUCH
  Liverpool Polytechnic
Simin DAVOUDI*
  University of Newcastle upon Tyne
Jon DAWSON
  Liverpool University
Richard EVANS
  Liverpool University
Steven FOWLES
  Liverpool Polytechnic
Alan HARDING
  Liverpool University
Graham HAUGHTON
  Leeds Polytechnic
Patsy HEALEY*
  University of Newcastle upon Tyne
Colin JONES
  Paisley College of Technology
Tony KEY
  Investment Property Databank
Chris LAW
  University of Salford
Greg LLOYD
  Aberdeen University
Rupert NABARRO
  Investment Property Databank

Mo O'TOOLE*
    School of Advanced Urban Studies, Bristol
Jim PATRICK
    Glasgow City Council
Kevin ROBINS
    University of Newcastle upon Tyne
Solmaz TAVSANOGLU*
    University of Newcastle upon Tyne
David USHER*
    Durham County Council
David WHITNEY
    Leeds Polytechnic
Sue WILKINSON
    University of Newcastle upon Tyne

* Editors

PREFACE

This book is the product of a seminar held in March 1990 at Newcastle University on Property-led Urban Regeneration. The seminar brought together researchers and academics concerned with aspects of property development and urban policy to discuss research findings in the light of contemporary trends in development activity and public policy. The seminar, part-funded by the Economic and Social Science Research Council, followed an earlier one held in March 1988 on Land and Property Development Processes in a Changing Context, since also published as a book (Healey and Nabarro, 1990).

The present text provides an opportunity to present the findings of a range of ongoing research projects. The authors of the papers selected for inclusion in the book have each revised their paper with considerable care to update it and relate it to the themes of the book. The editors have also sought to provide continuity through introductory and concluding chapters, and editorials for each of the main sections.

It is hoped that this book will contribute to debates on how to sustain the economic health, environmental quality and social justice of our cities into the next century. The editors have sought to keep in mind the interests of an international, interdisciplinary audience. While the focus of the book is on recent experience in the UK, this should be of wider interest in places with parallel experiences, notably within the European Community and other parts of Europe, in Canada and the United States, and in Australia. Explanations of particular UK initiatives and approaches are provided to help readers from elsewhere. It is anticipated that the book will be useful to those in public agencies and local authorities, consultancies and professionals concerned with urban regeneration and property development, and students of planning, estate management, urban studies and urban geography.

The editors, and the Newcastle authors who contributed papers, are all members of a research group focusing on Urban Regeneration, the Development Industry and the Urban Fabric, funded by the University of

Newcastle. The group consists of core researchers (Simin Davoudi, Patsy Healey, David Usher), advisers and PhD students from the Departments of Town and Country Planning, Architecture and the Centre for Urban and Regional Development Studies.

The editors would like to thank the ESRC for sponsorship of the seminar, the University of Newcastle's Research Committee for sponsorship of the research group, all those who have contributed to the book and put up with our editorial demands, to Rupert Nabarro and Tony Key, who contributed an additional paper especially prepared for the book, all other participants at the seminar, whose rich discussion contributed to the thinking in all the papers in the book, and to Doreen Bell, who has managed us so carefully through the seminar and the production of the book, and whose skills as a research secretary have been invaluable to us throughout.

PART ONE ———————

INTRODUCTION

1

REBUILDING THE CITY

Patsy Healey, Simin Davoudi,
Mo O'Toole, Solmaz Tavsanoglu and
David Usher

This book explores the development activity surrounding city rebuilding in the UK in the 1980s, the institutional relationships which have evolved to support this, and the impact of public policy aimed at promoting such activity. Drawing to a large extent on recent empirical research, it focuses on the operation of land and property markets, development processes and the development industry, and on the agency relations and public policies designed to promote what became known in the 1980s as **urban regeneration.**

1.1 CONTEXT

Urban regeneration as an idea encapsulates both the perception of city decline (in local economies, in the use of land and buildings, in the quality of the environment and social life) and the hope of renewal, reversing trends in order to find a new basis for economic growth and social well-being (Parkinson, 1989). Rebuilding the city, clearing away obsolete buildings and vacant sites, and producing new building forms and designs symbolized the renewal in action (Fig. 1.1).

Behind this encompassing notion, which came to describe urban policy in the 1980s, are major changes in economic, social and political organization. These have had significant spatial consequences, both in the relative fortunes of different urban regions, and in the internal organization of cities. Urban regeneration, in its city clearance and rebuilding aspects, has been a response to both the problems and the new demands created by these changes.

Economic change has been paralleled not only by the physical reshaping of the city. It has been accompanied by an institutional restructuring, the

Figure 1.1 Derelict land becomes Meadowhall Shopping Centre, near Sheffield
Source: DoE, 1990, p. 32

product both of pressures internal to economic activity (the rise of new firms, new working practices and relationships designed to exploit new market opportunities) and of the deliberate restructuring of the State during the years of Margaret Thatcher's Premiership, through strategies of deregulation, privatization and government centralization.

1.2 ECONOMIC CONTEXT

Within the economic sphere, the transition from mechanical mass-production technology in manufacturing (known as 'Fordist' production processes) to the more flexible and customer-sensitive processes enabled by electronic technology has had a major impact on the spatial and social relationships of many cities (Cooke, 1990; Piore and Sabel, 1984; Amin, 1990). Accompanying the new technologies of production have been new strategies for managing production and distribution, and new spatial divisions of labour (Massey, 1984). Throughout the industrialized world, industrial cities have suffered as 'rustbelt' industries – steel, vehicle manufacture and mechanical engineering in particular, but also textiles and chemical production – have been rationalized in the face of foreign competition and new production relations. Redundancy and unemployment have been mirrored spatially in the decline into dereliction of the production and distribution sites associated with the old production technologies and relations. Meanwhile, the growing activities – electronic engineering, high-technology, producer services (particularly the financial sector) and consumer services – have expanded, creating opportunities for new kinds of building forms (e.g. shopping/leisure complexes, science/business parks and 'intelligent' office buildings) in new locations. Thus the landscapes of 'Fordist' production are devalued, made redundant, while urban-regeneration policies promote the imagery of 'post-Fordist' production and consumption (Harvey, 1989a; Parkinson, 1989; Chapters 9 and 17 in this volume).

These changes penetrate into the daily detail of people's lives, transforming their household economies and life opportunities, breaking up established patterns of life and business relations on the one hand, and generating opportunities for new ones on the other. So, too, the physical environment has changed around people and firms. Terraces where people once lived within the smoke, noise and traffic of adjacent industry now enjoy peaceful inactivity around them. Firms may find themselves isolated among abandoned factories, or vacant shop units, a prey to theft and vandalism. This generates pressure for action to provide improved opportunities for people and firms, and for neighbourhood renewal. Competition for resources arises between the neighbourhoods which have lost investment and position ('devalued' places) and those which are gaining them through the new production and consumption relations (the 'revalued' places).

Over and above this competition for attention between places within the city, urban regions themselves are positioned in competition with each other for economic opportunities in national, macro-regional and global space. The quality of cities, in terms of physical, social and cultural infrastructure and environmental assets has emerged in this competition as of parallel importance to production factors (labour cost and quality; access to raw materials; site and building quality and cost). It is sometimes argued that in this new world of interregional competition, the key players are urban regions and their elites, able to capture investment opportunities and position their city on the global economic stage (Piore and Sabel, 1984; Blakeley, 1989). If so, local institutional relations are a critical ingredient to local economic success (Piore and Sabel, 1984; Cheshire, 1990).

However, claims for such opportunities for 'localism' (local determination of economic futures) must be treated with caution. Any gains from astute economic positioning must be set against the strong globalizing forces within the corporate economy, dominated by the multinational company which is easily able to switch investment between places (Harvey, 1989a; Soja, 1989; Amin, 1990). Post-Fordist production may be more Fordist than it appears, merely customizing for discriminating markets, while generating efficiencies by ever more sophisticated approaches to corporate control of business conglomerates (Amin and Robins, 1990).

The economic activity of land and property development is locked ultimately into this contemporary dialectic between globalizing and localizing forces. On the one hand, its level of activity and its products are strongly influenced by changing patterns of demand from occupiers in a specific region, i.e. **user demand**. Economic restructuring has removed some demands and hence development opportunities and created many new ones. The volatility of investment and user demand from economic activity creates pressures for effective local responses to rapidly changing requirements. On the other hand, land and property markets are driven increasingly by the dynamics of the **investment value** of land and property. As barriers to global capital flows are removed, much real estate investment and development activity has itself become globalized (Harvey, 1985; Healey and Barrett, 1990). The property development industry in the UK, traditionally highly organized and oligopolistic, with a strong emphasis on the investment role of property, has been challenged to respond to international competition and to a much closer relationship with the financial sector (Nabarro, 1990). Thus within urban regions, in reacting to opportunities and problems, firms within the development industry have had to balance both the relative merits of different projects across national and sometimes international space, while at the same time adjusting to the different indications of 'user' and 'investor' demand (see Chapter 4 in this volume). The industry is thus itself restructuring, both in relation to its products and internal organization, and its institutional relations.

1.3   SOCIAL CONTEXT

Changes in social organization, which interrelates in a complex way with economic restructuring, have also had major implications for city rebuilding activity in the 1980s. Two are of particular significance. The first is what may be termed the 'post-modernist' differentiation of lifestyles (Dear, 1986; Punter, 1988; Cooke, 1990). Once again, global homogenization is combined with individual and group assertion of differences. With more disposable income, large numbers of people seek out an exploding diversity of leisure activities and experiences, and pursue cultural interests of many

kinds, creating pressure groups to defend and promote particular environmental facilities and qualities, and market opportunities for providers of
these. This produces a demand for diversity of locales in cities, yet cities
themselves become more similar, with similar collections of locales in many
cities. This diversity of affluence is combined with the appreciation of more
deep-seated causes of differentiation, particularly with respect to gender,
colour and ethnicity.

There are many dimensions to the differentiations that result. Economically, they create market opportunities for the development industry,
constructing facilities and neighbourhoods to express particular lifestyle
qualities (the 'yuppie' environment; the 'healthy' new settlement project).
Socially, differentiation easily slips into segregation, as groups associate
with those with similar lifestyles and seek to defend environments from
intruders. The 'politics of turf' thus becomes more refined, subtly played
out in many a middle-class suburb. Culturally, the city comes to be perceived
as its elements, its projects, zones and neighbourhoods, rather than as a
coherent, integrated entity. The image of the postmodern fragmented city
replaces that of the modern functionally integrated city.

This helps to reinforce the second significant social change of the 1980s,
the steady increase in income disparities. In 1986, the top 20% of households
in the UK deployed 42% of total disposable income (compared to 38% in
1976), while the bottom 20% of households deployed only 6%, compared
to 7% in 1976 (*Social Trends*, 1989). Catastrophically affected by the collapse of established industries, with household economies then faced with
repeated reductions in welfare supports due to changes in government
social policy, many poorer people have found themselves marooned in
neighbourhoods of poorly maintained housing, with diminishing public
transport opportunities and declining facilities. As old institutional relations
and spatial organization in the city have broken down, so such groups
typically have lost their established connections to economic opportunity,
social support and political influence (see for example, the cases in Cooke,
1989). Institutional restructuring has tended to demolish old relationships
and create new ones to which such groups are only remotely connected.
Some public policy initiatives have sought deliberately to foster new connections (e.g. Estates Action, and Inner City Task Forces).

Most urban policy in the 1980s, however, has emphasized economic regeneration. The theory here is that economic benefits will filter down to all
groups in due course. But evidence for such filtering of benefits to the
poorest groups is difficult to find. The distance between the new, buoyant
activities within a city, and the lives of the poorest citizens has instead
tended to increase. It is not surprising if many poor people then feel excluded.
Concentrated in parts of the city, poor neighbourhoods then come to be
regarded as a threat by residents in other neighbourhoods, fearful of theft,
vandalism and mugging and of declining property values, despite evidence

that it is the residents of the poor neighbourhoods themselves who suffer most from these changes. The segregation of poor neighbourhoods thus adds to social differentiation of the city, and highlights tendencies within the post-modern city for deliberate urban design strategies to represent neighbourhood qualities and defend one neighbourhood from another.

This socio-spatial differentiation within the city raises critical questions with respect to who benefits from city rebuilding projects (Robinson, 1989a). Yet the rhetoric of postmodernism, which emphasizes the project, the event and the individual, rather than the collective community and the strategic plan, coupled with the theory of the filtering down of economic benefits, has allowed the conditions of the poor to remain persistently invisible. The environmental movement, with its emphasis on intergenerational equity and the urban ecosystem, barely influenced urban regeneration activity in the 1980s. As a result, the critical issue of who benefits from urban regeneration was asked and answered very narrowly in the 1980s.

1.4   POLITICAL CONTEXT

Associated with these economic and social changes, the 1980s saw a dramatic shift in urban governance. This is partly the result of the broad project of dismantling the UK postwar welfare state, to replace it with public and private agencies responding to market signals of demand and need. Privatization initiatives have encouraged new forms of provision and new relations between public and private agencies with respect to a wide range of urban services and activities. Harvey argues that the approach to urban governance has been shifted from a managerial to an entrepreneurial form (Harvey, 1989b). At the same time, efforts have been made to reduce the degree of regulation over, for example, land and property development, and to change the criteria used in such regulation to benefit market processes. These shifts are quite widespread in 'Western' economies. Specific to the UK has been the attack on local government. The aim has been both to restrict local government's powers and role in economic development, and in land and property development, and to foster the parallel development of new centrally directed initiatives (most notably the Urban Development corporations, Enterprise Zones, City Grant, City Action Teams and Inner City Task Forces).

These new initiatives have changed the institutional relations through which government grants and other support have become available within urban regions. In effect, government policy has promoted institutional restructuring actively in cities, through its various urban policy initiatives as well as its wider economic and social programmes.

In political rhetoric, the private sector was presented as the key actor in the city rebuilding project, leading a new partnership between state and market. Central and local governments meanwhile competed for public acclaim over their roles in urban regeneration. To this rhetoric of responsibility was added a rhetoric of economic promotion, as central government agencies and local elites promoted individual places in the competitive struggle for economic opportunity between urban regions (Chapter 9).

Such rhetorical promotion is inherently speculative in nature. With respect to city rebuilding, it was aimed at property developers and, particularly, the archetypal speculative entrepreneurial developer. Government urban policy in effect reflected a tension between encouraging local entrepreneurs to invest and providing a bridgehead into urban regions for national and international property investors and developers (Chapter 2).

1.5 THE CITY

These forces for change all came together in the arena of the city. City structures and relationships were themselves being restructured. In the 1960s, the objective of urban regional management was to transform the spatial structure of the city comprehensively, to facilitate industrial production through efficient infrastructure, and effective environments within which workforces could live, get trained and get to work. The 1980s has seen, in contrast, the emergence of a highly fragmented postmodern city (Soja, 1989). This new round of transforming energy has been accompanied by the breaking up of past land-value patterns in cities, with struggles to redefine land-value patterns enmeshed in volatile market processes and the highly complex politics of turf.

Yet the 'new' spatial patterns, of critical significance for the internal organization of regional land and property markets, are very difficult to conceptualize and identify. It is just possible to perceive the following emerging 'structure' to restructured urban regions. Centrality, differentiation, dispersal and fragmentation are perhaps the key elements. The city centre or downtown, has been strengthened. Urban peripheries have witnessed an explosion of projects: business parks, new settlements and retail complexes. In the UK, their location has been managed carefully by green-belt policy. The remaining existing fabric is a territory of volatile differentiation. This includes the highly unstable new symbols of: successful 'regeneration'; a few well-publicized horror stories of poverty and neglect; many more neighbourhoods with similar conditions but which are largely forgotten; and all kinds of monofunctional and multifunctional variety in between (Soja, 1989). Within this city of bits and pieces, people and firms put together particular spatial patterns and institutional relationships to meet their possibilities and purposes. They compete to define advantageous positions in the uncertain land-value map and struggle to establish use values and social meaning for spaces and places.

The trends discussed above have affected most urban regions in 'Western' economies. How have they affected cities whose present scale and form is the product of Fordist and pre-Fordist industrial activity? The economies, social life, political relationships and spatial organization of these cities have been broken up, fragmented, by the various dimensions of restructuring. Unless well placed within new economic opportunities, they have then been left adrift in a sea of fragmented uncertainty, exposed to new competitive pressures as new firms and agencies enter the arena of urban action but with limited and often fragile bases for building new economic growth opportunities. The winds of restructuring in such regions may easily destroy new local efforts at economic regeneration as they drive out the obsolete and redundant. Effective urban regeneration in these areas thus requires great sensitivity to the local particularity of activities in places.

In this context, how has the property development industry responded to the opportunities created by government promotion of urban regeneration through private sector property development? How far has local initiative been fostered to engage in the city rebuilding project? How far has the property dimension of urban regeneration been dominated by major national and international investment interests, or the concerns of multinational rather than local companies? How far have agencies locally regrouped to provide a cohesive institutional response to guide urban region change in the fragile local economies of older industrial areas? How far have national initiatives taken the lead, sweeping away or reasserting local firms and local public sector activity? What have been the consequences for the long-term economic health, social opportunities and political organization of urban regions with fragile economies and 'thin' property markets? How are the trends developed in the 1980s changing as these cities enter the 1990s?

1.6   THEMES

This book explores the above questions. Based around current empirical research, it focuses on three main themes.

1. The dynamics of the development industry and property development processes in urban regions with fragile local economies in the 1980s;
2. The changing institutional relationships within and surrounding the development arena in such urban regions; and
3. The nature and effects of urban policy initiatives in the 1980s, and the interplay between urban policy and the development industry.

A number of issues recur throughout the chapters, reflecting the changing situation of the city, as outlined above.

1. The significance of spatial variation: in land and property markets, development activity, in institutional relations, and the potential and actual effects of urban policy (both within urban regions and between them);

2. The significance of temporal variation, and specifically the impact of the cyclicality of property development activity, as reflected in the booms and slumps in property prices, as these work themselves out in different urban regions, and within urban regions; and, in parallel, the significance of the history of institutional relations in urban regions for present strategies and outcomes;

3. The interplay between changes in land and property markets, development industry relationships, and the user and investor needs and demands of the changing city; how does one help to shape the other?

4. The distribution of costs and benefits from development activity in fragile urban regions in the 1980s, as this has interrelated with urban policy intiatives. What has been the balance of risk and reward between public initiative and private action? How far can private sector development activity come to replace facilities, infrastructure and environmental qualities provided by the public sector? How far do the benefits of development activity accrue to urban regions where the activity takes place? Who have been the principal beneficiaries of development?

5. The interplay of the specific history and geography of particular urban regions, and the efforts of locally based initiatives, the localizing forces, and the globalizing tendencies of corporate conglomerates and oligopolistic relations (Amin, 1990), international capital flows and investment patterns, and national and supranational political initiatives.

Underlying these themes and issues is a broader question concerning the general impact of development activity and urban policy on the local economies of fragile urban regions, those most in need of urban regeneration in the 1980s, and on the spatial and institutional organization of the city and urban governance. How far has the urban regeneration activity of the past decade equipped such urban regions, economically, socially, environmentally and institutionally, for the conditions of the 1990s? What do we mean by the 'city' and the 'urban' at the end of the twentieth century (Chapter 14)?

Although the authors of the chapters address these issues from a range of perspectives, the predominant approach involves an institutional perspective on land and property development processes (Healey and Barrett, 1990). This focuses on the actors and agencies involved in development activity, their strategies and interests, the networks of relationships through which they operate and the power relations which these express. This links together the concern with property development processes and institutional relationships. The authors generalize from their material in various ways, but the editors have tried to draw out of the material, in editorial comment and in conclusions, how the varied experiences presented can be used to develop our understanding of the nature of cities and their governance.

1.7   THE ORGANIZATION OF THE BOOK

The book consists of five parts. This first part sets the context. Chapter 2 reviews the relationship between urban policy and the development industry. It sets the scene for much of the rest of the book by reviewing the strategy of urban regeneration through private sector property development. It then explores four models which offer a rationale for such a strategy. From this, hypotheses are generated as to the forces driving development activity in urban regions with declining or restructuring local economies, and the potential impact of urban policies of the kind pursued on the development industry.

Part Two focuses on the characteristics and dynamics of land and property markets, in different urban regions. It aims to set the context for the discussion of the actors and agency relationships which cluster around particular development projects. The key issues explored are the way development activity has varied over time during the 1980s, and how the patterns of activity have varied between development sectors and between and within urban regions.

Part Three examines development projects. The emphasis there is on the processes through which individual elements of the city are produced, and the imagery through which urban regeneration initiatives are presented. Key issues explored are the nature of the actors and agencies involved and the relationships through which development takes place, their local specificity and global links, and the relative importance of different factors, including urban policy, in driving development activity. The material presented here links back to the discussion in Part Two with respect to land and property markets, notably with respect to attempts to revalue locations, and forward to the discussion of partnerships in Part Four.

Part Four focuses directly on the institutional relationships of urban regeneration, through an examination of various aspects of partnership arrangements. It focuses particularly on the power relationships and politics surrounding development activity, and the rhetoric through which projects and institutional arrangements are presented.

Part Five sets the project of urban regeneration through rebuilding fragments of the city in the wider context of debates on the meaning and imagery of urbanity and the city. Robins argues that current urban regeneration initiatives reflect a postmodern view of the city, in which the search for place identity coexists with a disjunction between universalism and particularism. The city is not a distinctive territory with its own relationships, as modernist planners tended to think until the 1970s, nor a collection of distinctive particularities, as the postmodernists have celebrated, and as urban regeneration policies have often sought to cultivate in the 1980s. For these particularities crop up all over the world in cities, reflecting the universalizing tendencies of global economy and culture. The final chapter then seeks to draw together the main findings from this collection of papers with respect to the themes and issues presented here, and to look forward to directions for urban policy in the 1990s.

2

URBAN REGENERATION AND THE DEVELOPMENT INDUSTRY*

_____ *Patsy Healey*

> Under capitalism, there is . . . a perpetual struggle in which capital builds a physical landscape appropriate to its own conditions at a particular moment in time . . . only to have to destroy it, usually in the course of a crisis, at a subsequent point in time.
>
> (Harvey, 1985, p. 25)

In the 1980s, the primary thrust of urban policy in Britain was urban regeneration through private sector property development (Solesbury, 1990; Robson, 1988; Lawless, 1989b). Such a policy requires a major effort by the development industry, that broad collection of agencies – landowners, financiers, builders, developers, property consultants, property marketers and managers – who organize the conversion of land and property from one form of physical development to another. How effectively has the industry responded to this challenge? How far has it been changed by the various policy initiatives? And, given government claims that the strategy will achieve broader economic and social ends, what have been and could be the economic, social, physical and environmental consequences of urban regeneration specifically focused on property development?

This chapter first reviews the strategy of urban regeneration through property development. It then evaluates this in the light of four models of the property development process. It concludes with hypotheses about the driving forces of the development industry in fragile urban economies.

* A different version of this chapter appears in _Regional Studies_ Vol. 25(2).

2.1   THE STRATEGY OF URBAN REGENERATION THROUGH PROPERTY DEVELOPMENT

There are a number of excellent accounts of urban policy since 1945 (Gibson and Langstaff, 1982; Lawless, 1989b; Robson, 1988; Home, 1982). They record a restless and often ill-focused search for a way of addressing urban issues which many would argue are symptoms of general social and economic dilemmas in our society, rather than having their locus in the urban (Peterson, 1985). The emphases of urban policy have varied, shifting between a focus on the built environment and environmental quality (in the 1950s and 1960s), to a social emphasis in the late 1960s, an institutional emphasis in the mid-1970s, and an economic emphasis by the late 1970s. The economic emphasis has remained dominant since then.

The development industry was offered many opportunities by the urban redevelopment strategies of the 1950s and 1960s, both in the sphere of construction and in property development (Marriott, 1967). The industry had much less of a role in the social and institutional policies of the late 1960s and early 1970s. It was through the economic emphasis of urban policy that the development industry re-engaged with urban policy. Local authorities in regions with depressed economies had had a long history of promoting industrial estates, to subsidise firms which would create jobs. In the 1970s, Rochdale District and Tyne and Wear County experimented with Industrial Improvement Areas, a way of assisting industries *in situ* to stay in business or to stay in the inner city. Under the 1977 Inner City policy initiative, more such improvement areas were promoted, as well as the provision of small start-up premises. While local authorities focused on the smallest units, developers came in to offer a slightly larger size of unit (2500–5000 sq. ft), for which there was a reasonable market, although one the private sector had previously neglected (Boddy, 1982; Barrett and Whitting, 1983). Meanwhile, developers who offered job gains were generally welcomed, even if these tended to be in the retail and warehousing markets. Local authorities were nevertheless cautious about retail and warehousing projects. Industrial development was preferred, as providing more appropriate local employment. Non-centre retail projects threatened existing city-centre investments in which local authorities often had an interest as landowners and joint developers.

In parallel, initiatives were taken (primarily at central government instigation) to encourage private sector housebuilders back into the inner city. In such deals, the public sector usually provided a subsidy in some form, via land costs, infrastructure provision or accepting some of the stock for council or housing association purposes. There is little information on which developers and investors were involved in such projects (but see Nicholls *et al.*, 1980; Healey *et al.*, 1988; Boddy, 1982; Barrett and Whitting, 1983).

In the housing field at least, the major national and regional builders seem to have been the most active, perhaps because they could afford to carry the risks. Nevertheless, there may have been investors and developers who would have taken on projects had there been less of a public sector land monopoly and more opportunity sites. The Land Register initiative of 1980 certainly assumed so (Ibbott, 1984). It is also possible that the big builders might have moved in on the market without inducements, but most became cautious after early experience (Brindley *et al.*, 1989, Chapter 8; Cameron, 1987; Bradford and Steward, 1988), and did not enter this market substantially until they reorganized their firms to create specialist urban renewal sections, and moved in on rising property markets.

In the 1980s, the economic emphasis of urban policy moved to centre stage. No clear urban policy was articulated until 1988, but the thrust represented in the various initiatives was clearly towards property development, with the private sector cast in the lead role. Initiatives were consolidated into a major urban policy thrust as a result of Mrs Thatcher's profiling of the inner city after the 1987 general election. In the 1988 policy statement, *Action for Cities*, the objectives of urban policy were stated as:

'– to encourage enterprise and new businesses, and help existing businesses grow stronger
– to improve people's job prospects, their motivation and skills
– to make areas attractive to residents and to businesss by tackling urban dereliction, bringing buildings back into use, preparing sites, and encouraging development; and
– to make inner-city areas safe and attractive places to live and work'
(Cabinet Office, 1988, p. 2).

This suggests a concern which is broader than the economic, within which property-based initiatives are only one among several strands of policy. However, when analysed in terms of expenditure, the primacy of the economic emphasis is obvious, and the dominance of property objectives within this emerges clearly (DoE, 1988), thus justifying the characterization of the urban policy of the 1980s Conservative administrations as **urban regeneration through private sector property development**.

The main urban policy activities during the 1980s have been of four types: (dates refer to primary legislation or date of announcement of the initiative).

Reorientation of existing programmes and mechanisms

1. *Urban Programme*: special funds for the most disadvantaged areas, continued from the 1970s, but switched to a predominantly economic emphasis;

2. *Derelict Land Grant*: emphasis switched in reclamation from environmental schemes to property development projects in urban areas;
3. *Land Registers (1980)*: local authorities and other public agencies exhorted to dispose of land rather than assemble it for public purposes;
4. *Planning Regimes*: exhorted to promote development and operate by market criteria, rather than by traditional needs-based principles.

Special financial incentives to facilitate private sector property development

1. *Enterprise Zone Incentives (1980)*: (rate relief , 100% capital allowances for industrial and commercial buildings);
2. *Urban Development Grant (1982)* (later City Grant): to provide gap finance to enable projects to proceed. Often used in conjunction with other urban policy mechanisms.

Replacing local authority control with zoning regimes or central government agencies in specific parts of the city

1. *Urban Development Corporations (1980)*: with specific budgets and some planning powers; agents for City Grant in their areas;
2. *Enterprise Zones (1980), and Simplified Planning Zones (1987)*: replacing local authority planning control with zoning regimes giving development rights to landowners;
3. *Housing Action Trusts (1988)*: to take over and improve local authority housing estates, and pass them on to private landlords; with budgets for improvement and some planning powers.

Task Forces and other initiatives:

(a) Merseyside Task Force (1981);
(b) City Action Teams (1985);
(c) Inner City Task Forces (1986);
(d) Garden Festivals (Liverpool 1984, Stoke 1986, Glasgow 1988, Gateshead 1990 and Ebbw Vale in 1992).

This last group were variously focused around large projects aimed to change the image of an area to which government funds were targeted (Garden Festivals), co-ordinate central government activity within urban areas (City Action Teams), and foster business initiative and job take-up in development projects in areas of high unemployment (Inner City Task Forces).

In parallel with these primarily property related initiatives were a further range of initiatives emanating mainly from the Department of Trade and Industry designed to increase employment and assist businesses. By 1989, the Audit Commission for Local Government referred to a 'patchwork of central government programmes' focused on urban regeneration (Audit Commission for Local Authorities, 1989, p. 4). Table 2.1 summarizes these.

Collectively, these initiatives demanded a substantial involvement from the development industry. They created considerable opportunities, but also generated uncertainties. The relationship between the public and private sectors was changed, with new principles and rules undermining established relationships and encouraging new ones. The proliferation of initiatives and the problematic co-ordination between them further exacerbated this uncertainty, as the nature of opportunities changed. The implicit assumption informing this strategy was that the development industry could be a lead sector in urban regeneration, but is held back from this by supply-side factors, notably: 1. institutional factors, especially the dominance of the public sector; and 2. the adverse image of older industrial conurbations, with working-class attitudes and labourist/unionized politics and workforces, with little entrepreneurial initiative. The strategy may be summarized as:

1.   economic development,
2.   targeted to local/urban economies,
3.   via property development,
4.   through private enterprise,
5.   targeted to sites/zones, and
6.   expressed via projects/entrepreneurs.

While encompassing a wide range of interventions in the development process (see Table 2.2), it is primarily targeted at:

1.   Unblocking supply-side constraints on the development potential of land and property and removing difficulties with respect to ownership, ground conditions, site conditions, planning policy and infrastructure. The objective is to make **brownfield sites** as attractive in cost and location terms as **greenfield sites** on urban peripheries, with their low development costs and access to road networks.
2.   Publicizing the qualities and opportunities of sites and locations previously neglected by the private sector development industry. The assumption here is that developers and investors have failed to notice real economic prospects, or have been put off by past policies and experiences of low rates of return on investment, and therefore need to be made aware of the impact of the new strategy. The imagery and rhetoric of regeneration is seen as important not just as political publicity, but to regenerate confidence in the property development possibilities of older industrial cities.

The objective of the strategy is to achieve local economic growth by providing the physical structures and locales appropriate for the new kinds of economic activity which will replace the old manufacturing industries. The imagery stresses high-technology, science-based industries; financial services and other new producer services; new industrial opportunities such as providing locations for Japanese firms seeking a European base; the new consumer services; and recreation and leisure activities. The strategy is targeted at transforming urban space to make it more appropriate for the hoped-for activity mix which will provide a base for a new self-sustaining local economy.

The private sector is not only being asked to take the lead in development, in contrast to the public-sector led industrial building programmes of the 1960s and 1970s. The strategy encourages the speculative private developer, providing property in the hope of future demand. The assumption here is that a developer's assessment of speculative risk is much better than that of public sector agencies focused on making land and property available to attract firms who will provide jobs for local needs. It focuses attention on the skills of the entrepreneurial speculative deal-maker, in parallel with the deregulated financial sector in the 1980s.

But the urban policy initiatives of the 1980s contained significant ambiguities. The rhetoric of policy presentation shifted between responding to market demand and market signals and making markets to which the private sector will respond (Davoudi and Healey, 1990). Urban regeneration is to be market led, yet the strategy involves public investment to lead the market. There is an important strategic issue here for urban regeneration through property development. If the public sector is to focus its investment to allow the market to lead, the timing of the switch from unblocking the constraints to publicizing the opportunities, in relation to overall economic prospects, may be critical. The problem for a national policy of urban regeneration is that it may lack the sensitivity to get the timing right.

The rest of this book illustrates, however, that the ability of the market to deliver the objectives of urban policy is not only likely to vary in time, depending on land and property market cycles. Land and property market conditions vary significantly both between urban regions and within them. Therefore the initiatives briefly summarized here may produce results in one place and period, but produce little result or actually impede the regeneration of local economies in other times and places.

2.2   THE IMPACT OF URBAN REGENERATION POLICIES ON LAND AND PROPERTY MARKETS

What then might be the effects of this strategy on property markets and development activity under different conditions and specifically those with weak local economies? It is a reasonable generalization that the land and

Table 2.1 Chronology of Central Government initiatives (England and Wales). The pace of central government initiatives is increasing (*Source*: Audit Commission, 1989)

Year	DoE	DE	DTI	Other
1981	LDDC and MDC set up First EZs set up Mersevside Task Force		Loan guarantee scheme for small businesses set up[†]	
1982	UDG introduced Additional EZ			
1983	Further 8 EZs designated	YTS introduced TVEI introduced		
1984	3 further EZs		New assisted areas Revized Regional Development Grant	
1985		← CATs set up WRNAFE programmes introduced	Wider remit for English Estates →	
1986		First 8 Task Forces*		

1987	UPMI introduced New UDCs announced URG introduced Simplified planning zones			Further 8 Task Forces*	
1988		←——————————————— Action for Cities ———————————————→			
	Further UDCs announced City Grant introduced Additional EZ announced	ET introduced 30 Inner City Compacts	Regional Enterprise Grants Enterprise Initiative RDG abolished	Welsh Valleys initiative Safer Cities Programme (Home Office)	
		←——— 2 more CATs set up ———→			
1989		←————————— Progress on Cities —————————→			
	Local economic development power	10 more Compacts	3 more Task Forces	2 more Safer Cities European Structural Forces reformed	

* Since transferred to DTI
† Since transferred to DoE

Table 2.2 Intervention in the development process: targets for urban regeneration through property development in the 1980s

Factor of production	Specific intervention	Emphasis of UR × PD strategy	Instrument
Land/property	Land tenure*	Transfer to private ownership	Land Register
	Land value*	Increase values to attract investment in land/property	Remove public sector provision of subsidized sites and premises
	Making land available for development:	Break public sector monopoly	
	land release†		Land Register
	site assembly*		CPO powers (by UDC)
	reclamation†		DLG
	provision of services*		LAs/public inquiry UDCs
	planning policy*	Relaxation of restrictions	Plans and development controls, EZs/SPZs
	Land development	Sphere of private initiative (compare 1960s)	Controls on local authority capital spending
	Property development		
	Land/property marketing		
	Land/property management		
Labour	Building industry	Sphere of private initiative and sectoral economic policy	
	Building materials industry		

Finance	For land/property purchase*	Indirectly, via cost of public land made available to private sector	Exhortation to LAs to dispose of land
	For land/property reclamation†	Grants largely justified in these terms	DLG/UDGs – City Grant
	For land/property development		UDG/City Grant/Urban Programme
	For land/property purchase		Relaxation of credit controls; low interest rates
Information	Development plans	Reduced in significance	Market criteria emphasized; EZs/SPZs
	Development frameworks† } Development briefs†	Becoming more important to help market sites to capture private sector interest	LA/UDC practices
	Property market analysis†		Property consultants' reports to UDC/LAs
	Publicity†	Less attention to broader economic context	
	Market analysis		LA/UDC, etc., promotional strategies

* Important in public policy in the 1980s.
† Very important in public policy in the 1980s.

property markets of older industrial cities in the UK in the early 1980s had the following characteristics:

1. Constrained by overall sluggish growth in the economy;
2. Relatively large amounts of obsolescent property, depressing property values;
3. Relatively small scale shifts to new forms of economic activity, whether industrial, service sector or leisure services;
4. Housing markets with a substantial public housing stock and low-cost private stock;
5. Substantial public sector land and property ownership, as a result of past efforts to improve the quality of the housing stock, regenerate local economies and remodel city centres;
6. A negative image of local development opportunities held by the London-based financial institutions, property companies and property consultancies.

By the late 1980s, all older industrial areas were experiencing an increased level of development activity associated with the economic boom and the substantial property boom. But, as Part Two shows, the property boom was markedly uneven in its inter- and intra-regional effects. The potential for a differential impact of urban policy on local land and property markets is now explored using four models of the property development process. Each emphasizes a different dynamic for land and property markets.

1. A concern with supply-side constraints on the production of land and property to meet demand; this derives from neoclassical economic models of property markets.
2. An emphasis on landowners' struggles to capture a share of the surplus value generated in production; this derives from early Marxist discussion of the relation between landowners and capitalism.
3. An institutional model of competition between local and national/international networks, linking capital to development opportunities; this derives from a focus on the role of actors, and interests, strategies and relationships in organizing land and property markets and development activity.
4. An emphasis on the dynamics of economic restructuring in a global production and consumption framework, and the role of finance capital and property as a financial investment in these processes; this derives from recent theorization in urban political economy.

(For an expanded discussion of the theoretical background to these models, see Healey and Barrett, 1990).

2.3   LAND AND PROPERTY SUPPLY AS A CONSTRAINT ON PRODUCTION

This model assumes that the development process is driven by the demand for land and property for production and consumption. Its capacity to respond to this demand may, however, be limited by supply-side constraints. Analysts of particular economic sectors disagree on the importance of land and property as inputs to production processes, and on whether land availability is ever likely to be a significant constraint. However, several authors have argued that land supply has been significant in industrial decentralization (Fothergill and Gudgin, 1982; Fothergill *et al.*, 1987). It seems likely that the extent to which land and property supply are a constraint on production varies between industries, times and places. Certainly, governments at both local and national level have assumed in the past that a good supply of land and property could attract economic activity (for example, in the building of industrial estates, and in industrial building programmes of various kinds).

Supply-side constraints with respect to the land and property requirements of production and consumption activities could occur with respect to all the factors of production listed in Table 2.2. The strategy of urban regeneration through private-sector led property development emphasizes site conditions, local conditions (with respect to infrastructure), inadequate information and monopoly control by public sector agencies.

The strategy assumes that the public sector has 1. been holding potentially developable sites off the market; 2. been holding rental values down below levels at which new provision can compete by past subsidies (particularly as regards industrial land) (Morgan, 1990), and 3. so dominated the development process that private sector entrepreneurs have been excluded. It requires that the development industry, either in the form of national and international companies, or local firms, is poised to move in on the opportunities created. It assumes that demand-side constraints (arising from the 'health' of the local economy and the relation between local demography, income levels and the housing market) are not a limitation on development activity. However, if the focus is on supply-side constraints, it may well be the case that other development industry factors than those considered by the strategy are important, notably:

1. Tenure patterns, involving private as well as public owners, and requiring legal support and resources for compulsory purchase. Private firms may well seek public agency partnership in some form to assist with this problem. There were many examples of this in town centre development in the 1960s (Marriott, 1967). The Urban Development Corporations have made significant use of compulsory purchase powers where their territory is in multiple ownerships.

2. Land values may be high because of private sector expectations. Adams *et al.* (1989) note this in Manchester in the 1980s, as landowners sought to maintain levels of land value established before the severity of the recession had bitten deeply into the local economy. It also seems likely that the publicity surrounding *Action for Cities* and the deliberate emphasis on publicizing opportunities, may have resulted in pushing private landowners' expectations up beyond values sustainable by economic conditions.

3. It may be necessary to reconstitute the locale in terms of environmental quality and design as well as service provision in order to overcome adverse labelling as wasteland, as is argued in recent reports on the relationship between urban regeneration and environmental quality (McLaren, 1989; also Chapters 7 and 8). Until this is done, local environmental conditions may produce a drag effect on local land values. Urban wasteland and images of economic decline may undermine investor confidence. Imagery and rhetoric may be insufficient in themselves to reverse this. The public sector may be called upon to take over sites with falling values, and help to reconstitute localities with investment in infrastructure and landscaping, and the production of development frameworks. Studies of land recycling in the Black Country and Manchester (Watson, 1986; Adams, 1990) suggest that in the 1980s, the public sector assisted in the process of writing down land values by purchasing sites from private companies and then passing them back at reduced values, often with considerable investment in reclamation and infrastructure reorganization. The Hebburn case in Chapter 8 provides another example of this.

4. Low levels of development activity in a locality in the past, coupled with the former dominant role of the public sector in the development process, may mean that local capability in both the building industry and the development industry are limited. This could lead to a slow local response to the release of supply-side constraints, an increased role for national/international firms, and rising building costs. In these circumstances, flagship projects and big-bang strategies could merely make an area more dependent on external enterprise rather than fostering local capability.

In conclusion, the strategy may appear to be grounded in neoclassical economics, but it is blinkered by the preoccupation with public sector constraints on supply and fails to consider the range of possible constraints which may affect the building and development industry in a locality. It may be hypothesized therefore that locality-specific supply-side constraints will limit the effectiveness of the strategy and lead to local modifications to it. In general, neo-classical models would urge caution about the scope for significant urban economic benefits from property-led urban regeneration, except where an urban economy is basically robust. If it is economically still fragile, then the strategy could at best have very limited multiplier effects and at worst adversely destabilize local land and property markets, unless accompanied by other strategies to strengthen overall levels of demand.

2.4 LANDOWNING CAPITAL AND RENT

In Marxist economics, value is created by labour expended in production. Capital, which organizes the production process, struggles to gain control of the 'surplus value' left over from that required to sustain and reproduce labour. Landowners struggle to extract a share of this surplus value from capital and labour in terms of rent, either as a capital sum on sale or as a flow of rents. Essentially, the struggle centres on whether user or investor/renter criteria prevail in determining land price. Rent is analysed into three components: **absolute rent**, reflecting the overall limited supply of land; **differential rent 1**, attributable to location; and **differential rent II**, attributable to investment in sites and services. In Marxist critique, only the last is 'legitimate', since it is a product of the expenditure of labour. For the present discussion, the key issue is the problems landowners may face in conditions of urban decline, and how the strategy of urban regeneration through property development could help them. Table 2.3 suggests some possibilities.

All those with land and property investments in older industrial areas suffered in recent years as local economies sunk further into decline. In the US, the response seems to have been substantial inner city abandonment, notably in the housing stock (Smith, 1979; Berry, 1985; Fainstein *et al.*, 1986). In the UK, with more oligopolistic land and property markets, the tendency has been to hold on to property waiting for better times, thus masking a downward creep in property values (Watson, 1986; Adams, 1990), although there are small pockets of abandonment in most cities, and several local authorities have been implementing a careful policy of demolishing the worst council stock, i.e. 'controlled abandonment'. Planning policy has tended to benefit inner city land and property owners by preventing the massive decentralization possible in the US, i.e. by limiting overall supply substantially. Landowners thus collectively have an interest in any intervention which strengthens the local economy, and in planning policies which limit the conversion of land to urban uses. Landowners also collectively benefit from reducing the overall stock of urban land. Abandonment could 'contaminate' adjacent sites. Rather than letting sites and zones slip progressively into obsolescence, a more satisfactory approach for landowners would be to replace oversupplied stocks of urbanized land with positively designated open areas. Serving the interests of urban landowners can thus provide a justification for urban greening strategies such as the new Urban Forestry initiative. All this demands a strategic framework to focus investment (which

Table 2.3 Landowners' problems in realizing rent in conditions of urban regeneration

Type of rent	Landowners' interest	Problems generated by urban decline	Appropriate public policy interventions
Absolute rent	Overall conditions of the local economy	General decline affects overall level of rents attainable	Strengthen local economy Reduce supply of stock (i.e. help landowners adjust) Limit increases in supply (e.g. green-belt policy)
Differential rent I	Attributes of location	Spreading 'islands of decay'	Reconstitute and revalue locations infrastructure environmental investment labelling (imagery)
Differential rent II	Site conditions	Obsolete physical structures Contaminated land Access difficulties Service constraints	Reclamation Infrastructure provision

is difficult to envisage without some local political coordination). This suggests that the greater the fragility of local land and property markets, the stronger is landowners' interest in a strategic and coordinated approach to managing local land and property markets, and the more damaging are initiatives which generate uncertainty and encourage the speculative deal-maker with little long-term interest in a project.

If the overall level of demand for land and property in a local economy is relatively robust, then landowners' concerns are likely to focus more on the changing fortunes of locations within urban areas, and the development possibilities of particular sites. The strategy addresses the former by its emphasis on the opportunities available in development zones (i.e. marketing), either former industrial wastelands, or areas of neglected historic heritage. This is supported by some infrastructure provision and the breaking up of institutional constraints on development in the public sector. But landowners concerned about location may also appreciate environmental investment, and be concerned that their location is not contaminated by conditions elsewhere. This may lead to an emphasis on the production of development frameworks which emphasize the distinctiveness of zones and their segregation from neighbouring areas, particularly where these are yet more industrial wasteland, or areas of council housing.

The strategy delivers most to landowners with respect to site conditions, with a strong emphasis on reclamation and infrastructure provision. Thus the strategy removes land preparation costs from the private sector, so that landowners need only bear development costs, while retaining the profits which may result from the collective investment of the public and private sectors. The scale of such land value increases has been widely publicized in the London Docklands case.

In this analysis, 'landowners' include those whose concern is to realize returns from their assets over the long-term, financial institutions who may want to enter a local property market to become such landowners, and property companies who may purchase (or purchase options on) sites expecting to realize development gains on completion of the project (McNamara, 1983), i.e. with a short-term interest. Does the strategy of urban regeneration through property development favour one type of interest more than another, for example financial institutions and property companies seeking to enter a local land and property market? Does it favour existing landowners, and under what conditions might it do this? Does it favour the speculative entrepreneurial developer (O'Donnell, 1989), who enters a market at rock bottom, when no one can imagine a development opportunity, and manages to use public policy combined with energetic publicity to promote a project, which is then sold on to long-term investors? John Hall, at Metrocentre, provides an archetypal example of this strategy. The strategy's intention may have been to favour those who wish to enter a property market as long-term investors, such as the financial institutions. However, these will be concerned with future rates of return and cautious about both the overall health of the local economy and the future quality of locales. Financial institutions in the 1980s were generally very cautious about property investment (See Chapter 3). John Hall was astute in his exit strategy from Metrocentre, selling on to the Church Commissioners. Its long-term future is by no means assured.

This example highlights the importance of identifying not only agents, roles and relationships in the development process, but the interests involved, in terms particularly of the timescale over which rates of return are to be realised (McNamara, 1983). The strategy as it evolves in action in particular places may well serve primarily to benefit certain interests within land-owning capital. Whether these will benefit interests primarily rooted in a locality is likely to vary with place and time.

2.5 INSTITUTIONAL RELATIONS WITHIN THE DEVELOPMENT INDUSTRY: COMPETITION BETWEEN NETWORKS

The previous two approaches tend to assume a self-contained local economy. An institutional approach focuses on the nexus of relationships between those involved in the development process and the way these connect to other sectors of a local economy, and to regional, national and international financial and development interests. Its starting point is the institutional articulation of the industry and the patterns or networks of relationships this generates. An institutional map of the development industry would show a concentration on the oligopolistic nexus of property companies, financial institutions and property consultants which operate out of London. This has in the past been linked to local areas via relationships between local and national property consultancies (Nabarro, 1990; Leyshon and Thrift, 1980; McNamara, 1984; McNamara, and Turner, 1987). However, this map has been changing in recent years, restructuring the institutional nexus. Financial institutions have moved into the estate agency business, consolidating this into vast interlinked networks. The London-based property consultants have diversified both internationally and regionally (Leyshon and Thrift, 1990). As with estate agencies, many local consultancies have been taken over by national companies (for example Chesterton's absorption of many regional agencies). Local banks were long ago consolidated into national banking chains. Previously, it was probably the case that a few local property consultancies acted as gatekeepers, mediating relations between landowners, financiers, developers and end-users within an area, and the relations between national and local companies (McNamara, 1984). Relations with local government would have been valued for this purpose, and the key representatives of the industry probably worked closely in a stable network combining public and private sector agencies. There is every likelihood that these networks are now breaking up, partly as a result of the collapse of many local industries, and partly as a result of the progressive downgrading of the role of local authorities, and partly also as a result of the centralization within the development industry just described.

In this context, the strategy might contribute to local economic development by:

1. Encouraging more people in a locality to come forward to develop, or invest in development (a mobilization objective); and
2. increasing the density of local relationships, and hence the likelihood that local multiplier effects are generated (a synergy objective).

Through the Urban Programme and, to a lesser extent, the Enterprise Zones, the strategy enlarges the resources targeted towards property development by local authorities and could help to strengthen local networks within the development industry. There is some evidence that Enterprise Zones in particular (and GEAR in Scotland) have fostered the expansion of a number of local developers, often moving from land clearance and demolition work to development itself. But this tendency is counteracted by the regimes for Urban Development/City Grant and Urban Development Corporations, which allocate finance for development according to national criteria. There is evidence in practice of complex negotiations between established local elites and others brought in around these new activities for control of the deployment of City Grant and UDC resources, and outcomes could vary from place to place. Nevertheless it is possible that local elites whatever their success in gaining control may see the opportunities created by the strategy as a way of attracting outside investors and property companies into their locality. In particular, they may depend on these outsiders for finance. Institutionally, therefore, the strategy could be seen as a mechanism for opening up localities to national/international companies. Locally, it is targeted at reorganizing institutional relationships and changing attitudes. Nationally, it is marketed to the institutions and companies concerned.

This suggests that the driving force behind the institutional dynamics of local property development activity, in the present period at least, is the changing flows of finance into and out of the property sector. Local land and property markets are perhaps being opened up to enable ready access to these flows. But they then become exploitable yet marginal terrains, drawn into the nexus of national/international investment patterns when money is washing into property, but left above the tideline when the wave recedes. 1990 brought many examples of such beached projects.

2.6 FINANCIAL CRISES, ECONOMIC RESTRUCTURING AND SPATIAL TRANSFORMATION

The role of capital flows, and the tension between user and investor interests in land and property, in the organization of the development industry are central elements of Harvey's approach to the production of the built environment (Harvey, 1982, 1985). Investment in the built environment is generated by the needs of production, of consumption and of financial investment, where the built environment acts as a store of capital. Places may experience surges of building activity when local economic growth requires an appropriate spatial expansion and reorganization. The primary concern is with the value-in-use of property as generated by local production and consumption activity.

The value this generates however makes property attractive as investment in growth conditions. Thus the financial sector may seek to invest in property to store capital which has been accumulated elsewhere. As a result, capital flows from one geographical area to another, as is currently very evident in the global flows of capital in the 1980s. Harvey then argues that there are periodic crises of overaccumulation, operating nationally and internationally. It is in such periods that capital may 'wash around' the economic system, looking for investment havens. When it flows into land and property in particular periods, as in the UK in the Barber boom of the early 1970s, and again as a result of financial deregulation in the mid-1980s, it is not only likely to drive investment values in property ahead of use values sustainable by the local economy. It may also lead to booms in speculative overbuilding. In time, these booms are self-correcting in that values adjust and financial investment seeks alternative outlets. But the consequence for a local economy and local property markets may be periods of excess supply and depressed or falling property values, as overvalued assets are devalued.

This effect will be greatly exaggerated where local economies are relatively small, and lack a strong growth dynamic. In such fragile property markets, one large project, or a few mediumsized ones, could have a major effect on conditions in the market overall. Where local economies are in decline, small downward movements in values could all too easily escalate into a widespread value blight. This appears to have been a common trajectory in US rustbelt cities. In the UK, manufacturing firms in difficulties in the 1970s turned to their property assets to raise capital, only to find the value of these assets falling in the 1980s, increasing the threat of bankruptcy for many firms. As firms restructured to escape from this situation, they then sought ways to realize the capital value of their properties. But their ability to do this was threatened by crises in all the 'circuits of capital' as Harvey describes them. With a local economy in recession, producers are not interested in new space. Consumers cannot afford new space, and the financial sphere is cautious about investment in property. These are exactly the property market conditions experienced in the UK's older industrial cities in the early 1980s, and which are reappearing in 1990.

There are two ways out of such a value trap. One is to pursue a vigorous policy of stock reduction, and of writing down values in many areas. This has the effect of concentrating a lower quantum of value on a smaller area, thus re-creating development opportunity. Some cities have attempted this strategy, a good example being Manchester City Council's approach to its City Centre Local Plan (Healey, 1984). The second way is to strengthen the local economy and attract financial investors back into property. This began to happen in the UK's older industrial cities in the late 1980s as a result of the backwash of a revitalized Southern economy, financial deregulation and the end of the long bull market in equities in 1987.

But Harvey, and others writing on local economic change (Massey and Meegan, 1982; Cooke, 1983), emphasize that local economies did not just experience a major contraction in activity followed by some expansion. They were actively being reorganized, with new forms of economic activity, production enterprises using new technologies and new labour practices, and an expansion of both producer and consumer services. Such processes meant that while some properties and locations were abandoned and their values written down, demands for new properties and locations were created (see Chapter 1). Spatial restructuring and the reorganization of local land

and property markets took place in parallel with economic restructuring and the reorganization of local institutional relations.

There is considerable discussion at the present time about the directions of this restructuring. One argument claims that the changes are driven by pressures to open up local economies as sites available for use by international production enterprises (Massey and Meegan, 1982) or to finance capital. In other words, they reflect globalizing tendencies. A counter-argument claims that local economies can be more independent in the present period, as they play for position in the international economy (Piore and Sabel, 1984), i.e. a localizing dynamic. A more perceptive interpretation is that localities are experiencing a complex interplay between both tendencies. Harvey (1985) argues that localities have choices about how they insert themselves in national and international economies. He goes on to indicate that the role of the built environment and the intervention strategies required with respect to the built environment will vary according to the strategy adopted.

This model develops many of the points already emphasized by the models previously discussed. It suggests that the most appropriate package of the various land and property interventions listed in Table 2.2 to assist spatial restructuring objectives will depend on the potential of the local economy and its particular land and property market history and conditions. What this approach emphasizes more than the others is the need not only for a **development strategy** for the local economy, but for a strategic approach to managing the built environment. This needs to pay attention to amounts of stock in different categories, infrastructure opportunities and constraints, the location of major new investments, and the reconstitution of locales within the urban structure, in terms of their utilities, environmental qualities, and place in the value map.

It is this strategic dimension that the strategy of urban regeneration through private sector property development specifically avoids. The intention is that the market will indicate the new qualities of location, and will generate by its incremental operations the new spatial structure. Thus the strategy focuses on zones and sites. The strategy in its current form hardly addresses the demands of industrial and financial capital with respect to the spatial restructuring of cities with fragile economies. The evidence from several US cities and from Glasgow suggests that co-ordinated long-term investment by the public sector in spatial reorganization is a precondition for levering in the industrial and financial investment out of which active markets in older industrial cities will once again be made (Donnison and Middleton, 1987; Barnekov and Rich, 1989).

These four models have all looked at local economic change, the impact on land and property development and the urban regeneration strategy from an economic point of view. Although different economic interests will seek different things from state intervention, as has been illustrated, each perspective has assessed the strategy in terms of economic returns. This is of course justified in view of the strategy's primarily economic focus. Its utility in economic terms is however compromised by its internal ambiguities. These reflect both its experimental nature and the real conflicts between economic interests (within capital, as much as between capital and labour). But the strategy is not driven purely by economic considerations. It is also strongly coloured by several strands of thought which derive from the political philosophy and strategy of the Conservative administrations of the 1980s, notably:

1. The privileging of the private sector over the public sector in all spheres, as a result of the concern to break up the centralized public-sector dominated welfare state established in the 1940s;
2. The negative view of local authorities, as symbols not only of welfarism but of the 'dead hand' of bureaucratic municipal socialism and 'new left' alternative economic strategies;
3. The 'new right' liberal model of markets based on individual incremental decision-making by economic actors. This has inhibited the development of ideas about how to co-ordinate public and private action around urban regeneration activity and promoted over-simple notions of partnership and entrepreneurial activity.

With the deliberate objective of breaking the postwar political consensus, the Conservative administrations have sought to establish a hegemonic position for their philosophy (Gamble, 1988). For this purpose, they have deployed publicity with great skill. Urban policy has been no exception. Urban regeneration through property development has the tactical advantage that it produces powerful political imagery. Reconstituting the urban landscape can symbolize the restructured and prosperous economy. The strategy is thus about political publicity as well as real economic effects in localities. Such policy initiatives are also seen as a way of enlarging the basis for Conservative party support by the disbursement of material benefits as well as by ideological strategy. Thus the strategy may be seen as a means of extending central government (and hence Conservative) control over land and resources into the urban heartlands of Labour support. These political functions of the strategy may best be understood in terms of the shift towards a more populist form of politics in the UK.

2.7 CONCLUSIONS

A broad array of hypotheses has been presented about what structures the development industry and land and property markets, about the relation of property development to local economic development, about the significance of variations in the organization of the development industry and the

Table 2.4 The driving forces of the development industry under conditions of urban regeneration

Model	Driving force
Supply-side constraints	Underlying consumer demand
Landowning capital and rent	'Landowners' search to safeguard rates of return on land and property investment
Institutional relations	Competition between local interests and national and international financial and property interests
Financial crises and economic restructuring	(a) Flows of finance capital on a national/international scale (b) Spatial restructuring for economic restructuring

characteristics of land and property markets, and about the consequences of such variations for the production of the built environment and who benefits from this.

The four models discussed offer alternative ways of approaching these hypotheses concerning the relations between economic development, the development industry and the political sphere. Each suggests different driving forces for change in the development industry in a locality, and consequently different ways of predicting and explaining the potential impact and relevance of the strategy (see Table 2.4).

Each model also generates different hypotheses with respect to spatial and temporal differentiation. This reinforces the need for fine-grained local analysis in order to understand the potential effects of the strategy and explore what alternative strategies might be appropriate in different places.

The research presented in this book provides examples of the fine-grained empirical research which is needed for this purpose.

PART TWO ———————

THE DYNAMICS OF LAND AND PROPERTY MARKETS

3

EDITORIAL

_____ *Simin Davoudi and Patsy Healey*

3.1 PROPERTY MARKET TRENDS

Land and property markets mediate the relationships between those seeking to supply sites for use and development, and those in search of sites
and properties, for occupation, investment and development. But what
exactly do such markets consist of? How do they operate? How have conditions changed in the 1980s, and what has been the impact specifically in
urban regions with fragile local economies?

The most striking phenomenon in land and property markets in the late
1980s was a roller-coaster swing from slump (low transaction levels; stagnant or falling values; high investment yields) in the early 1980s to boom,
followed by a further slump which, by 1990, threatened to be at least as
serious for the development and construction industry as the previous
collapses of 1973–4 and 1981–2 (*The Economist*, 1990a). This section of the
book explores how this cycle has varied between types of market and
between regions, and how the experience has affected particular urban
regions. The papers raise questions about the impact of such swings in
development activity in regions with fragile local economies and thin property markets, i.e. those with relatively few transactions and low levels of
demand. In such conditions, it is difficult for buyers and sellers to assess
what an appropriate price for a site or a future development might be,
creating informational uncertainties to compound those created by a local
economy with uncertain prospects of future demand. How does this affect
the level and location of development activities and the nature and relationships of those who engaged in development projects in urban regions?

Nabarro and Key's paper (Chapter 4) draws on data from Investment
Property Databank to provide an outline of investment trends in commercial property to the end of 1990. This serves as a context for much of the
research which follows. They first stress the inherent cyclicality of property
investment, echoing Barras (1985). They then show that these short cycles
were swamped in the late 1980s by a massive boom in construction which,

they argue, was the result of the coincidence of a short and longer, 15-year cycle. The result was a record peak in construction activity in 1989, producing a very large amount of new development on the market in 1990. Their paper shows dramatically how banking finance fuelled this recent boom.

Their paper illustrates the variation in the scale and financing of the boom in different property market sectors and in different parts of the country. Retail investment slowed down relatively early. In the office sector, there has been a massive growth in supply, which began to level off by 1990. Other cities look set for an increasing supply into 1991. The boom was least pronounced in the industrial sector, with construction orders for industrial space still rising in the Northern industrial regions in 1990. This provides an interesting complement to evidence of a shortage of industrial space recorded by Law in Chapter 4, and Usher and Davoudi in Chapter 5. Generally, property investment yields were rising by 1990. Faced with this prospect, Nabarro and Key predict a low level of investment in new commercial development for the next few years.

3.2 REGIONAL PROPERTY MARKETS

The next three papers explore development activity in three different urban regions. In Chapter 4, Law examines development trends in Inner Manchester. This is an area which has had a range of national urban policy initiatives, with an Enterprise Zone and two Urban Development Corporations in an area which was also designated as an inner city partnership authority under the 1978 Inner Urban Areas Act. After a brief review of government urban policy over the last decade, and of the policies pursued in Inner Manchester, he examines zones which have been the focus of development activity or planning attention. He argues that, while policy initiatives affect the location of development in an urban region, the amount of development depends on the state of the property market. The efforts of Manchester City Council in the early 1980s had limited success because of slack market conditions. New central government policy initiatives coincided with boom conditions, particularly in housing and office markets. Law shows how this produced a rash of proposals, and some construction projects. As a result, the downturn in the property market and the economy in Manchester coincided with a tendency towards oversupply in local property markets.

Law also shows how development activity centred primarily on housing and services, although others have argued that there was also an upturn in industrial development markets in the region in the late 1980s (Adams, 1990). Law illustrates the complexity of relations between public and private sector agencies, and central and local government initiatives.

In Chapter 5, Usher and Davoudi review development activity across a whole conurbation from 1984 to 1989. As an urban region, its local economy suffered more from the collapse of heavy industry, and had less buoyant conditions in the housing and service sector. Nevertheless, development activity followed a similar cycle to that illustrated by Law, although its upturn came later. Recent evidence, supported by Nabarro and Key's assessment in Chapter 3, suggests its downturn was also delayed, not becoming obvious until mid-1990.

Usher and Davoudi provide a valuable comprehensive picture of development activity across the conurbation. Housing was the dominant sector, with development spread through the conurbation, and particularly, inner zones and the periphery. Development in inner areas and riverside locations was strongly associated with public sector development activity or urban policy financial incentives. Office development concentrated in Newcastle, as the centre of the city region, and retail activity in the city centre, in the huge Metrocentre project in the Dunston Enterprise Zone, and in a scatter of peripheral locations and district centres. Industrial development was concentrated in the Enterprise Zone, the Nissan car complex and a few peripheral estates. It is clear that the intra-urban pattern of development activity has been very uneven.

Usher and Davoudi show clearly the extent to which public policy influenced the spatial pattern of land and property markets. Their findings parallel accounts of the effects of urban policy in US cities in the 1970s (Giloth, 1990; Frieden, 1990).

In Chapter 6, Couch and Fowles focus on Liverpool, and describe a property market which seems barely to have benefited from the boom conditions of the late 1980s. They discuss the issue of land vacancy, which they view as an indicator of problems in structural adjustment within markets. As with unemployment, high vacancy rates are considered to indicate weak demand, or a failure on the supply-side to reduce land costs in line with what purchasers are prepared to pay. Their study seeks to identify the scale and causes of the vacancy. They conclude that functional causes were the main problem in the early 1980s, with landowners taking time to adjust to deteriorating market conditions. Urban policy initiatives such as Enterprise Zones and Urban Development Grant, Couch and Fowles argue, could alleviate such problems. But by the end of the decade, the overall problem appeared to be declining demand. This may be contrasted with Manchester, and Tyne and Wear, where there was evidence of growing user demand as well as investment interest, although the basis of the assessment of demand is different from the Liverpool study. Couch and Fowles therefore claim that the causes of land vacancy in Liverpool shifted during the decade from functional to structural causes. If this conclusion is correct, then it illustrates the spatial unevenness of urban regeneration at the inter-regional scale, to compound that at the intra-regional scale identified by Usher and Davoudi.

These papers emphasize the impact on urban region land and property markets of both temporal shifts in the scale of development activity, oper-ating across national space, and the relative success of different urban re-gions in sustaining and expanding their local economies. Law, and Usher and Davoudi, also highlight the significant role of public policy and of the committed and well-organized actions of particular agencies in both the public and private sectors in changing intra-regional patterns in local prop-erty markets. This aspect will be explored further in Part Four.

3.3   PROPERTY MARKET DIFFERENTIATION

An important analytical issue to emerge from the papers is the need to differentiate among land and property markets. Markets for new and exist-ing properties may behave differently from markets in development op-portunities, and the tension between use value and investment value in property is now widely recognized.

Markets in different sectors of property behave differently over time, as Nabarro and Key show. This could allow developers in urban regions to switch between sectors over time in order to sustain their scale and capacity of activity. In the past, a more likely shift was between development activity, new construction work and refurbishment, with established developers tend-ing to concentrate in particular market sectors. A new phenomenon of the 1980s has been the large mixed-use project, promoted by either very large conglomerates or a development consortium. In this case, it is possible to renegotiate the mix of uses in a scheme as market conditions change.

There is certainly much evidence of such renegotiation. During the 1980s, there was a general shift to business use and office content in industrial projects, as rates of return in these other sectors rose above industrial levels. Nevertheless, in the three conurbations examined here, the significant sec-tor was housing. Switching between housing and other uses in a develop-ment is difficult in any case, due to planning regulations, the expectations of purchasers and the distinctive traditions of the residential development sector. In any event, by 1990, all markets were in recession, with the prospect of stagnation in development activity for the next few years, as the confidence of the 1980s ebbed away. This raises the possibility that these large schemes, often promoted by developers and investors from outside a region, may have crowded out more locally based initiatives.

The papers also illustrate the complex differentiations with respect to type of property and location in each of the market sectors. There is not in effect one housing market, or industrial property market in an urban region, but several. In buoyant conditions, excess demand from one segment can flow over to revive conditions in a secondary office market, create market interest in poorly located vacant sites, or provide resources for refurbishing premises with modern office or industrial facilities. In urban regions with fragile economies, there is much less demand to go around. This appears to have the effect of making market segmentation more obvious. For some types of property and some locations, there may be no market, even in boom conditions. Where efforts are made to revive market activity, labelling locations and establishing clear boundaries between new environments and adjacent properties with quite different market prospects may be critical to the success of a scheme. The large mixed-use scheme has great attractions in this context. The imagery of urban regeneration, with its waterfront projects, business parks and leisure schemes, has a critical role to play in 'revaluing' locations. However, it can easily be undermined by oversupply and overenthusiasm, and, evidently, by recession in development activity.

3.4 DO BOOMS PROMOTE LONG-TERM URBAN REGENERATION?

This suggests that the effects of substantial cyclicality could be particularly serious in urban regions with thin property markets. Law argues that national property market booms arrive late in peripheral areas, and wane early. In Tyne and Wear, boom conditions certainly came late, but did not level off until mid-1990. Was this because in Tyne and Wear, industrial and commercial demand in the local economy actually remained buoyant for longer, benefiting partly from foreign investment in the region in preparation for the Single European Market, and from a significant shift of industrial and commercial enterprises out of the high costs and congestion of the South? Has the North benefited from its export-oriented production economy, thus avoiding the full impact of cutbacks in domestic demand? Whatever the reason, property markets in the North-East have now joined the rest of the country into stagnation. What will be the effect of this on schemes underway and in plans? In particular, how will the Urban Development Corporations be able to achieve their development objectives?

All the papers in this part urge caution with respect to future prospects for local land and property markets, and raise questions about whether the urban policy initiatives of the 1980s have actually strengthened local development capacity. The city rebuilding project may turn out to have been an episode of the 1980s, with little but cautionary lessons for those preparing for the next upturn in development activity.

Which parts of the city have benefited from development activity in the 1980s? Law, and Usher and Davoudi, confirm that activity has been concentrated in city centres, some parts of the urban periphery and zones targeted by urban policy. In effect, this represents a significant restructuring of city space, although not necessarily in consistent directions. The private sector's attention has been focused on city centres and parts of the periphery with good transport and good services. Urban policy incentives have been available in city centres (City Grant, UDCs), and areas of obsolete industrial land. Projects in these locations are often in competition with peripheral sites. This suggests that the degree of public sector commitment, investment and subsidy needed to sustain active market interest in substantial sites which are neither in the periphery nor in and around city centres may be very substantial indeed. Without the help of boom conditions, such significant 'market restructuring' may be very difficult to achieve in Britain's former 'rustbelt' cities.

3.5   STATE AND MARKET IN THE DEVELOPMENT PROCESS

This raises important questions as regards the relationship between state and market in the development process. Until the mid-1970s, private developers and building firms could rely on a public sector which regulated development opportunities reasonably effectively through the planning system, organized and provided physical and social infrastructure, gave a flow of contracts to local builders and, in urban regions with fragile economies, on the whole provided support to development firms. In the 1980s, the state's role in providing a flow of work and in stabilizing market conditions through a clear framework of development opportunities has been radically restructured. Structure plan policies which provided a framework for the level and location of market activity have been undermined substantially, while public investment has been reduced, and shifted from general provision to project and zone subsidy. The result has been much greater uncertainty in property markets in fragile urban economies, to compound that arising from lack of strength in user demand and relatively limited information. These sources of uncertainty are all likely to have serious effects in the 1990s.

However, in the 1980s the property boom, with government subsidy, and the efforts of many agencies both in championing and managing projects, has produced substantial investment in new development. Improvements in local economic conditions have helped to make this happen. While the intra-regional location of this development activity has been strongly influenced by urban policy, and the type and design of that provision has been shaped by fashions in building style and layout, this activity has added significantly to the amount and variety of the stock of premises available in urban regions. It remains an open question, however, whether this stock is appropriate in amount, location, style and terms of access to the user demands generated by the local economy and local consumption patterns. Urban policy in the 1980s may have achieved the objective of releasing supply-side constraints in development markets. It is not at all clear that this has made local land and property markets work more efficiently over the long term from the point of view of user demand.

4

CURRENT TRENDS IN COMMERCIAL PROPERTY INVESTMENT AND DEVELOPMENT: AN OVERVIEW

_____ *Rupert Nabarro and Tony Key*

4.1 INTRODUCTION

By early 1990 the boom in commercial property development was levelling off. What were the prospects for future levels of commercial property development? Were conditions similar to those in 1974 when a rise in interest rates and a check on demand had brought a hitherto unprecedented development boom to a sharp end? Did, alternatively, high levels of development over 1986–9 represent a period of catching-up after depressed commercial building levels had lasted throughout the previous decade? How specifically did national events relate to property markets in the regions? Commercial development had only recently shown signs of recovery in Liverpool, Glasgow and Newcastle. Could this continue as the clouds of recession started to settle on the new growth sectors of the South-East; or would the regional markets be pulled down by the national trend?

This chapter attempts to provide a context for events described in later chapters by discussing shifts in the national economy and property markets. It was written at the end of 1990 and thus benefits in part from hindsight: the rapidly deteriorating economic prospects of the second half of the year; the Gulf crisis; and in the domestic property market, the bankruptcy of some of the big development players of the mid-1980s.

The chapter is presented in two parts. In the first we look at the mechanics of the property cycle, and attempt to show how movements in the economy are transmitted and amplified in the property sector. In the second, we take a closer look at the point in the property cycle at which we now stand. The section is introduced by a brief discussion of property funding changes, which have had a significant impact on the strength of the recent boom. The work draws heavily on the work of Investment Property Databank both in developing a basic description of the property market, and in analysing and modelling some of the key relationships within it. It takes as read two earlier papers by the authors (Nabarro, 1990; Key, Espinet and Wright, 1990).

4.2 THE BIG DIPPER: THE ECONOMY AND PROPERTY CYCLES

Changes in the supply of space to meet occupier requirements must, in the nature of the property industry, lag behind the economic cycle. To meet rising demand, new developments have to be planned and constructed – a lag from inception to completion of one or two years, or longer. As an economic upswing strengthens, and any surplus capacity in the existing stock is absorbed, rental growth will strengthen until the new supply of space begins to come through the pipeline.

If, with the development lag, this takes two years, rental growth will accelerate right up to the peak of the economic cycle. Surging rents stimulate still further new development, up to, and perhaps after, demand has turned down. It becomes near-inevitable that the peak of supply will come after the economic cycle has turned down and demand is cooling.

An inherent cycle in the user market – in demand, take up, new supply and rental values – may be magnified by other factors operating in the investment market. In the first stages of an upswing in the economy – the end of the last trough in the cycle – interest rates are likely to be low as policy seeks to stimulate the economy. Low interest rates, and low inflation, make for low property yields.

In the property upswing, tight markets and accelerating rental growth make property investment more attractive, pull down the yield again, and add capital appreciation over and above rental growth to the attractions of both investment and new development.

At the top of the market cycle, these factors go into reverse: inflation rises and interest rates are hiked up; yields are pushed up. The property yield is further affected by the evidence of rising new supply against the prospect of cooling demand, and capital values fall disproportionately to the reduction in rental growth.

For those involved in large-scale development programmes the turning points in the cycle are painful. High development profitability built on low

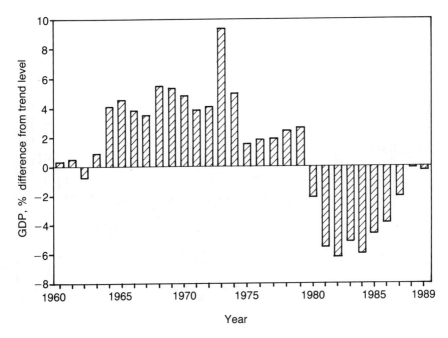

Figure 4.1   The economic cycle: Gross Domestic Product

site values, low interest charges, low construction costs and high sale values in the early phases of the cycle are shifted to low profitability for the schemes started toward the end of the cycle as all the cost and revenue influences become negative.

Figures 4.1 to 4.4 plot how the property cycle has actually run. We show various components using indicators running from the early days of the modern investment property industry in the 1960s.

Starting with the economic cycle (Fig. 4.1), the course of the economy has been dominated by the major recessions of the mid-1970s and early 1980s. Divided by a period of weak growth in the late 1970s, these slumps left the economy in its deepest postwar trough in 1982. Although the eight years since 1982 have seen strong growth, they have done no more than fill in the hole left by the economic failures of the previous decade. So a long cycle of over 15 years' (decline from 1973 to 1982 and qualified recovery from 1982 to the end of the decade) has swamped the 'normal' four-year business cycle.

The impact of these economic trends on property development is shown in a matching long cycle (Fig. 4.2). Building rates fluctuated around a fairly stable level in the 1960s through to the early 1970s. We can see a rough four-year cycle closely related to the economy's business cycle. Poor economic performance over the decade from 1973 then pushed development down to historically low levels, although the four-year cycle was still weakly

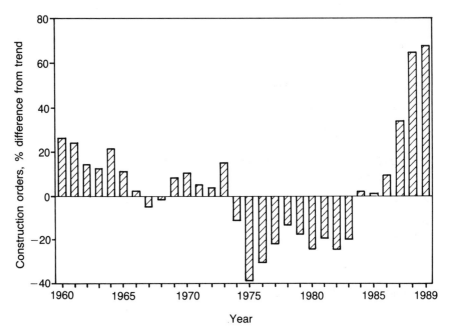

Figure 4.2   The development cycle: construction orders

evident up to the early 1980s. For 10 years, old building stock was not being replaced, and the supply of modern building was exceptionally low.

From 1982 onward, a sustained year-by-year rise took development to an all-time record high in 1989. This was a year after the peak in the economic boom (in late summer 1988). The chart shows development contract starts, not completions, so supply of space from the high peak of 1988 and 1989 is still flooding on to the market, and will continue to do so for another 18 months.

Putting demand and supply together produces rental growth (Fig. 4.3). Here again the short cyclical pattern of growth fluctuated through the 1960s and early 1970s without major booms and slumps. This was followed by weak demand right through from the mid-1970s to the mid-1980s, with real rental values falling in 10 out of the 11 years. 1984 to 1988 saw a sustained improvement in rental growth every year, peaking at a record level in 1988 – right at the peak of the economy. The chart includes IPD's estimate for 1990 – effectively zero real rental growth.

The last component of the clockwork property cycle was movement in yields (Fig. 4.4). This shows the impact of yield movements on real total return, so a rise in yields is negative, a fall in yields is positive. Through the 1960s and 1970s, the yield cycle again shows the four-year pattern. Through this period, yields generally fell a year or so before the peak in rental

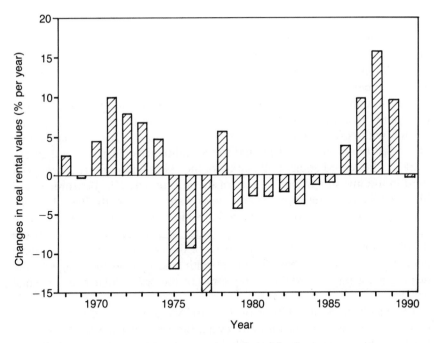

Figure 4.3 The rental cycle: changes in real rental values

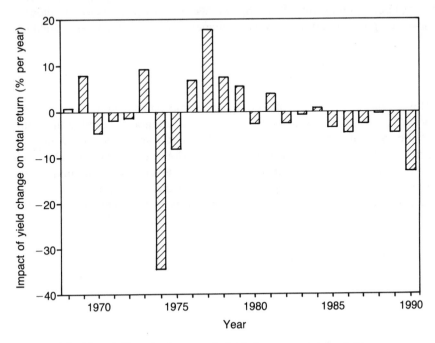

Figure 4.4 The yield cycle: impact of yield change on total return

growth. This might lead to the surprising conclusion that property investors have excellent foresight. More likely, it is because financial markets in general anticipate movements in the economy by a year or so, with equity prices falling as profit expectations are written down, and bond yields rise as government monetary policy begins to tighten.

But through the 1980s, the expected pattern has failed to appear. Property yields rose modestly but consistently through the 1985–8 boom (although with considerable differences across sectors). This unusual feature of the last boom may be attributed to two influences. First, in the financial markets, the record equity bull market of the 1980s left property a very poor third in the investment preferences of the institutions. The 1980s regime of high real interest rates (apart from a downward blip in early 1988) has also tended to keep yields up. Second, perhaps more speculatively, the investing institutions may have become rather better at reading the cycle than the development sector. Through the peaks of the boom, the prices they have been prepared to pay have been set with one eye on the bulge in the development pipeline, discounting some of the spectacular rises in rental values.

This has been a Grand Tour of the past. We are firmly of the view that there is a strong inherent property cycle, but that over the last 15 years it has been swamped by an unusually long cycle. An exceptionally long and deep trough has been followed by an exceptionally long upswing and a record peak in rents and development. We must expect this to be followed now by a protracted downward adjustment in rental values and new building.

4.3 WHERE ARE WE NOW?

The previous section has offered a simple, mechanistic view of the operation of the property cycle. In this section we attempt to describe the point of the cycle at which we now stand. We start with a brief description of property funding flows, for there can be no doubt that the ease with which bank money was made available to property developers in the mid to late 1980s gave a significant supply-side push to the development boom. We then describe supply and demand conditions in the main sectors of the market. Finally, we speculate about the future trend of development.

4.3.1 Property finance in the 1980s

Figure 4.5 shows the different sources of finance which make up the net injection of funds into the property sector between 1980 and 1989: the net investment of UK institutions; borrowing and capital issues on the stock market by development companies; and bank lending. A significant

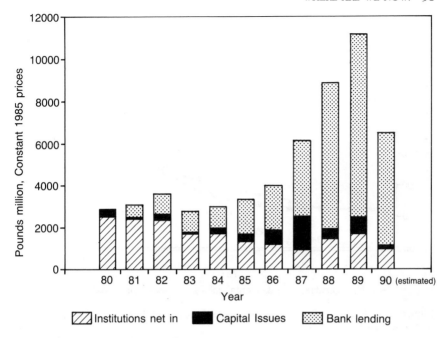

Figure 4.5 Property funding flows: constant prices. Source: IPD from CSO data

contribution to these funds came from overseas investment in the UK property market. No definitive figures are available for this, but it is thought that some £3 billion was injected by overseas investors in 1990.

Figure 4.5 illustrates the colossal rise in total funding available to finance the development boom. Moreover, the boom has been financed largely by bank lending, which has grown from negligible levels at the start of the decade to over £30 billion in loans outstanding at the end. At the same time the contribution of financial institutions to net investment in property has fallen more often than it has risen in the 1980s, and for the last three years of the decade was half that of the first three.

These trends can be taken as evidence of a diminishing institutional interest in property – which might not be surprising given that the property returns over the decade ran at an annualized 13.9% a year against equities (21.4%) and were barely above gilts (13.5%). More pressingly, however, they demonstrate the extent to which quite unprecedented levels of bank debt were made available to developers in the late 1980s. The chart lends itself to alarming comparisons: the outstanding bank lending on property is over half the total value of institutional portfolios; institutional refinancing of that debt at recent rates of net investment would take upwards of 20 years. And there is considerable evidence that institutional investment in property largely dried up in Spring 1990 and has yet (January 1991) to reappear.

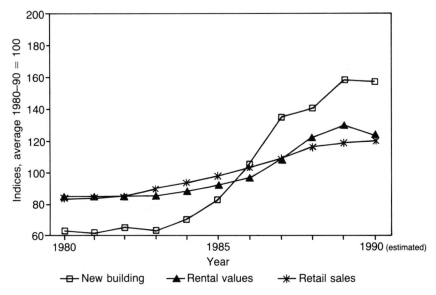

Figure 4.6 Retail market indicators: demand, new building and real rents. Source: IPD, CSO, DoE

4.3.2 The state of the markets

The retail market

Figure 4.6 provides a simple overview of trends in the retail market since 1980. It shows retail sales and the flow of new construction on to the market. These are plotted alongside the IPD index of retail rental values. All three series are shown in constant prices and indexed with their own average values for 1980–90 set at 100. Estimates for 1990 are based on the latest figures (to October) on retail sales, construction orders and rental growth from the IPD Monthly Index.

Looking at the chart suggests that the retail market has passed through three main phases in the past 10 years:

1. The early 1980s up to 1982, characterized by sluggish retail sales, no real rental growth and low levels of new buildings;
2. A sustained five-year period of growth from 1983 to 1988, through which retail sales grew on average by 5.3% per annum, real rental growth soared from 0.2% to 13.3% and the amount of new space built each year more than doubled; and
3. A period of retrenchment starting in 1989, which so far has seen retail sales growth slow down to only 1% per annum, a small drop in the volume of retail schemes being built and, once allowance is made for inflation, falling rental values.

According to IPD's Monthly Index the peak in rental growth in the retail property market occurred in July 1988. After that, the massive expansion in new space began to take its toll on rental values and this dampening effect has been compounded through 1989 and 1990 by the rapid slowdown in retail sales.

By the early months of 1990, the rental growth rate dropped to around 5% a year in cash terms, but it then stabilized at around this level for the rest of the year up to October. Over the 12 months to December 1990, rental growth now seems likely to turn out at about 5% in current prices and in real terms to fall by about 5%.

In all regions, except the North of England, the supply pipeline measured in terms of construction orders shrank over the 12 months to mid-1990. Judging rental growth potential, it is possible to split the regions into three broad groupings.

1. The North-West and South-West show a relatively attractive combination of a significant drop in orders, against already strong demand pressure.
2. In East Anglia, London, the West Midlands, the rest of the South-East and Scotland, the supply pipeline is now tailing off rapidly, so that the position of oversupply which has emerged in these regions should not deteriorate further.
3. Despite weak demand pressure, the supply pipeline in the North of England is still expanding, the worst possible combination. Yorkshire and Humberside, where construction orders are only now peaking, appears as the next weakest region.

The office market

Figure 4.7 provides an overview of developments in the office market at a national level over the past 10 years.

The rapid expansion of the financial and business services sector during the 1980s is clearly illustrated by the chart. In addition to the major banking and financial institutions, the sector also includes the accountancy, legal and property professions plus a wide range of rapidly growing newer business services such as advertising, computer services, consultancy, design and marketing. Between 1980 and 1990:

1. Financial and business services output grew by 6.9% per annum, almost twice the rate of growth in retail sales over the same period and virtually four times the annual average increase in manufacturing output.
2. The sector's output doubled. Financial and business services now account for 12% of employment, more than half of manufacturing's share.

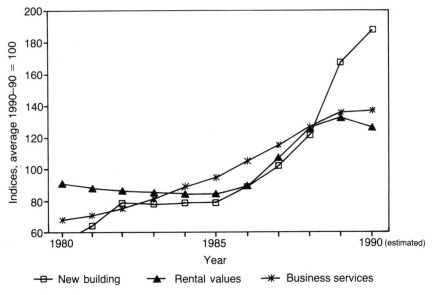

Figure 4.7 Office market indicators: demand, new building and real rents. Source: IPD, CSO, DoE

The boom in demand has in turn been followed and eventually outstripped by a three-and-a-half-fold increase in supply:

1. In the first half of the 1980s, the supply of new development picked up from the depressed level of the late 1970s, reaching a level close to its long-term average.
2. From 1986 development activity took off exponentially, leaving new supply in 1990 at double the level of the last major peak of the office cycle in 1973.

These demand and supply trends have produced a very mixed rental performance through the decade:

1. Despite the strong growth in demand in the first half of the decade, a combination of oversupply inherited from the 1970s and the revival in new development kept real rental values on a downward trend.
2. The acceleration in the growth of the financial and business services sector to 10% in 1986 triggered a substantial increase in real rental values of nearly 60% between 1985 and 1989.
3. The massive expansion in supply, coupled with the rapid slowdown in growth in this sector in 1990, has resulted in a new downturn in real rental values.

The IPD Monthly Index shows July 1988 as the high peak in office rental growth – the same turning point as in the retail sector. At that peak, rental growth was running at an annual rate of over 30%, dropping sharply to 20% by the end of the year. Since growth in the financial and business sector was still strong, it appears that the main factor initially dampening rental performance was the supply pipeline.

From the end of 1988, the continued expansion in the amount of new office space built, together with the added downward influences of a loss of momentum in the financial and business services sector, pushed the nominal rental growth over 12 months down to 15% for 1989, then to 8% by October 1990. With inflation at over 10%, real rental values have started to slide, and are likely to show a fall of 5% through 1990 as a whole.

How the financial and business services sector will perform in the early 1990s against the background of a sluggish economy poses some problems of prediction. Part of the sector's spectacular 1980s growth was the product of one-off changes, such as the drive to cut corporate overheads by contracting out, financial deregulation and the arrival of cheap personal computers. Whilst such windfalls may not recur in the next few years, it seems probable that, as interest rates decline and business spending revives, the sector should maintain its 20-year unbroken record of outperforming the economy as a whole. Best estimates suggest growth fluctuating between 3 and 5% over the next couple of years, still above the growth of the economy as a whole, but half its rate over the last 10 years.

Against weaker but still expanding underlying demand, immediate prospects for the supply side of the market can be judged from the relationship between construction orders placed and the amount of completed space built.

1. After holding up in the first months of the year, new orders for offices have fallen sharply, and in 1990 will probably drop by 15% compared with 1989.
2. Nonetheless, the year or so lag between start and completion of schemes means that the volume of new completed offices will rise by 12–15% in 1990.
3. Space actually reaching the market will not begin to fall until 1991, and then probably by no more than 15% from its 1990 peak.

It seems doubtful that this supply correction will be sufficient to check the downward trend in rental growth over the coming year. The cut in construction volumes to date remains modest against that seen in the retail sector.

At a regional level there is a large measure of correspondence between our assessment of the underlying market conditions and recent movements in new supply.

1. London appears as an extreme case, where the growth in employment of the office sector has been swamped by the massive development

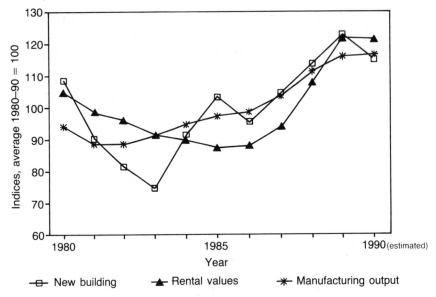

Figure 4.8 Industrial market indicators: demand, new building and real rents. Source: IPD, CSO, DoE

boom of the past four years. Reflecting this oversupply, London was the first region to see a drop in new office construction orders, down by 20% on the last 12 months' figures.
2. By contrast, new office orders are still on a rising trend in many regions (see Chapters 4 and 5) and only in East Anglia and Scotland is the pipeline definitely showing signs of shrinking. A downturn in new space reaching the market in most major provincial centres is therefore unlikely before 1992.

The industrial market

Figure 4.8 traces development in the industrial market over the last 10 years. It uses manufacturing output as an indicator of the demand for space, with the supply of completed industrial building measured by construction values, and the rental result shown in real terms by the IPD index.

The 1980s opened with a slump in manufacturing output, which matched in scale the Depression years of the 1930s. On the demand side of the market:

1. Manufacturing output remained depressed throughout the early 1980s, having fallen by 14% between 1979 and 1981;
2. Between 1983 and 1986 output rose steadily at an average rate of 1.7%. There then followed a brief three-year spurt ending in 1989, during

which manufacturing output increased by 18%, an average rate of 5.6% per annum; but

3. 1990 has seen a very sharp check to the boom with manufacturing output either static or falling marginally.

The supply side of the market has tended to track the three-to-four-year cyclical pattern of manufacturing growth. Looking at both the supply side and rental values:

1. New development collapsed by 40% in the first three years of the 1980s. In the subsequent three years the volume of completed industrial space rose more or less in step with manufacturing output.
2. Despite the dramatic cutback in development at the start of the decade, real rental values drifted lower through to 1985 due to the presence on the market of the oversupply inherited from the 1970s.
3. The shift from recovery to boom in manufacturing precipitated a corresponding increase in development which rose by 30% between 1986 and 1989.
4. Whilst this took industrial development to a new peak, the growth in development was relatively modest against the massive booms in retail and office building.
5. Real rental values rose steeply from 1987 to 1989, as the oversupply of space from the 1970s was finally absorbed and as the expansion in demand for space mushroomed.
6. 1990 has seen both the volume of completed industrial space and rental values fall back slightly from last year's levels, as manufacturing growth has ground to a halt.

The relatively muted response of supply to the strong growth in manufacturing output explains why rental growth in the sector has held up relatively well through 1990. The IPD Monthly Index shows that the peak of the industrial rental cycle (at a rate of well over 30% a year) was reached in the autumn of 1988, a few months behind the peaks in the retail and office markets.

The deceleration has been less severe than in the other sectors, with nominal rental growth (measured quarterly) holding up at around 20% a year into the early months of 1990. In recent months, however, growth has been cut severely by the downturn in manufacturing industry. The current underlying growth rate, at 6% a year, is only marginally better than the 3–4% a year for offices and retail investments. In nominal terms, industrial rents are likely to rise by around 10% on the year, against 5% for both retail and office investments.

Immediate prospects for the industrial market have been the most severely affected by emerging economic trends through the year. The standstill in manufacturing in 1990 activity envisaged in the Spring now looks almost certain to extend well into 1991. The more pessimistic fore-casters now see a fall in manufacturing output in 1991, and a much weaker recovery in 1992 than previously anticipated.

All regions shared in the industrial boom between 1986 and 1989. Gen-erally, performance was stronger in the traditional industrial regions of the Midlands, northern England, Scotland and Wales. In these regions manu-facturing output increased by over 7% per annum in the three years through to last year. By contrast, in the southern regions manufacturing output grew over the same period at the slower, though still respectable rate, of around 5% per annum.

Over the past 12 months developments at the regional level in the industrial markets have loosely mirrored the pattern of growth in manufacturing. The regions of lowest output growth in southern and eastern England, and highest supply in the early and middle 1980s, have now seen a downturn in development, while construction in other regions is still rising. The in-dustrial market is now showing a reversed North–South divide from that of five years ago. Thus:

1. While in East Anglia, London, the rest of the South-East and the South-West the demand pressure index is well below the national average, in the Midlands and northern regions of England, Scotland and Wales it is either close to the average or well above.
2. Throughout southern and eastern England, new industrial orders are either static or declining. Conversely, outside the South, the pipeline has only dipped in Scotland and Wales. In every northern region of England orders are still rising.

Investment markets

It may be argued that the reduction in rental growth that has occurred during 1990 might readily have been foreseen from the high rates of growth recorded in 1986–9, and the huge construction boom that was triggered. A rather unexpected feature of 1990 has been rapidly rising yields – which have converted a downward slide in user markets to a fully blown slump in the investment markets with yields moving out to a new historic high.

1. Yields in all three sectors began to move sharply upward from Novem-ber 1989, initially at a slightly faster rate for retails than for offices and industrials.
2. For all three sectors, the rate of increase in yields hit its peak in mid-Summer 1990, when they were rising at no less than 0.2% per month.
3. Despite the 1% cut in interest rates of early October 1990, the most recent figures give only the most tentative signs of an end to the rise,

with retail and office yields still rising but at half the rate of the Summer, and industrial yields perhaps beginning to stabilize.

The rise in yield since late 1989, despite a measure of variation in rental trends and perhaps also in future prospects, shows little differentiation between different areas of the country. In the retail and industrial sectors, yields have risen at the same rate across all three broad regions. In the office sector, the rise in yields in London has been the same as in the provincial markets. This appears at odds with the differences in rental performance, possibly because London's yields did not adjust downward through 1988 in line with the rest of the country. The most severe rise in office yields has been in the South of England.

Combining the effects of the rental slowdown and rocketing yields, property returns in 1990 will be the second worst on record, with only 1974 seeing a more severe slump.

4.4 CONCLUDING COMMENTS

We argued in the first part of this paper that the recognizable cycles of both the economy and the property industry had been greatly elongated in the 1970s and 1980s. We have attempted to show how rapid economic growth from the early 1980s was only slowly converted into new increased commitment to development in the mid-late 1980s and how the rapid increase in rents gave a further push to the development boom already well underway by 1987.

During 1990 many chickens came home to roost: a check in the economy reduced the demand for new space; buildings under construction were leading to unprecedented levels of new space coming on to the market; high interest rates placed continuing pressure on the costs of many developers; rapidly rising yields reduced or eliminated the profitability of many development schemes. Within this broad picture particularly severe problems were felt by the development sector in retail property and/or southern (and particularly London) offices.

Temporarily, the property market at the end of 1990 has come to a halt. Banks, who have financed much of the development boom, are faced in many instances with non-performing loans and severe losses. Institutions are unwilling to purchase at present prices or to take on the losses left by the boom in the rest of the industry. At a low point in the economic cycle, lettings of new space are very low. The prospects for commercial development, perhaps for three to four years, seem dismal.

Editor's note: This chapter was written in March 1990, and lays the ground for the subsequent collapse of the property market, although possibly underestimating the extent of this movement.

5

PROPERTY-LED URBAN REGENERATION IN INNER MANCHESTER

Chris Law

The last five years have witnessed a spate of developments and proposals in the inner-city areas of our major cities which has not only contrasted with the stagnation of the previous 10 years but has been encouraging to all those who wish to see these districts revitalized. Until mid-1989 the government could claim some credit for this achievement both from providing an environment of national economic growth and from putting in place urban policies which appeared to stimulate development. However, some of these proposals are bound to be put in doubt by the prospects of slower economic growth and when some of the gilding has been removed from the apparent success of inner-city policies there will inevitably be questions asked about the nature and direction of these measures. During the last 10 years the Thatcher government has shifted policies towards an emphasis on land and property development, which like all sectors responds to and is shaped by market forces. However, there may be particular disadvantages arising from land and property development concerned with the glut-to-famine (hog) cycle type of phenomenon which is inimical to long-term economic regeneration.

In this paper I shall review briefly these ideas which are basic to the theme of this book. The main part of this paper will examine development trends in Manchester, one of the UK's major provincial centres situated in northern England, capital of North-West England with a population of 6.5 million and with its own conurbation having a population of 2.5 million (Fig. 5.1). In particular the paper will examine trends in Inner Manchester, a shorthand term which refers to the inner areas of Manchester City, Salford City and Trafford Borough (Old Trafford and Trafford Park) (Fig. 5.2). After

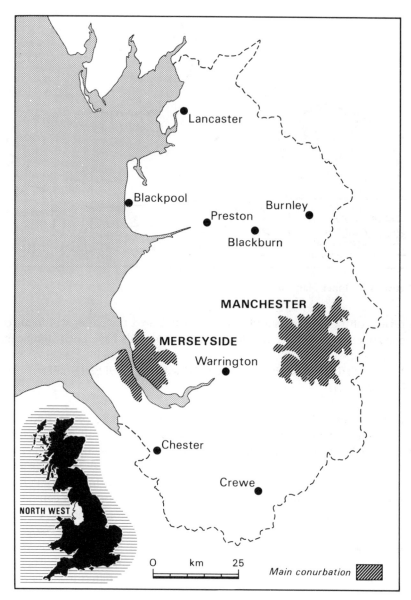

Figure 5.1 Manchester and North West England

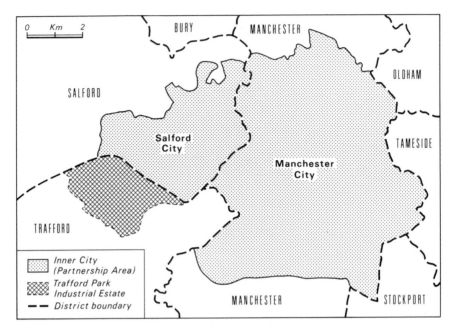

Figure 5.2   Inner Manchester

a review of the problems and policies for this area the paper will focus on those zones where either developments or proposals have been significant.

5.1   THE SHIFT OF URBAN POLICY TOWARDS PROPERTY-LED DEVELOPMENT

The last 11 years have seen significant changes in urban policy under the Thatcher government. This is not the place to recount all the measures, which has been done admirably elsewhere (Lawless, 1989b; Robson, 1988) and earlier in this book. Here it is sufficient to emphasize the shifts away from the 1978 Inner Urban Areas Act which established Inner City Partnerships in our major urban areas. In these partnerships between central and local government, funds were provided to the latter for economic, environmental, housing and social projects. Whilst property and land development were by no means excluded, social projects such as crèches for young mothers and clubs for senior citizens were significant. Under the Thatcher government the emphasis of these programmes has shifted towards economic projects and, subsequently, funds have been diverted to newer forms of urban policy, such as Urban Development Grants.

Various new policies have encouraged land and property development. City Grants (formerly Urban Development Grants and Urban Regeneration Grants) are usually obtained for property schemes, although the number of jobs created may assist a project to obtain a grant. Enterprise Zones, created in 1980, include a tax concession of 100% capital allowances on both industrial and commerical buildings which benefits developers but not necessarily the occupiers of the premises who may not own them. Derelict Land Grants, made available in urban areas in 1982, favour 'hard' projects where there is property development as opposed to 'soft' ones which may merely provide open space or an enhanced environment. Urban Development Corporations, created in 1980, appear to be established to create an environment in which property development will occur and one criterion for measuring their success is the amount of such investment leveraged.

It would be wrong to suggest that the Thatcher government's urban policy is solely concerned with land and property development. Task Forces and City Action teams seek to encourage enterprise and training. However, the importance of property development within urban policy can be gauged when a comparison is made with the revisions which have been made to regional policy where the size of grant given has been related not to the scale of investment but to the number of jobs created. Whilst within urban policy there is a clear expectation that jobs will be created, there is no direct mechanism to ensure this outcome and jobs are frequently perceived as the fortunate by-product of property development. Insofar as urban agencies are pro-active there is the opportunity to influence economic trends and achieve particular objectives, but frequently there is the presumption that once the right environment is created it is up to developers to put forward projects. All such projects must be profit making. There is little place for non-profit-making activities such as housing for low income groups, social facilities and even key publicly subsidized tourism attractions.

5.2   PROPERTY-LED DEVELOPMENT AND MARKET FORCES

It is axiomatic that property development will reflect market forces and that without intervention it will not necessarily achieve the social objectives of inner-city policy. General government economic policies can affect the rate of growth in the national economy, and thus trends in property development and these will be reflected differentially in local economies according to their strengths and weaknesses. Whilst urban policy can stimulate development activity through creating a framework and environment and by giving grants, it cannot significantly affect the local market in which developers operate. Environmental improvements may over a period make an area more attractive for development whilst grants may bring forward schemes that otherwise would be delayed. However, in the short term developers will be very much influenced by the state of the local market. Only through regional policy, i.e. the inter-regional shift of economic activity,

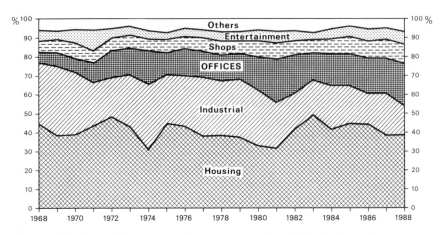

Figure 5.3 Great Britain private-sector construction 1968–88: shares by sector

can government policy significantly enhance property development through increasing demand. Thus the scale and form of development activity will be determined by the state of the local market and the types of demand which exist within it.

The property market can be disaggregated into different components such as housing, industry, offices and retail, although, of course, individual projects may include more than one type. The demand for these different components varies over time, reflecting both internal and external factors so that the composition of total demand may change from one year to the next (Fig. 5.3). During the last 20 years the importance of office investment has increased whilst that of industry has diminished within the total. All sectors will be affected by external factors such as the state of the economy and interest rates so that there is a tendency to cyclical development, although not every type of investment will necessarily follow the same cycle (Fig. 5.4).

For some types of property development the cycles of output may exaggerate the cycles of demand akin to the famous hog cycle in economic literature. During periods of rapid growth there is an imbalance between supply and demand which cannot quickly be bridged because of the time necessary to realize projects. Rising rents will encourage developers to propose many schemes, not all of which will be proceeded with. Actual construction is likely to exceed demand, producing oversupply. This in turn will cause a fall in rents which will discourage any further investment except in very favoured areas. When demand has absorbed this supply, returns will begin to improve and this will encourage another round of investment (Barras, 1979). The length of the downswing will depend on the state of the local economy. In a vibrant local area the fall may only last a short time, but in a depressed one it could last many years. As developers become aware

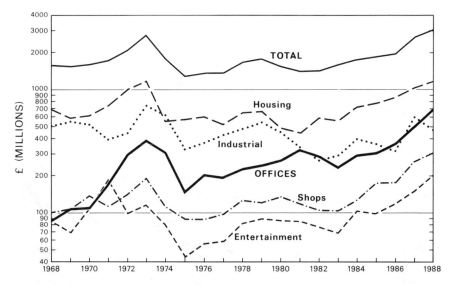

Figure 5.4 Great Britain private-sector construction 1968–88: investment by sector at constant prices

of rival proposals there may be a scaling down of schemes, and less viable ones will not be proceeded with. However, oversupply may result in some poorly located newly built properties remaining empty for some time and in older and/or less well located properties becoming vacant as occupiers move upmarket and into core zones.

The spatial aspects of property development are important. The components of demand vary from one area to another depending on the character of the local economy. These differences are inter-regional (Fig. 5.5) with London and the South-East usually leading the upswing in the cycle, as well as intra-regional, and in particular we can note the differences in demand between the inner and outer areas of cities. These patterns are not fixed: there is continual change and to a certain extent places are in competition with each other. Urban policy can influence the location of property development since it usually operates within discrete spaces. Insofar as urban policy stimulates property development we could expect to witness certain areas benefiting more than others from each round of development activity.

However, there is probably a limit to how far urban policy can influence the type of investment undertaken, since this will be shaped by general market conditions. Accordingly, some commentators have suggested that the role of Urban Development Corporations is one of pragmatic opportunism. The outcomes of urban policy are likely therefore to be highly variable depending on the state of the market when measures come into operation and the characteristics of the local geography. These processes can now be illustrated by reference to Inner Manchester.

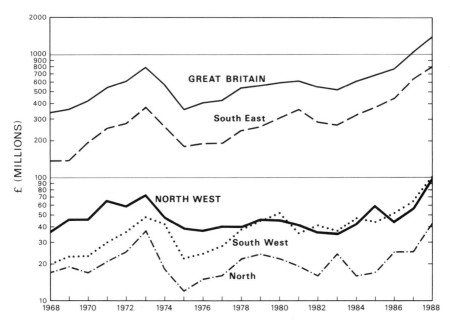

Figure 5.5   Great Britain private-sector construction 1968–88: investment by region at constant prices

5.3   THE PROBLEMS OF INNER MANCHESTER

Manchester is a classic industrial city and its problems are typical of those of many northern towns. The following account can only highlight the main difficulties which it faces. After 150 years of rapid growth the population of what is now the core reached about one million at the time of the First World War. Since then there has been extensive decentralization so that by 1981 the population had fallen to about 300 000. As elsewhere most of the people remaining living in this area were from the lower socio-economic groups. This situation had been reinforced as a consequence of massive slum clearance which had been replaced by public housing. In the early 1980s it was difficult to sell new housing for owner occupiers. As a result of employment decline, recession and occupational shifts in the jobs available there was in the area unemployment which was substantially above average, which was associated with significant deprivation.

From the 1950s to the early 1980s there was also a high rate of employment decline in this area caused by *in situ* job losses in firms, closures and decentralization. Jobs in industry, warehousing and transport disappeared on a large scale. The role of the regional centre suffered both from the running down of industries in the region and the shifting of control to London. Retailing in the city centre suffered from the decline of population in the core area and the growth of sub-regional centres in outer Greater Manchester where the population was growing. At the same time office functions in the city centre were subject to competition from new centres developing in the southern suburbs close to the main higher socio-economic group residential areas.

During the 1970s and early 1980s the responsible authorities became very concerned about the decline of the core area. One of its clearest and most visible expressions was seen in the amount of vacant, derelict and underused land, and in empty buildings. All these features were evident and extensive in the zone around the city centre. To the west the docks area was becoming derelict by the late 1970s and by the end of the 1979–82 recession about one third of Trafford Park Industrial Estate was unused. The eastern industrial area was also laid waste at this time. As elsewhere much of the modern high-rise housing stock was also causing concern. Lack of funds to renovate the building coupled with an unwillingness of people to live in these areas meant that much of the stock was unused. Whilst this state of affairs caused concern in the early 1980s, given the depressed state of the national economy it was not clear how the area could be regenerated.

5.4 THE POLICY ENVIRONMENT IN INNER MANCHESTER

Once again it is only possible to give a brief account of the evolution of policies which have been covered elsewhere (Law, 1989). In 1974 the reform of local government placed the responsibility for dealing with these problems with the Greater Manchester Council (GMC), a new upper-tier authority, and three lower-tier municipalities, Manchester City, Salford City and Trafford Borough (Fig. 4.2). Between these bodies there was clearly some scope for different views about the nature of the problems and their solutions, a feature further emphasized by the different political complexions of the various authorities. In 1978 a Manchester and Salford Inner City Partnership was established. The GMC gave great weight to maintaining the role of the regional centre, regenerating the inner city and concentrating development (including retailing and offices) in existing centres, objectives which were incorporated into the county structure plan. It also became actively involved in urban revitalization through its purchase of the Central Station site, the Liverpool Road Goods Yard and the Midland Hotel. With Manchester City Council it produced a plan for the city centre and created the Castlefield Urban Heritage Park. Perhaps its misfortune was to exist (1974–86) in a period of low development activity so that except for the G-MEX exhibition centre, the refurbished Holiday Inn Crown Plaza Midland Hotel, the Greater Manchester Museum of Science and Industry in Castlefield, and road improvements in the city centre it had little to see for its endeavours. Other achievements included the establishment of the Greater

Manchester Economic Development Corporation (which continued to 1990) and through G-MEX and Castlefield, the beginning of tourism development in the city.

Salford and Trafford were both successful in moving development forward. Together they successfully bid for an enterprise zone for the decaying docks area and the Trafford Park Industrial Estate. Salford went on to launch a dockland redevelopment scheme at Salford Quays (see below) and also to sell run-down council owned flats to construction firms for rehabilitation. Trafford also persisted with its attempts to revitalize Trafford Park which came to fruition with a development corporation in 1987 (see below).

Meanwhile, Manchester City's actions were more eclectic. With the Chamber of Trade it launched a City Centre Campaign in 1982 to bring back activities to this area. It also worked with the GMC on Castlefield and later became active in tourism initiatives. However, it resisted the idea of either an enterprise zone or a development corporation for the run-down east Manchester area with the consequence that regeneration here has been much less impressive than on the western side. Neither did it welcome the establishment of the Central Manchester Development Corporation (CMDC) in July 1988 covering the eastern and southern fringes of the city centre, although it has subsequently co-operated with this body. Compared to other cities, such as Birmingham, it did not actively seek out projects suitable for a UDG award, with the consequence that few were won.

Since the mid-1980s there have been several changes in the planning environment. The abolition of the GMC has weakened a comprehensive approach to the region's problems and encouraged a more competitive spirit between the metropolitan authorities. The strategic plan updating GMC's structure plan, although in theory upholding previous principles, in fact allows deviations where there is good reason, such as urban regeneration, so that almost anything is possible and is becoming so (DOE, 1989a). The idea promoted by the central government, that planning should not restrict either growth or competition has again weakened controls. In particular, it appears likely that an out-of-town regional shopping centre will be built on the west side of Manchester. Earlier restrictions on office development to particular zones have almost entirely been removed.

5.5   THE DEVELOPMENT CONTEXT

The period from 1985 to mid-1989 was one of accelerating development activity. Since mid-1989 there has probably been a downturn but this has affected the various sectors of the market differently. For Manchester this development boom has been the first since the early 1970s and has thus been welcome (Catalano and Barras, 1980). Numerous proposals have been made, although it is not clear whether all will come to fruition.

The boom is most clearly seen in the office sector. In 1987–8 it became apparent that the demand for office space in Greater Manchester was increasing and exceeding supply. The accompanying rent rises provided an incentive to developers to build new stock, as well as reconstruct or refurbish existing buildings in the city centre core. Hitherto development activity had generally been restricted to this core or the burgeoning office centres in the southern suburbs such as Altrincham, Sale, Stockport, Cheadle, Cheadle Hulme and Wilmslow. During the boom developers were encouraged to put forward schemes in all these areas plus the city centre fringe and two new zones, Salford Quays and the Airport. Between 1987 and 1989 annual planning permissions for offices (full and outline) in Greater Manchester County increased from approximately 2 840 000 square feet to 9 290 000 square feet (Source: Greater Manchester Research and Information Planning Unit). By late 1989 there was either under construction or proposals for between nine and eleven million square feet of office space, which compared to a maximum take-up (absorption) rate under good conditions of 600 000–750 000 square feet a year. It was therefore apparent to all that a condition of oversupply would emerge unless, of course, the region could suddenly start to attract office-using activities on a large scale from outside the region, and particularly from southern England. Surprisingly, in view of the region's previous lack of success in this respect, many chartered surveyors considered this a possibility given the overheating of the South-Eastern economy.

During this period, investment in private housing was also high and for the first time made itself present in the city centre and inner-city areas. Since the rise in interest rates in mid-1989 demand has slackened, no doubt dampening developer activity. The growth of retail spending for most of this period also encouraged investment and this was experienced mainly in the form of retail parks and supermarkets, although there were proposals for out-of-town shopping centres, as mentioned earlier. Demand for industrial space increased but this has not been high. Whilst the public sector has suggested schemes for leisure and tourism, private sector investment has been limited in this area. These developments can now be discussed in terms of the principal areas affected.

5.6   SALFORD QUAYS AND THE ENTERPRISE ZONE

Once again, it is only possible to give a brief resumé of changes in this area and readers are referred to the authors' earlier works (Law, 1988a and b). During the 1970s the trade of Manchester Docks declined disastrously and it was clear that there was little likelihood of a revival, so raising the issue of the future of the docks. In 1981 a small part of the docks was incorporated into the Enterprise Zone together with Manchester Ship Canal Company

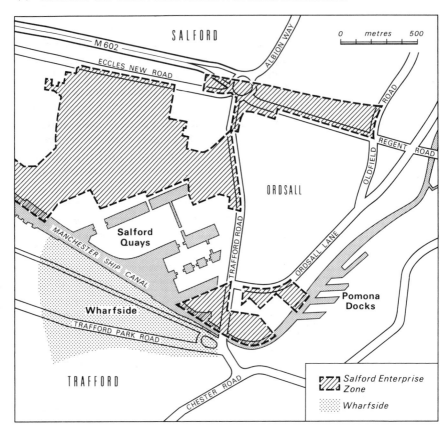

Figure 5.6 The Salford Quays/Trafford Wharfside area

(MSCC) land north of Dock 9 which had been kept in reserve in case of port expansion. The Enterprise Zone also included a strip along the main A57 road (Fig. 5.6). Early developments in the EZ consisted mainly of light industry, warehouses and some retail warehouses (on the A57). The development of the docks themselves for other uses was perceived to be difficult without environmental and infrastructural improvements which the MSCC did not consider would be justified by the likely returns at this time in the early 1980s. Since it was felt that a public subsidy would be necessary to redevelop the docks, these were sold to Salford City for £1.5 million. In 1985 a plan for Salford Quays was prepared and at the end of the year the Government gave approval for £25 million of assistance over five to six years from the Urban Programme and Derelict Land Grant, to be spent on infrastructure and environmental improvements. Salford City Council agreed to involve the private sector and subsequently sold part of the southern area to Urban Waterside. The basis of the overall plan was for one third of the zone to be used for residential, one third for employment activities and one third for leisure facilities.

The effects of the recession were still present in the mid-1980s and Salford felt pleased with the launching of the scheme in 1986–7. Initial projects included a cinema, hotel, housing and offices. The latter were small scale, perhaps reflecting the fact that the area was not a traditional office zone, as well as the state of the market. With the completion of the first phases of the scheme, which were highly praised, and the upturn in the office market, the development environment changed. By 1988 it would have been possible to rezone the whole of the Quays for offices and obtain much developer interest. Urban Waterside pulled down the remaining transit sheds which had been used by a boating company and replaced them with offices. The developers of Waterfront 2000 on Pier 7 sought to increase the amount of office space as well as upgrading the quality of the office buildings. The MSCC came in with proposals for two office buildings in front of the Dock Offices, and for Harbour City on land it had retained on the north side of Dock 9, where it proposed 750 000 square feet of mainly office development. At the head of Dock 9 Salford City was able to auction the site for what is to be a 250 000 square feet predominantly office complex. Housing has proceeded satisfactorily, but the leisure proposals have faced problems. Salford City would like activities which serve a social function but for which there may not be a commercial market. A performing arts centre may eventually be built, but only if a developer can offset the costs with office development.

Meanwhile, in the rest of the EZ, which will end in 1991, there has been a rush of office developments to be completed in time to obtain the tax benefits. These are mainly either near the end of the M602 or on the riverfront, such as the 500 000 square feet Exchange Quay. During the office boom this latter scheme was increased in size by 200 000 square feet. On the opposite bank, in the Pomona Docks, the MSCC, who were keen to start office development immediately in spite of the desire by the two development corporations for leisure uses, have commenced construction of 47 000 square feet of offices. Thus a significant part of the activity in the burgeoning Salford Quays office area is tax driven/supply led.

5.7 TRAFFORD WHARFSIDE

Trafford Park, created in 1896 to assist the trade of Manchester Docks, can arguably claim to be the world's first industrial estate. Linked by railway to the docks as well as providing some direct waterfront access it attracted many but by no means all port-related industries. Employment increased steadily; some reports suggest a maximum of 75 000 jobs during World War Two. By 1965 it had fallen to 52 000 and by 1985 to 24 500. By this time only a handful of firms had links to the Ship Canal and Docks. The recession of 1979–82 hit the estate badly as the job losses show. It also left about one-third of the area derelict and empty with the quality of the environment decaying rapidly. This was a great concern to the local council, Trafford, which considered it did not have the resources to improve the area, and also, to the firms on the estate (a mixture of manufacturers and whole-salers). They felt that the decaying environment would discourage new entrants to the estate, make existing tenants wish to leave and not provide a milieu attractive for staff or clients. Jointly with the DOE a study was undertaken by Roger Tym and Partners (1986), followed by a request for government support to implement the proposals. In February 1987 the UDC was established with £160 million to spend over 10 years.

The task of the UDC was to improve the environment, enhance the infra-structure, engage in special area projects and seek to attract 16 000 addi-tional jobs during its lifetime. In some respects its task could be seen as the management of the UK's largest industrial-improvement area and it could have been expected to attract a mix of activities similar to those already existing, namely manufacturing and distribution. However, the timing sug-gested otherwise. The emerging Salford Quays directly opposite the eastern end revealed an environment very different from that of an industrial estate, whilst the burgeoning office market in Greater Manchester suggested an alternative. The Roger Tym report had suggested the possibility of some offices on the waterfront, quoting a figure of 175 000 sq. ft, but this embryo idea was blown up to become a flagship project – Wharfside, with 2 million square feet of offices set amidst additional canals and a high quality envir-onment (Fig. 5.6). To offset the criticism that offices might attract activity from the city centre, the maintenance of which was part of the structure plan, it was argued that high-quality offices in this setting would attract tenants from outside the region. For the UDC the prospect of at least 10 000 jobs in the area would go a long way to achieving its target of 16 000 jobs.

5.8 THE CITY CENTRE

For nearly 30 years the problems of the city centre have been most evident in the decaying 'collar'. These problems have been due to the *in situ* de-cline of activities, the decentralization of firms, the lack of dynamism in the regional centre increasingly overshadowed by London, and the high cost of conversion of derelict sites and empty buildings. Proposals had been put forward to encourage residential schemes and tourism but progress was either slow or non-existent. In the early 1980s the investment climate was not conducive to encourage investors even with UDGs available. However, from the mid-1980s conditions began to change. Around 1985–7 there was a small hotel boom possibly connected with the opening of G-MEX in 1986. The Phoenix Initiative stimulated developer interest in the conversion of warehouses on the Whitworth Street corridor conditional upon government funds being available. In order to provide a framework in which such support could be given the CMDC was established in 1988. Amongst its aims was to reclaim 24 acres, create 6000 jobs, increase local residents by 2000, enlarge Manchester's international role and expand tourism.

Concurrent with the launch of the CMDC the office boom was getting under way. The prospect of government support has certainly encouraged many schemes but it is significant how many of these contain an office component. The proposals around Picccadilly Station, the International Trade Centre and Piccadilly Harbour both had a major office component (Fig. 5.7). The Grand Island Scheme (ex Gaythorn Gas Works) is basically an office-development site and is now secured through the proposed British Council move. Granada's Media City on both sides of the Irwell again has a large office component, as will the Northern Gateway project astride the Irwell near the Cathedral. Significantly, two projects which are likely to proceed (the Concert Hall initiative and the Great Northern Festival Market Place) both contain a significant office element which will in effect sub-sidize the leisure component. However, the Castlefield Urban Heritage Park, for tourism, which does not contain an office component, has attracted very little private investment. On the northern side of the city centre office schemes are once again being considered for Victoria Station and the zone north of Shudehill, but unless the office boom continues and/or the Metrolink light rail project significantly enhances the accessibility of these areas, it is doubtful whether any development will materialize.

Following the success of the 1985 conversion of the Granby House ware-house into flats (one of the first schemes in Manchester to receive a UDG) there has been increased developer interest in similar schemes as well as some new building. Under the Phoenix Initiative several proposals were put forward for warehouse conversions in the Whitworth Street Corridor, and subsequently these have come under the umbrella of the CMDC. The components of this programme are either completed or well advanced, including Granby Village (211 flats), India House (140 flats) and Lancaster House (115 flats). Some of these properties are for sale whilst others have been retained by housing associations as affordable housing. Another con-version, Chepstow House (76 flats) is proceeding without subsidy. New-build properties are in progress or planned for Piccadilly Village, Piccadilly Harbour, Great Bridgewater Street and Castle Quay, usually involving a direct or indirect subsidy.

5.9 CONCLUSION

The conjunction of an office boom and an urban policy geared to prop-erty development produced a rash of proposals in 1988–9 and some

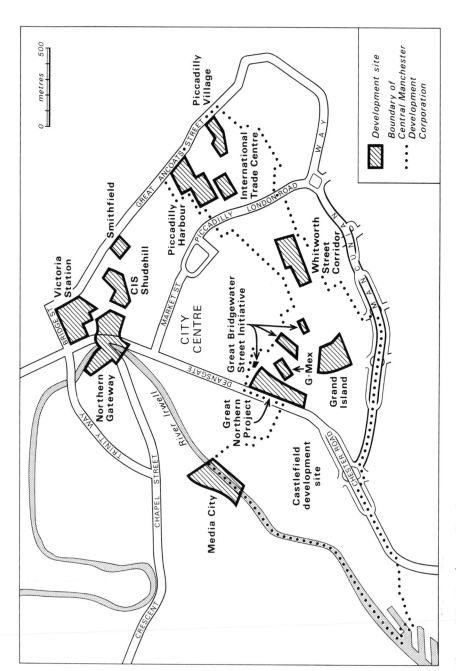

Figure 5.7 Manchester City Centre

construction in Inner Manchester on a scale not witnessed for over a decade encouraging the heady prospect of substantial urban regeneration. However, this has not been without its problems.

The scale of the office proposals, suggesting oversupply, and the fear that the boom may be coming to an end, has meant that some developers are now hesitant about proceeding with their schemes. In the city centre most of the office proposals on the northern side are in obeyance, a situation reminiscent of the mid-1970s. Development is proceeding and is most likely to continue to do so on the south side where there is a combination of natural trends towards the southern suburbs and assistance from a development corporation. In the docks area office development is proceeding rapidly in those parts included within the enterprise zone in order to get the tax benefits before they expire in 1991. The 1–2 million square feet of offices now in the pipeline have appeared to blight the Trafford Wharfside scheme, which is mainly outside the EZ with the result that the development corporation has had to revise the proposals, phasing them over a longer period with a delayed and smaller start.

Second, it is apparent that many schemes involving leisure, tourism, retailing and residential components, activities considered desirable for urban regeneration, are in fact underpinned by office development. If the office boom collapses will these whole schemes collapse, and if so how much will this harm the urban revitalization process?

Third, the property market is highly selective in terms of sectors. Investment has been heavily biased towards office activities. These provide white-collar jobs involving a high skill component. Whilst these should not be discouraged, they do little for most residents of the inner city who are looking for low-skilled jobs, such as are found in industry, distribution and, possibly, tourism.

Fourth, as in US cities, property investment is highly selective geographically. The city centre is the favoured location, although in the case of Inner Manchester, a new focus has appeared in the former docks area, aided by inner city policy and now perceived as prestigious. However, most of the inner city is neglected, and this includes east Manchester where over 20 000 jobs were lost between 1971 and 1985.

If the prospect of a downturn in development was only temporary, say a year or two, before the market picked up again, then there might be little to worry about, but if, as previously, Manchester must wait another decade, then it is a cause for concern. The problem which Manchester faces is typical of many northern industrial cities in the UK. As the rate of growth in the economy improves it is first manifest in London and the South-East and only subsequently trickles down to other regions (Fig. 5.4). However, just when the effects are beginning to be felt in the peripheral regions, the national and South-Eastern economy overheats and the government has to apply the brakes. Consequently, the boom for cities like Manchester is soon over. Provincial cities need policies which will divert economic functions away from the South East towards them and on a long-term and sustained basis. Property and land development, and environmental improvement are not inimical to long-term policies of growth for these cities, indeed they have an essential part to play, but need to be incorporated within a wider perspective. Within Inner Manchester there are three local authorities, two development corporations and a burgeoning private sector, all wishing to play a role. Even if a national strategy existed, it is not clear how co-ordinated policies would emerge in this area, although happily in recent months there has been improved co-operation. Certainly, a strategy for Inner Manchester needs national, economic and social as well as property development components.

6

THE RISE AND FALL OF THE PROPERTY MARKET IN TYNE AND WEAR

David Usher and Simin Davoudi

6.1 THE CONTEXT OF TYNE AND WEAR

Tyne and Wear is a classic industrial conurbation with all of the implications of that term for inner-city problems. Located in the North East of England it consists of the five districts of Newcastle, Gateshead, North and South Tyneside and Sunderland. In common with several other industrial conurbations the area suffered devastating manufacturing decline which reached its nadir in the early 1980s. The manufacturing sector, based upon coal, shipbuilding and heavy engineering, experienced the loss of 70 000 jobs in the period 1971–84, representing a decline of 43%. In a similar vein, Greater Manchester lost over 73 000 manufacturing jobs in the period 1971–81, a fall of 51%. Manufacturing job losses have been partially offset by the proverbial shift in the balance of the economy away from manufacturing towards services, and especially producer services (Cameron, 1990). Tyne and Wear contains a total population of just over one million, of whom 332 139 were in employment during 1984. There were 59 078 unemployed persons in Tyne and Wear (as at January, 1991) representing an unemployment rate of 12% which was almost twice the national average of 6.6%. Whilst unemployment fell from a high of 20% in 1985 there are indications that it is set to rise once again during the early 1990s, in line with national trends and as a consequence of national economic slowdown.

For some commentators the malaise represented in the decimation of the manufacturing industry was seen as terminal whilst for others the prescription of improved land and property markets in the late 1980s provided the antidote which averted administering the *coup de grâce* to a very sick conurbation. At the same time the vocabulary used to denote the economic situation has shifted from terms such as 'problem' and 'decline' to 'potential' and 'opportunity'.

6.2 URBAN POLICY SHIFTS TO BUSINESS AND PROPERTY INTERESTS

Urban policy directives exhorting government and business to become the dominant partners in regenerating local economies reached their apogee in the glossy brochure *Action for Cities* published in March, 1988. This publication was the first strategy document to address the Conservative government's concern to prioritize the solution of the inner-city problem. Nationally, this has resulted in a significant policy shift from the local to the national elected body (Harding, 1989b). Simultaneously, representatives of indigenous business communities have been exhorted to adopt corporate social responsibility for the regeneration of local economies (Judd and Parkinson, 1990).

In Tyne and Wear, which is characterized by a relatively narrow economic base, the same 30 business leaders are inevitably asked to sit on every government-appointed board ranging from direct policy interventions such as the TWDC (Tyne and Wear Development Corporation) TECs, (Training and Enterprise Councils) CATs (City Action Teams) and the CTC (City Technology College), to CBI-inspired initiatives such as the The Newcastle Initiative (TNI) and The Wearside Opportunity (TWO). If the private sector is to adopt a higher profile in the regeneration of the local economy then the agenda in Tyne and Wear is likely to be dominated by a narrow range of personnel drawn from a combination of banking, brewing, engineering and construction interests.

As with other industrial conurbations, the role of land and property development, induced by the backwash effect of the national property boom, represented a key strategy in the spheres of urban policy and economic development during the 1980s. As Law suggested in Chapter 4, it would be wrong to suggest that the Thatcher government's urban policy was concerned solely with property development. However, the emphasis upon levering private sector investment through public subsidy and the creation of frameworks (such as UDCs) in which property development was likely to occur took precedence over the encouragement of enterprise and training. This was reflected in the relative weighting of public monies made available to UDCs which became the major institution for the achievement of urban regeneration. For these reasons the link between local economic development and property development was strengthened as private investors were attracted to property development which came to represent a tangible symbol of regeneration serving to create confidence in the area. Mega-development projects representing 'monuments to Thatcherism' symbolized the economic prosperity which the Conservative administration aimed to deliver prior to the collapse of the property boom. In the context of Tyne and Wear, the Metro Centre, a 185 800 m² shopping mall located in the Tyneside Enterprise Zone, epitomized such a symbol and provided a profitable route into property development for local entrepreneur John Hall who backed the project.

6.3   INFLUENCES UPON LAND USE CHANGE AND DEVELOPMENT

This chapter aims to evaluate the impact of private-sector property development upon Tyne and Wear as the one example of the experience of an older industrial region of the regime of property development. There are many factors which promote land use change and development. These include the state of the property market, prevalent urban policy directions, the availability of finance capital and the type of property developer operating within a region. In Tyne and Wear all of these factors have influenced development activity, although the interaction of the local property market with policy measures has been especially important. As Law suggested, whilst government policy can stimulate development activity through creating a framework and environment and by giving grants, it cannot significantly affect the market in which developers operate. The success of urban policy during the 1980s has been heavily dependent upon improved local property market conditions. In the early–mid-1980s all sectors of the property market were stagnant with the possible exception of retailing which remained consistently buoyant. Private-sector investment was sluggish, hit by the deep industrial recession of the same period. By the mid-1980s, there were signs of an economic upturn, but this did not lead to increased development activity in the Tyne and Wear conurbation until the late 1980s. The most dramatic upturn was observed in the office market and was triggered by high demand throughout 1987–8 which began to exhaust existing office space. During the late 1980s office rents doubled, and in some cases tripled, from £4 per square foot to £12 per square foot. Tyne and Wear possessed a total office stock of just over 371 600 m² in the period 1980–5 (TWDC, 1989b). The upturn in the office market led to proposals to provide a further 325 150 m² of either newbuild or refurbished office space by late 1989. In theory this would have almost doubled the supply of available office space although many of these proposals were rescheduled in response to concerns about oversupply and economic slowdown.

Meanwhile, industrial property development was characterized by the least buoyant market conditions, although evidence of an improved market led to an increased level of private-sector property development. The industrial sector was dominated by a public-sector development agency, English Estates, which deliberately built low-cost premises in order to attract industrial development. This led to oversupply at low rents (Morgan, 1990). The sale of Washington New Town's industrial property to the London and Edinburgh Trust and a programme of rent increases by English Estates at the behest of central government served to increase the interest of local private developers.

Aside from impending supply shortages in the commercial and industrial sectors caused by the absence of newbuild activity in the early 1980s backwash effects from the South East's economic boom and international marketing strategies by Japanese companies both led to the attraction of new commercial and industrial users from outside the conurbation. During 1990, AA Insurance Services and British Airways announced intentions to relocate part of their business operations to Newcastle. Prior to this, the Japanese car manufacturer, Nissan, located its major assembly plant near Sunderland in 1985. In the period 1984–9, almost half of the new industrial floorspace completed in Tyne and Wear was built for the Nissan car plant and its component suppliers, providing evidence of the conurbation's narrow economic base.

6.4   URBAN POLICY IN THE 1980s – THE ENHANCED URBAN PROGRAMME

As suggested, the interaction between property market performance and public policy have been central in determining the success of the latter. Tyne and Wear has experienced virtually every kind of urban and regional policy ever implemented in the UK, with each policy variation being tested to destruction in its metropolitan laboratory (Robinson, 1989a). Early initiatives in the 1980s were the declaration of the Tyneside Enterprise Zone followed by the availability of Urban Development Grant (1982) renamed City Grant (1988). The progress encountered by these initatives was slow, due partly to their experimental nature, but mainly because private-sector investment was hit by the stagnant property market. The Tyneside Enterprise Zone was designated in 1981 and is one of the largest enterprise zones, covering 1120 acres on the north and south banks of the River Tyne and the southern end of the Team Valley Trading Estate. With the exception of the Metro Centre, other forms of commercial development only began to emerge in the late 1980s after the state of the property market improved.

In the case of City Grant, around 56 UDG/City Grant projects were approved in the period 1982–9 involving £26m of public grant aid in the Northern Region (Usher, 1989). Many of the UDGs were for housing projects although the incidence of commercial schemes grew in conjunction with improved demand after 1987.

By 1987, the Tyne and Wear Urban Development Corporation had come on the scene with the objective of further promoting private investment in urban regeneration projects and a budget of £180m over a 10-year period. This intervention raised considerably the profile of public policy and its impact upon development activity, although this was also premised upon an upturn in the property market. Whilst TWDC provided a strategic framework in which development could occur, the achievement of its targets became hostage to the misfortunes imposed by national economic slowdown. Some developers working on TWDC projects experienced financial difficulties with both short- and long-term implications for large-scale property ventures. Rosehaugh Stanhope Developments, whose subsidiary company Shearwater Property Holdings is involved in the £140m East Quayside Scheme, raised £125m through a rights issue during February 1990, reflecting the pressure experienced by the property industry. Meanwhile, Rush and Tompkins, a national contracting company with strong interests in Tyne and Wear, in general, and the TWDC-backed Closegate Hotel, in particular, went into receivership during April 1990; while Stanley Miller, a North-East contracting company and former partner with Shearwater in the East Quayside project, suffered a similar fate during May 1990. This series of events did not negate the relevant projects but highlighted the difficulties encountered by public policy during a period of market uncertainties.

Major commercial schemes were proposed for 54 sites in Newcastle by the end of 1989. Taken in conjunction, there were speculative proposals for the provision of 241 540 m^2 of office space in Newcastle and a grand total of 325 150 m^2 proposed for Tyne and Wear. Twelve of the schemes proposed for Newcastle were backed by TWDC, whilst a further five were enabled by City Grant. However, the remaining 37 schemes seem to have been proposed without an identifiable fix of public subsidy indicating the level of confidence in the market. Public subsidy gained increased relevance in the case of larger TWDC-backed projects. However, the need for City Grant and its forerunner UDG, may have been offset by improved property market conditions as higher development values were realized. On the other hand, the availability of City Grant, which is administered by TWDC within its boundaries, proved important given the problems encountered in reclaiming some riverside sites and their relative inaccessibility. As would be expected, the availability of larger amounts of subsidy through TWDC has served to increase the size of development projects proposed for the early 1990s. The proposed £140m East Quayside project, containing an element of around £34m of subsidy would not have emerged in the absence of the Tyne and Wear Development Corporation.

6.5 LURING THE FINANCIAL INSTITUTIONS

The availability of finance capital and the type of developer operating in an area are further related determinants upon the form and scale of land use change and development. Half of the property dealings by financial institutions in 1987 were in London. Fifty-one per cent of institutional property holdings are in London and a further 20% in the South East (*The Independent*, 1988). The corresponding figure for Tyne and Wear is less than 1%. When viewed in terms of the established hierarchy of investment by financial institutions in British cities it is perhaps remarkable that an increased level of institutional investment has been forthcoming in Tyne and Wear. A few investor-developers had entered the planning framework of TWDC by the early 1990s and this in turn reflected the size of schemes proposed. For example, the East Quayside project contained proposals for 20 902 m² of office space. Avatar were at advanced stages of proposing the 9290 m² refurbishment of the Royal Exchange Buildings on Newcastle's central Quayside, also for office space during 1990.

Institutional interest also became evident in the industrial property market with investors such as London and Edinburgh and Scottish Provident providing the financial backing for major industrial ventures on the north bank of the River Wear near Sunderland. These plans included 11 148 m² of business space at Hylton Riverside (London and Edinburgh Trust) and 13 935 m² at Castletown (Scottish Provident). Both projects were underpinned by public subsidy in the form of TWDC monies and Enterprise Zone status, the latter being designated for Sunderland during 1989. Industrial projects within the conurbation seem to have been influenced considerably by access to public subsidy reflecting the less confident nature of the industrial market. Industrial developments have tended to cluster in peripheral locations at the fringes of the conurbation in a variety of traditional industrial estates and new locations facilitated by public policy in the form of TWDC, City Grant and Enterprise Zone status. This is in contrast to office and retail developments which concentrated in central Newcastle and at the Metro Centre in Gateshead.

In spite of the evidence for increased institutional investment in the commercial and industrial sectors by the late 1980s, future escalation of this activity is questionable given the realities of local demand and economic slowdown in response to the high interest rates which characterized this period. Further, this scale of investment has only been observed in isolated flagship projects and these do not reflect the broader base of smaller developments undertaken by developers indigenous to the Northern Region. Of the 54 office developments proposed for central Newcastle, 38 (or 70%) were in the size range of 186–3716 m² and these were proposed mainly by local development companies. Seven projects of 9290 m² or more were proposed (or 13%) and were contained mainly within TWDC boundaries. These tended to be undertaken by national developers. Notwithstanding this, consortia of local developers also figured prominently in some of TWDC's flagship projects including the Newcastle Business Park and Royal Quays on the River Tyne and North Haven on the River Wear. National developers seem to have entered the conurbation on the back of an initial surge of development by local developers.

Retailing activity remained strong throughout the 1980s and this was premised upon the implications of lower housing costs for disposable incomes within the Northern Region. Development interest in the retail sector was maintained throughout the 1970s and 1980s manifest in Newcastle's Eldon Square Shopping Centre and Gateshead's Metro Centre, respectively. Apart from the Metro Centre most of the major retail schemes were undertaken by national and international retail developers and were enacted in central Newcastle, which acted as the region's retail and office capital. The 4645 m² Eldon Garden opened in Newcastle during 1989 and the majority of available units were let by the end of that year. A further 11 148 m² retail scheme was completed by the St Martins Property Group at Northumberland Court on Blackett Street. Meanwhile, proposals were at an advanced stage for a 16 722 m² redevelopment of the Haymarket site by Slough Estates and for the still more ambitious redevelopment by Guinea Properties of existing shopping facilities covering some 74 320 m² on Market Street. This latest proposal induced concern amongst retail estate agents about potential oversupply in the retail sector (*Estates Gazette*, 1990).

6.6   THE SPATIAL IMPACT OF PROPERTY DEVELOPMENT

Analysis of the impact of private-sector property development and its principal determinants highlights strong spatial differentiation within the conurbation. Whilst Tyne and Wear contains the major centres of Newcastle and Sunderland, Newcastle was undoubtedly the major beneficiary of the dramatic upturn in office and retail activity proposed during the late 1980s. This assertion is corroborated by updated work on the performance of major urban regions in Europe (Cheshire, 1990). This study indicated the substantial difference in the problem rating of Sunderland compared to Newcastle and the more rapid deterioration of Sunderland during the study period. Out of 117 European urban regions, Sunderland was rated at 113 whilst Newcastle was located at position 98. With the exception of industrial property, Newcastle maintained its dominance over the office and retail sectors during the 1980s. Whilst Sunderland's designation as an Enterprise Zone in conjunction with TWDC may pull development activity toward the district during the 1990s this will mainly affect industrial development and there is no reason to believe that the traditional role of Newcastle will be undermined. The chapter now turns to specific examination of the amount and type of development activity in the period 1984–9, based on original data obtained from the five Tyne and Wear District Planning Authorities (Davoudi and Usher, 1990).

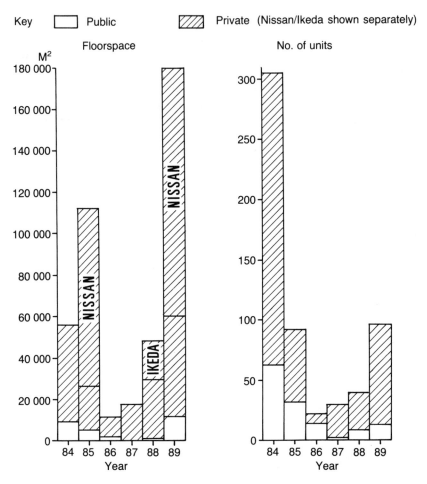

Figure 6.1 Units of industrial floorspace completed in Tyne and Wear 1984–9. Source: Local Authority Planning Department records

6.7   INDUSTRIAL DEVELOPMENT

6.7.1   Building trends

During the study period (1984–9), over 425 483 m² of industrial floorspace were completed in Tyne and Wear (Fig. 6.1), almost half of which was built for the Nissan car plant and its component suppliers on the site of Sunderland Airport. However, despite the Nissan development, the average annual rate of industrial completion in that period was reduced by 20%, compared with that of the previous five-year period (1979–83). The take-up for development of industrial land totalled about 607 ha or an average of about

51 ha per year between 1978 and 1989, which was far less than the County's Structure Plan forecast.

The amount of land allocated for industrial use but developed for alternative uses has also grown considerably since 1984, which reflects the process of de-industrialization that occurred. The largest of these sites are in Gateshead: 47 ha for the Metro Centre at Dunston and 10 ha for Retail World at the Team Valley. Both developments are in the Tyneside Enterprise Zone, where rates exemptions and capital allowances have also encouraged industrial developments, especially advance units.

The amount of vacant industrial floorspace, particularly among larger units, has been accelerating since 1982 and reached a peak in 1985. Although the demolition of some significant large, older premises in 1986 led to the reduction of the amount of space available, between 1986 and 1987 vacant industrial spaces virtually doubled. By 1989, however, they fell by about one sixth.

The considerable reduction in the average annual rate of industrial completions during the study period is mainly due to the decline of public-sector activity, whilst the average rate of private-sector completion has increased from 39 000 m^2 per year during 1979–83 (Tyne and Wear County Council 1981, 1982, 1983, 1984) to 66 072 m^2. During the study period, 94% of the total industrial floorspace was completed by the private sector. This shows an increase of over 50% on the previous six-year period when the private-sector share was only 44%.

By the early 1980s the provision of industrial property in Tyne and Wear, as elsewhere in the North East, was dominated by the public sector and particularly by English Estates and the Washington Development Corporation. In 1983, out of a total of 58 000 m^2 of new industrial development nearly two-thirds was developed by the public sector (Tyne and Wear County Council 1981, 1982, 1983, 1984). In 1988, the public-sector share was only 2%. While the winding up of Washington New Town and cutbacks in expenditure by English Estates and the local authorities severely reduced the public sector contribution, the designation of the Enterprise Zone stimulated private-sector interest.

Within the study period, industrial development experienced a V-shaped pattern: falling between 1984 and 1986 (excluding Nissan), and rising steadily afterwards (Table 6.1). However, the downward trend of the mid-1980s had started after a peak in 1981 when the Washington Development Corporation and English Estates were the main developers. This trend is illustrated by Fig. 6.2 after excluding the amount of floorspace provided for Findus (in Longbenton, North Tyneside) and Vickers (at Scotswood, Newcastle) in 1982. The latter was transferred from one part of the Enterprise Zone to another area.

With regard to the contribution of each district, Sunderland possessed the bulk of industrial floorspace completed between 1984 and 1989, of which

Table 6.1 Industrial floorspace (m²), completions by year and sector (*Source*: Local authority records)

Sector	1984	1985	1986	1987	1988	1989	Total
Private	46 516	105 050	9 739	17 651	47 343	168 137	396 436
Local authority	9 210	5 191	1 828	*	1 022	11 796	29 047
Total	55 726	112 241	11 567	17 651	48 365	179 933	425 483

* Two units were completed by the local authorities for which the figure for floorspace areas were not available.

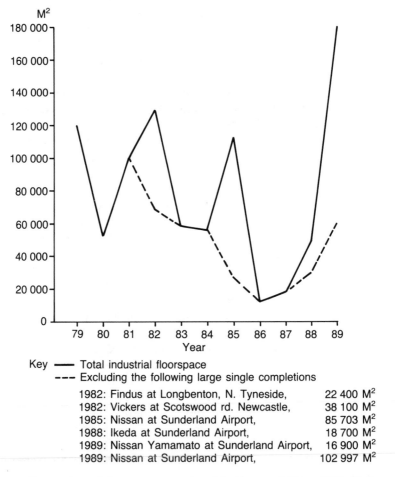

Key —— Total industrial floorspace
‐‐‐ Excluding the following large single completions

1982: Findus at Longbenton, N. Tyneside,	22 400 M²
1982: Vickers at Scotswood rd. Newcastle,	38 100 M²
1985: Nissan at Sunderland Airport,	85 703 M²
1988: Ikeda at Sunderland Airport,	18 700 M²
1989: Nissan Yamamato at Sunderland Airport,	16 900 M²
1989: Nissan at Sunderland Airport,	102 997 M²

Figure 6.2 Industrial floorspace completed in Tyne and Wear 1979–89. Source: 1979–83 figures from Tyne and Wear County Council, 1981, 1982, 1983, 1984; 1984–9 figures from Local Authority Planning Department records.

Table 6.2 Industrial floorspace and number of units in each district, 1984–9 (*Source*: Local Authority records)

	Newcastle	Gateshead	N. Tyne	S. Tyne	Sunderland	Total
Total floorspace (m²)	43 114	64 409	27 438	18 748	271 774	425 483
% of all Tyne and Wear	10.10	15.10	6.40	4.40	63.90	100.00
Total number of Units	124	178	74	83	126	585
% of all Tyne and Wear	21.20	30.40	12.70	14.20	21.50	100.00

224 300 m² were concentrated in three large units. If these units were excluded, Sunderland would drop to second position after Gateshead (Table 6.2).

The annual distribution of industrial floorspace completed in each district shows signs of increased activity in recent years, particularly in Sunderland and Gateshead, the former benefiting from new inward investment and the latter exploiting the advantages of the remaining tax-free life of the Enterprise Zone which ended in 1991.

6.7.2 Spatial distribution

The map of floorspace completed between 1984 and 1989 (Fig. 6.3) points to the significance of two major locations in Tyne and Wear, which attracted the bulk of recent industrial development: Sunderland Airport, a flat greenfield site close to the A19, and the Team Valley Enterprise Zone. Of the total industrial development in Sunderland, 77.4% is located at Sunderland Airport and is occupied by Nissan and its component suppliers. By the end of December 1989, 291 ha of land were made available for Nissan on this site, and a further 86 ha are being prepared to accommodate the future expansion of the Nissan plant and its component suppliers. The Team Valley Enterprise Zone has attracted 86.3% of total industrial floorspace in Gateshead. The proportion of Enterprise Zone completions to the total for Gateshead increased during the study period.

In addition to these two major locations, other major industrial developments are located either along the banks of the River Tyne or at peripheral locations in northern Tyneside. Boldon Business Park also became an attractive location for industrial development. Forty-three ha of land were prepared in this location in 1986, but they were not developed until 1988 when 1022 m² were completed by South Tyneside Council. Later in 1989, a further 4692 m² were completed by English Estates.

Among the peripheral locations in northern Tyneside, the Airport Industrial

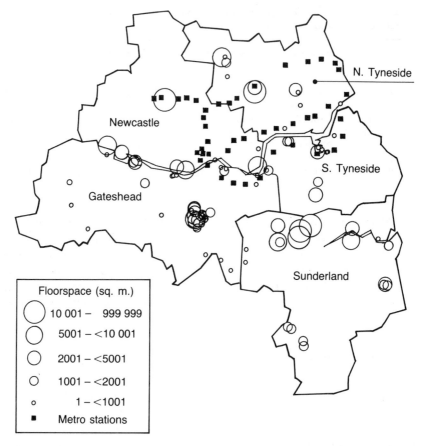

Figure 6.3   Industrial floorspace completed in Tyne and Wear 1984–9. Source: Local Authority Planning Department records

Estate and the North Tyne Industrial Estate are the most important, with Killingworth and the West Chirton Industrial Estate coming next. Some of the important sites along the Tyne include the Armstrong Centre at Vickers Elswick, the Newburn Industrial Estate, and the Walker Naval Yard.

6.8   RETAIL DEVELOPMENT

6.8.1   Building trends

During the study period more than 265 207 m² of new retail floorspace were completed in Tyne and Wear, of which 56% was completed in 1986–7 (Table 6.3).

The high level of completions in 1986–7 is due to the construction of

Table 6.3 Annual completions of retail floorspace (*Source*: Local Authority records)

	1984	*1985*	*1986*	*1987*	*1988*	*1989*	*Total*
Total floorspace (m²)	18 004	26 700	71 207	75 169	37 729	36 398	265 207
% of total	6.80	10.10	26.90	28.30	14.20	13.70	100.00

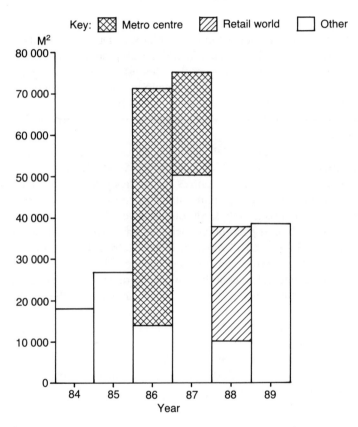

Figure 6.4 Retail floorspace completed in Tyne and Wear 1984–9. Source: Local Authority Planning Department records

phases 1 and 2 of the Metro Centre in 1986 and phases 3 and 4 in 1987, in the Enterprise Zone. However, as Fig. 6.4 shows, 1987 witnessed a substantial increase in new retail floorspace even outside the Enterprise Zone, although the largest proportion of it is still elsewhere in Gateshead. Completions in 1988 are dominated by the floorspace provided in the Team Valley's Retail World. Overall, more than half of Tyne and Wear's retail developments between 1984–9 were completed in Gateshead (Table 6.4).

Table 6.4 Retail floorspace by districts, 1984–9 (*Source*: Local Authority records)

	Newcastle	Gateshead	N. Tyne	S. Tyne	Sunderland	Total
Total floorspace (m²)	38 223	142 719	14 737	34 174	35 354	265 207
% of total Tyne and Wear	14.40	53.80	5.60	12.90	13.30	100.00

Construction of the Metro Centre complex at Dunston, on the western side of Gateshead, and the Retail World development at the Team Valley, in south-west Gateshead, represent the greatest change to the retail system in Tyne and Wear in the 1980s. Both developments are within the Tyneside Enterprise Zone where the tax concessions available within the Zone and freedom from structure plan control played an important role in stimulating development.

The Metro Centre and Retail World together account for 84% of new durable goods floorspace provided during the 1980s. However, at the same time, other established main centres, apart from Newcastle, have either remained stable or declined, particularly in terms of durable floorspace. Vacant floorspace also doubled. Although Newcastle has the largest amount of vacancies, the largest percentage increases have been in Gateshead, North Shields and Killingworth (Tyne and Wear Metropolitan Districts, 1988a, 1989a). The same pattern has occurred in the secondary centres; a new centre has been established in Kingston Park whilst there has been an overall decline in floorspace in the existing centres, and an increase in the vacancy rate. However, the downward trend in secondary centres might change if new proposals in the pipeline for Boldon Colliery and Kingston Park go ahead.

By contrast, off-centre shopping development in Tyne and Wear witnessed major growth, especially for DIY goods, with an increase of some 65 030 m² since 1976/78, excluding the Metro Centre and Retail World (Tyne and Wear Metropolitan Districts, 1988a, 1989a).

6.8.2 Spatial distribution

As Fig. 6.5 shows, most of the new retail developments were located in the Enterprise Zone and other off-centre locations. Forty-one per cent of the Tyne and Wear completions were in the Gateshead Enterprise Zone, mostly at the Metro Centre. Outside the zone, the largest single development in Gateshead was the Interchange Centre on top of the Gateshead Metro Station, where 10 210 m² of commercial floorspace were completed in 1987.

After the Enterprise Zone, the second major location with regard to the proportion of new retail floorspace completed between 1984 and 1989 is

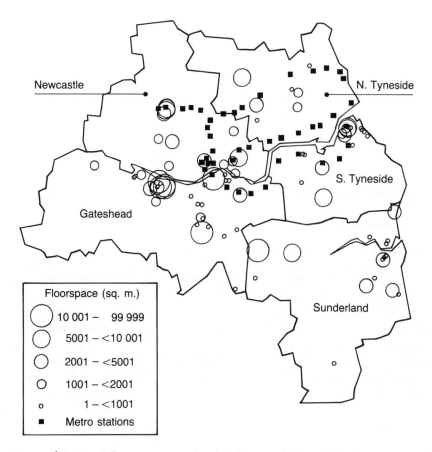

Figure 6.5 Retail floorspace completed in Tyne and Wear 1984–9. Source: Local Authority Planning Department records

South Shields which accounts for nearly 8.2% of total Tyne and Wear completions, and 63.8% of the total South Tyneside completions. Outside of South Shields, the most significant retail development within South Tyneside between 1984 and 1989 is at Boldon Colliery.

The third major location is Washington New Town, accounting for 7.8% of all Tyne and Wear completions and 58% of Sunderland's completions. The fourth significant location is Kingston Park which accounts for 6.2% of Tyne and Wear's and 43.2% of Newcastle's retail completions during 1984–9.

Apart from these clusters, other major shopping developments account for some 36.5% of the total Tyne and Wear completions during the study period. These mostly take the form of large freestanding units, with the exception of the Eldon Garden which includes 46 small units (4645 m²) added to the Eldon Square Shopping Centre in 1988.

Table 6.5 Annual completion of office floorspace (m²) (*Source*: 1984–7 figures, Tyne and Wear Metropolitan Districts (1988a, 1989a), 1988–9 figures, Tyne and Wear Metropolitan Districts (1988b, 1989b)

	1984	*1985*	*1986*	*1987*	*1988*	*1989*	*Total*
New build	6 032	10 274	5 289	12 386	11 536	79 000	124 517
Conversion	3 462	4 766	2 580	4 087	1 126	24 136	40 157
Total	9 494	15 040	7 869	16 473	12 662	103 136	164 674

6.9 OFFICE DEVELOPMENT

6.9.1 Building trends

During the period 1984–9 124 517 m² of office floorspace were completed in Tyne and Wear, almost entirely by the private sector. Over the same period 40 157 m² of office floorspace were provided by conversion or refurbishment of older premises (Table 6.5).

Throughout the early 1980s growth in office jobs, development and rental levels was substantially halted by the impact of recession. New office developments completed in the early 1980s but conceived in the more buoyant market of the late 1970s were slow to let. Therefore, the vacancy rate increased to its highest level (8.6%) since the mid-1970s. Hardly any development was started during 1981–3 (Tyne and Wear County Council, 1981, 1982, 1983, 1984). Consequently, 1984 witnessed a substantial reduction in office completions. This factor, together with an upturn in demand and the growth of office rents, led to the reduction of vacancy rates to about 6% of the total stock by the mid-1980s.

Further, a degree of economic recovery, especially in the service sector, resulted in a considerable upturn in the office market by the late 1980s. The revival of the office market in the late 1980s led to the quick reduction of the vacancy rate and saw increases in rentals from around £3 per square foot in the early 1980s to about £10–12 per square foot by the late 1980s. In 1989, the amount of new floorspace provided in the county rose to almost 79 000 m² which was the highest recorded in the period 1978–89 (Fig. 6.6). In addition to the completed schemes, there are several major office projects, either under construction, or at the proposal stage. If these projects materialized total office space in Tyne and Wear would be doubled. However, many of the proposed office developments are highly speculative and are unlikely to be built, or alternatively, may be scaled down.

Meanwhile, Newcastle city centre remained as the dominant office location in Tyne and Wear, serving as the regional capital. Almost 75% of office development in 1989 was located in Newcastle with the most significant development (37 160 m²) being located on the Business Park (Tyne and

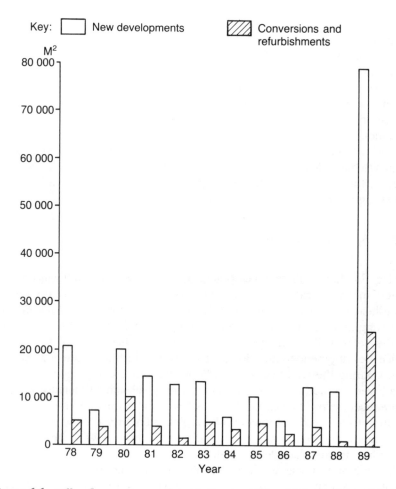

Figure 6.6 Office floorspace completed in Tyne and Wear 1978–89 (1978–87 figures from Tyne and Wear Metropolitan Districts, 1988a, 1989a; 1988–9 figures from Tyne and Wear Metropolitan Districts, 1988b, 1989b)

Wear Metropolitan Districts, 1988b, 1989b), where Enterprise Zone status and the Tyne and Wear Development Corporation's support had a major impact in stimulating development. Further, a large amount of office floorspace was provided by conversion, refurbishment and change of use in Tyne and Wear. In 1989, the level of refurbished office premises (24 136 m²) was the highest recorded in the period 1978–89. Over 51% of this refurbishment was carried out in Sunderland, 39% in Newcastle and the remainder in South Tyneside (Tyne and Wear Metropolitan Districts, 1988b, 1989b).

North and South Tyneside had a very low level of activity up until the mid-1980s. Between 1984 and 1989 there was only one office development completed in North Tyneside (Albion House) by English Estates at North Shields. In South Tyneside between 1978 and 1986, only two units were completed at the Denmark Centre as part of a mixed-use development in 1985. However, there have been signs of recovery, especially in South Shields town centre, notably through the completion of 1408 m² (20 units) at Cookson House in 1989.

Although Sunderland is defined by the structure plan as the main second-ary office centre in Tyne and Wear, the designation of the Enterprise Zone seems to have altered the balance in favour of Gateshead. During the study period, the amount of office floorspace provided in Gateshead was 2.6 times higher than that in Sunderland.

6.9.2 Spatial distribution

As Fig. 6.7 shows, office development between 1984 and 1989 was concen-trated in two locations (Newcastle city centre and the Team Valley, Gateshead). The city centre has continued to dominate the office market, attracting investment in both new building and refurbishment. In the case of the Team Valley, Enterprise Zone designation has attracted speculative office development to this long-established industrial estate for the first time. During the study period 86.8% of total office completions in Gates-head were located at the Team Valley, with a substantial increase in 1989. More recently, the Newcastle Business Park has become another significant location for office development. Although the Enterprise Zone status of the site ended in 1991, generous public subsidy from TWDC brought new incentives to stimulate development.

In addition to these key locations, Fig. 6.7 also indicates office develop-ments concentrating in a number of secondary centres such as Sunderland and South Shields, at out-of-town locations such as Washington New Town, and around the periphery of the city centre at Gosforth.

6.10 HOUSING DEVELOPMENT

6.10.1 Building trends

During the study period 17 876 dwellings were completed in Tyne and Wear, around 4000 fewer than in the previous six-year period 1978–83. The considerable reduction in the total number of dwellings completed is due mainly to the fall in public-sector house building in general and local au-thority completions in particular. During 1988, only 68 dwellings were com-pleted by the five Tyne and Wear districts, compared with 356 completions by housing associations and 2214 by the private sector (Table 6.6).

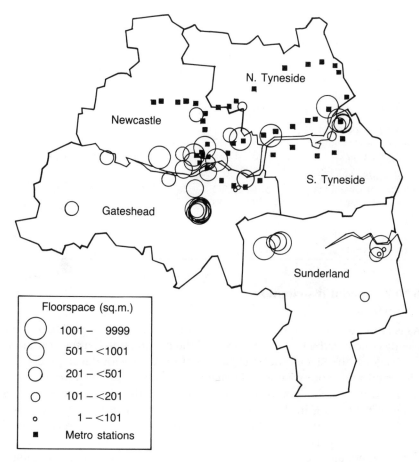

Figure 6.7 Office floorspace completed in Tyne and Wear 1984–9. Source: Authority Planning Department records

The private sector now plays the dominant role in house building, accounting for 73.4% of houses completed in Tyne and Wear between 1984 and 1989. This is a considerable increase on the previous six-year period when the private sector share was just 45%.

As Fig. 6.8 shows, public sector completions have steadily declined. This is largely due to the fall in local authority completions, as housing association building rates remained fairly constant. Meanwhile, private-sector completions fell in the mid-1980s and recovered afterwards, in line with a strengthening housing market and rising prices. In the late 1980s private house builders tended to move away from low-price/status schemes which they favoured in the early 1980s towards more expensive houses at the upper end of the market.

Table 6.6 Dwellings completed by sectors, and by year (*Source*: Local Authority records)

	1984	1985	1986	1987	1988	1989	Total
Private							
Number of dwellings	2 693	1 995	1 732	1 875	2 214	2 608	13 117
% of total year	69.60	68.70	70.00	67.50	83.90	81.10	71.90
Housing Association							
Number of dwellings	615	517	477	663	356	495	3 123
% of total year	15.90	17.80	19.30	23.90	13.50	15.40	17.70
Local Authority							
Number of dwellings	561	390	264	240	68	113	1 636
% of total year	14.50	13.40	10.70	8.60	2.60	3.50	10.40
Totals							
Number of dwellings	3 869	2 902	2 473	2 778	2 638	3 216	17 876
% of total year	100	100	100	100	100	100	100

6.10.2 Spatial distribution

As is illustrated by Figs. 6.9 and 6.10, whilst public sector completions were clearly concentrated in the inner areas of the conurbation (particularly along the banks of the River Tyne), the pattern of private-sector development was dispersed and more complex. Private-sector developers have traditionally favoured greenfield suburban sites, but since 1980–1 they showed greater interest in building in the inner areas for a number of reasons including: market demand (particularly for the low-price/starter-home sector); land availability (especially sites released by local authorities unable to finance development themselves); the availability of grants; the setting up of public/ private partnerships; and the changing attitude of developers toward developing brownfield sites. The proportion of private-sector completions in inner areas, as defined by the Tyne and Wear Structure Plan, to the total number of inner area completions increased from 48% in 1983 (Tyne and Wear County Council, 1981, 1982, 1983, 1984) to 73.8% in 1989. However, it should be noted that this increase was due largely to the fall in public-sector activities which were concentrated in inner areas. In fact, in 1989 only 29% of private-sector completions were located in inner areas, showing only a marginal increase (8%) since 1983. Thus, it can be suggested that the private sector predominantly still favours sites on the periphery of the built-up area.

6.11 CONCLUSIONS

The progress of private property development in Tyne and Wear during the 1980s was closely bound up with the rapidly changing fortunes of the

Key: ▨ Private   ☐ Public (LA and HA)

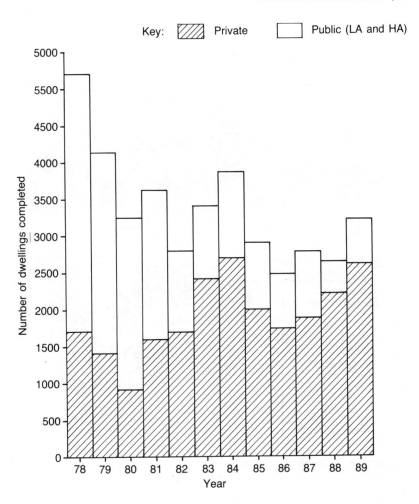

Figure 6.8 Dwellings completed in Tyne and Wear 1978–89. Source: 1978–83 figures from local housing statistics; 1984–9 figures from Local Authority records

property market. Urban policy initiatives introduced throughout the decade encouraged the speculative thrust in the property market which characterized the boom period. However, the momentum of this new development activity, which started late in the case of Tyne and Wear, was soon called into question by the economic slowdown of the early 1990s, although the impact of the recession was much less in the North East than in the South. Whilst development activity received a boost from the generous public subsidies available through the Tyne and Wear Development Corporation, the success of property development hinged upon the wider performance of the property market. Rental values proved to be a key determinant of the overall level of activity proposed within the commercial sector. Through

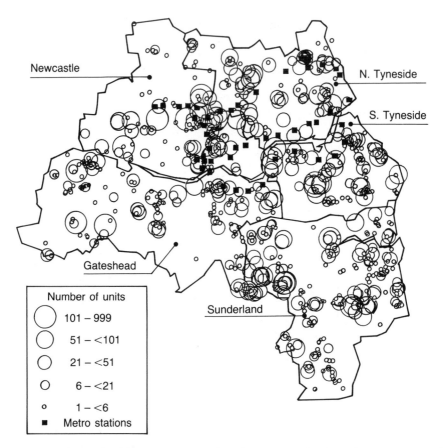

Figure 6.9   Privately developed residential units completed 1984–9. Source: Local Authority Planning Department records

the course of the 1980s the property market emerged out of a slump, then experienced a mini boom before reverting to uncertainty by the end of the decade.

The conurbation remained sheltered from the slowdown in inward investment and the collapse of the national property market, in contrast to the South East, up until the end of 1990. Further, by working closely with local developers, the Tyne and Wear Development Corporation was able to maintain the momentum of property development by fine tuning the level of development activity to potential demand from business relocators. This demand remained buoyant as a result of overheated conditions in the South East and international companies aiming to establish a foothold in European markets prior to the advent of the Single European Market in 1992. However, by the end of the 1990 there were clear signs that the property

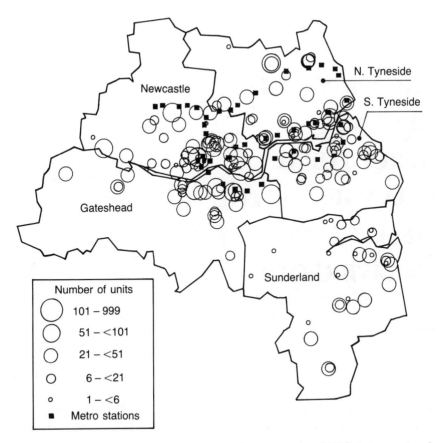

Figure 6.10 LA and HA developed residential units completed 1984–9. Source: Local Authority Planning Department records

market was stagnating once again, albeit in the context of enhanced property values. Additionally, as recession deepened the demand for new premises on a large scale became less certain. In these terms the tonic provided by a heightened level of development activity proved to be short lived as the Tyne and Wear Development Corporation reviewed its ability to deliver property-based performance targets during the first part of the 1990s. This necessitated the pursuit of alternative development agendas in the areas of business investment and environmental improvement as the property route to urban regeneration failed to deliver far-reaching change in the built environment. As the conurbation turned to face the 1990s the relatively limited level of land use change achieved during the property boom combined with the rescheduling of commercial projects raised major questions over the likely scale of development activity during a full-blown recession.

7

VACANCY AND RECENT STRUCTURAL CHANGES IN THE DEMAND FOR LAND IN LIVERPOOL

Chris Couch and Steven Fowles

In the development of urban policy the problem of derelict and vacant land has evolved, in the perception of government, from an issue of social expenses where reaction to public concern about environmental degredation and safety was the paramount concern, to a situation in which the issue of inefficiency in the economic use of scarce resources dominates. Government has increasingly become concerned to avoid valuable urban land being withheld from beneficial use, for whatever reason.

During the late 1970s the property development industry played an important part in changing perceptions through its lobbying of government, asking it to encourage local authorities and statutory undertakers to release unwanted vacant land for development and to be more 'realistic' in price negotiations. Such lobbying was influential in the creation of Public Sector Land Registers, Urban Development Corporations and other public policies intended to bring forward vacant public-sector land for private development in the 1980s.

According to the Department of the Environment's own estimates there is very nearly one hectare of derelict land in England for every 1000 inhabitants (Couch, _et al._, 1989). In a 1974 survey the DoE put the total figure at around 43 273 hectares, by 1982 and in spite of the reclamation of 16 952 hectares the figure had climbed to 45 683 hectares. The latest figures, based on a survey carried out in 1988, show a slight reduction to 40 489 hectares, with some 14 013 hectares having been reclaimed in the intervening period. (DoE, 1989b, p. 12 *et seq.*).

In spite of this quite high level of reclamation activity and the apparent recent fall in the amount of dereliction it has to be acknowledged that all these surveys considerably and consistently underestimate the scale of the overall problem of vacant and derelict land facing the country, for they exclude sites not falling within the statutory definition of 'derelict' (e.g. simply vacant urban land) and small sites. A further point is that this data relates to vacant and derelict land and says nothing about vacant buildings or parts of buildings, such as the upper-floor vacancy which is rife in many UK shopping streets. As a consequence of these omissions it is particularly urban vacancy that is underestimated.

Indeed, one of the features of urban dereliction and vacancy as an economic phenomenon is just how little is known. According to Cameron *et al.* (1988, p. 119)

> The biggest single research gap is that we do not know whether the vacant land problem is getting worse, or better, or staying the same.

A further major failing of existing literature and analysis is, according to the same report, that it fails to identify the relative importance and weight to attach to the various competing explanations and theories of dereliction and vacancy.

> We have found . . . that a whole host of different classifications of the cause of vacant land problems has been used. So we need to strive towards a more consistent approach to investigating the causes of land vacancy. The unemployment analogue has perhaps as much potential here as any other. We might ask whether vacancy is qualitative, frictional, demand deficient, cyclical or structural.
>
> (Cameron *et al.*, 1988, p. 120).

While it should be acknowledged that there are significant differences in the nature of land and labour as factors of production we would suggest that the way in which they are demanded and used in production is sufficiently similar to justify some further exploration of the analogy.

First, it is necessary to distinguish the causes of initial vacancy from the causes of continuing vacancy. Initial vacancy may be caused by: 1. a cyclical decline in the aggregate demand for goods and services, or; 2. the weak competitive position of an individual firm; or 3. a structural change in the demand for an individual firms's output; or 4. a change in the firm's means of production. Any of these changes may lead to a reduction in the area or intensity of land used in production and to total or partial vacancy. These causes of initial vacancy as the by-product of industrial change have been analysed in recent years and are generally well understood (Bruton and Gore, 1980; Markowski, 1978; MacGregor *et al.*, 1985). Our concern here is with the explanation of the causes of continuing vacancy, i.e. why this vacant land is not immediately returned to beneficial use. It is here that the unemployment analogy may be useful.

The major explanations of unemployment that may be of use to us here are 1. frictional reasons, 2. reasons of demand deficiency, and 3. structural changes in demand or technological conditions. Such an approach clearly sets our analysis within the context of neo-classical economics.

Frictional unemployment is usually defined as resulting from the time lags involved in redeployment. Time lags in the re-use of land may result from a variety of causes, such as poor marketing of land, slow decision-making procedures, and so forth. The primary characteristic of frictional unemployment is that it occurs in a situation where there is sufficient demand to absorb the available supply. Thus policies aimed at reducing friction in the land market will only work to the extent that there exists a potential demand for the land which can be turned into effective demand.

Structural unemployment occurs when there is some basic long-term change in the nature of demand or technological conditions. With regard to the 'unemployment' of land, Cameron *et al.*, 1988, p. 120 suggest that:

> The structural under-utilisation of land may, in this context, be caused by two different phenomena, the first being the long run substitution of land by capital so that the land to output ratio falls; the second being a shift in demand favouring different areas of the urban land market.

In our view the first of these phenomena is more useful as an explanation of cessation of use or initial vacancy but it is clearly not the case that the land-to-output ratio is falling in all market sectors (consider the differences between the increasing density of city centre office developments and the decreasing density of out-of-town hypermarkets). Therefore, as an explanation of continuing vacancy it is only likely to be of use in the rare situations where sectors of the land market are discrete and not subject to competitive demand from other sectors.

The second phenomenon can be perceived in urban areas where vacancy has resulted from: changes in locational preferences such as the increasing attraction of proximity to motorway junctions (and the decreasing attraction of proximity to railway access), or the greater importance attached to local environmental conditions rather than access considerations for some types of industry or services; and also changes in the type of premises demanded, which may lead to the rejection of very small sites, buildings of awkward shape or lacking certain characteristics. In contrast to the first phenomenon these are more likely explanations of continuing vacancy (structural) as some sites are deemed inappropriate by certain users.

The market demand for land is, of course, quite different from that emanating from an individual firm. Thus when a firm ceases to use a site for any of the reasons outlined above, it says nothing about the general market demand for land. If the market for land is buoyant the site is likely to be speedily re-used whereas in periods of slack land demand vacancy is more likely to continue. Even in circumstances where land is underused because of cyclical decline in aggregate demand for goods and services affecting all firms it does not follow that any vacant land that is released on to the market will necessarily face a sluggish land market: the movement of building cycles does not correspond well with trade cycles (but see Ball, 1988, p. 98) and the land market even less so. Nevertheless the point being made is that some land will remain vacant, not for frictional reasons, nor because of structural changes in the nature of demand for land but simply because it faces a low level of demand brought about by cyclical movements in the land market.

7.1 VACANCY IN LIVERPOOL

In this paper we are seeking to undertake some empirical testing of vacancy in order to begin to establish the amount of vacancy occurring within each unemployment category (frictional, demand deficient or structural), and to say something about the nature of the constraints upon re-use within each type. Our empirical work only considers trends in the City of Liverpool over the last 10 to 15 years and so cannot be taken as a strong indication of general patterns of vacancy occurring across the country. Nevertheless we feel that even this work reveals some interesting features of the local land market and offers some guidance for the direction of future research.

Liverpool first became significant as a city in the 18th century, as the port on the River Mersey began to expand with the growth of trade between Britain and its former colonies. The industrial revolution with the rise and concentration of economic activity in North-West England and Yorkshire led to rapid urban growth. The City of Liverpool reached a peak in terms of population size in the 1930s, while the conurbation (including suburban and peripheral areas beyond the city boundary) continued to grow well into the 1960s. However, dispersal of the population through housing renewal programmes led to a fall in population and economic activity within the administrative city boundaries. This trend was overlain by further out-migration caused by economic decline: the result of shifting patterns of national and international trade, decline of the region's manufacturing base, the increasing peripherality of the area for investment, together with substantial gains in the productivity of the port and associated industries.

The most dramatic loss of employment has occurred in the manufacturing sector, where the number of jobs in the city had fallen from 130 000 in 1961 to only 47 500 by 1985 (a drop of 64% and nearly twice the national average rate of change). Over the same period local employment in the growth sector of white-collar services (financial and business services, health, education and public administration) had increased by 31%, less than half the national average of 68% (Liverpool City Planning Department). Economic decline has not only led to labour unemployment but also to vacancy or unemployment in the stock of land and buildings.

In this work we have used three main data sources. The first is a register of void and vacant hereditaments maintained by Liverpool City Council Rating Section based upon their own and Local Valuation Office information. The data recorded includes use codes, date of first entry on to the register, and location. The advantages of using this data in our analysis were that the use codes, the method and purpose of data collection, and the responsible agency had been constant over a number of years. The disadvantages were that the use classification of each hereditament depends upon conventions which might vary between Valuation Offices and even upon the interpretations of individual officers, and that the size (floorspace) of vacant premises is not recorded. We analysed data from the registers for three separate years: 1981, 1984 and 1988. The information we were able to extract included the total number of voids in each year, the length of time a hereditament had been on the register (period of vacancy), the general location, and the use classification of each void hereditament.

Our second data source is the Land Availability Resource System (LARS), which is a periodically updated survey of land and buildings with development potential (vacant premises) undertaken by the City Planning Department. This system has been in existence for about 15 years but its use has diminished in recent years and there are reasons to suspect that its accuracy (particularly with regard to omissions) has also diminished. Our use of the LARS data has therefore been confined to using the 1981 data as an accurate record of a population of vacant sites from which we have drawn a 20% sample of 200 sites known to have been vacant at that time. This sample provides data on the location, size and ownership of vacancy at that time. Furthermore it provides the basis for our own 1989 survey. This involved checking the present condition of these sites to ascertain whether they have remained vacant or have been re-used for some beneficial use. Our basic findings are shown in Fig. 7.1.

Given that frictional unemployment results from the time lags involved in the redeployment of labour, then if we can identify the length of time land or buildings have been vacant it should be possible for us to distinguish short-term vacancy (which we might use as a proxy for the frictional unemployment of land) from other causes of vacancy. We acknowledge that this is a relatively weak proxy since it is possible for frictional problems to drag on into the long term and also that the amount of friction in the market is not entirely independent of the general level of market demand. Nevertheless it

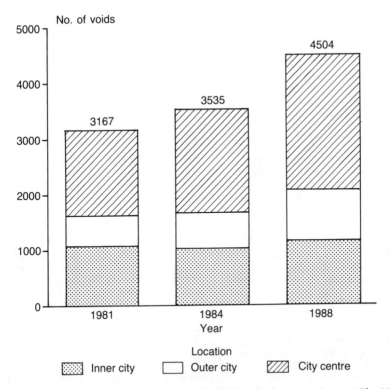

Figure 7.1 Void hereditaments in Liverpool 1981–8, by location. Source: The Void and Vacant Hereditaments Register, Liverpool Valuation Office

Table 7.1 · Void hereditaments and labour unemployment in Liverpool (1981–8) (*Sources*: 1. The Void and Vacant Hereditaments Registers for Liverpool, Liverpool Valuation Office. 2. Past Trends and Future Prospects, Liverpool City Council, February 1987)

	1981	Change 1981–4	1984	Change 1984–8	1988	Change 1981–8
Total voids	3 167	+11.6%	3 535	+27.4%	4 504	+42.2%
Labour unemployment	47 165	+18.3%	55 779	−3.2%	54 000*	+6.8%

* Approximate.

seems reasonable to assume that where land and buildings are vacant for longer periods of time they will tend to be in that condition because of deficiencies or structural changes in demand rather than for frictional reasons.

Table 7.1 provides some information of relevance. The first simple point of note is that the number of vacant premises in Liverpool has risen by more

Table 7.2 Total number of void hereditaments by year of first registration (period of vacancy) (*Source*: The Void and Vacant Hereditaments Registers for Liverpool, Liverpool Valuation Office)

Year of first registration	1981 No.	1981 %	1984 No.	1984 %	1988 No.	1988 %
1974*	549	17.3	349	9.9	239	5.3
1975	191	6.0	105	3.0	74	1.6
1976	234	7.4	134	3.8	99	2.2
1977	252	8.0	119	3.4	65	1.4
1978	370	11.7	147	4.2	69	1.5
1979	477	15.1	178	5.0	105	2.3
1980	1001 ⎫		272	7.7	144	3.2
1981	93 ⎬	34.5†	380	10.8	185	4.1
1982			572	16.2	237	5.3
1983			1093 ⎫		378	8.4
1984			186 ⎬	36.2†	500	11.1
1985					586	13.0
1986					792	17.6
					896 ⎫	
					135 ⎬	22.9†
Total	3167	100.0	3535	100.0	4504	99.9

* 1974 is the first year of listing on the new Registers; all pre-existing vacancies and voids are recorded as beginning in that year.

† The registers are compiled in April each year, the final 'annual' percentage given, therefore, relates to a 15-month period starting from January in the previous year. Table 6.2 should be read in conjunction with Fig. 6.2 which shows the cumulative total of voids.

than 42% over the study period, with a faster rise in the second half of the period than the first. Comparison with labour unemployment trends shows land vacancy continuing to rise after the rate of labour unemployment had begun to fall. Indeed the highest annual percentage increases in labour unemployment in Liverpool were the 47.3% (11 043) rise between 1975 and 1976 and the 21.4% (8310) rise between 1980 and 1981. This is consistent with the view that land and buildings are treated as a fixed cost of production and only given up or disposed of when a permanent decline or structural change in demand facing the firm has been established clearly, whereas labour is a variable cost increased or reduced in a much closer relationship with actual changes in production.

If we accept the idea of using vacancy of less than one year as a proxy for frictional vacancy then, according to Table 7.2, we can suggest that in 1981 frictional factors accounted for a maximum of 34.5% of all vacancy, rising slightly to 36.3% in 1984 and falling sharply to 22.9% in 1988. The significant change is this recent sharp decrease in frictional vacancy. What may have been happening is that the recent increase in total vacancy may have been caused as much by a reduction in the rate of re-use as by any increase in the rate of vacancy creation. If this is correct it indicates that the nature of the problem in Liverpool is changing so that the city is being faced increasingly with the problem of a hard core of vacancy caused by long-term decline or structural change in demand rather than frictional factors relating to the mechanisms of the land market. Another interpretation of this change which needs further investigation is that those government policies which are aimed predominantly at frictional issues (such as public land registers and simplifying the planning system as in Enterprise Zones and Urban Development Corporations) are beginning to have some effect.

7.2   SOME STRUCTURAL CHANGES IN THE LOCAL LANDMARKET

Under this heading we consider the extent to which location, size and ownership have been related to vacancy or re-use and, therefore, the degree to which structural changes in market demand have left some premises with the wrong location, size or ownership.

Two data sets are available to help in this analysis: voids register data on vacancy for 1981, 1984 and 1988 and our study of the present (1989) condition of LARS sites known to have been vacant in 1981.

In using the voids register it must be remembered that the data refers to the numbers of premises and gives no indication of size. Thus, while it is possible to say that around half of the vacant hereditaments are located in the city centre these are likely to comprise a larger number of small units, many of which are likely to be only parts of buildings. In contrast the one-fifth of vacant hereditaments located in the outer city are likely to comprise very much larger units. Nevertheless, if we make the assumption that the size composition of vacancy within each part of the city has remained reasonably constant over the period, then we can make some comments about the changing position of each area vis-à-vis the others.

On this basis Table 7.3 suggests that the biggest increases in vacancy have occurred in the city centre and the outer city areas. Similarly Table 6.4 shows that 72.1% of inner city sites that were vacant in 1981 had been redeveloped by 1989, whereas only 16.0% of outer city sites vacant in 1981 had been redeveloped. Table 7.4 also shows a considerable divergence between the north of the city, where only 15.8% of sites had been redeveloped, and the more favoured south where 66.3% of sites had been returned to use.

This leads us to suggest a number of hypotheses which might justify further consideration. First, the differences between the north and south of the city could be explained by two factors: 1. that (as is shown below) much of the re-used land has been redeveloped for housing and, certainly as far as the private sector are concerned, housing demand and prices are higher in the south of the city than the north, and 2. that the south of the

Table 7.3 Total number of void hereditaments by area (*Source*: The Void and Vacant Hereditaments Registers for Liverpool, Liverpool Valuation Office)

Area		1981	% change 1981–4	1984	% change 1984–8	1988	% change 1981–8
City centre	Number	1540	+21.2	1867	+30.5	2437	+58.2
	%	49		53		54	
Inner city	Number	1072	−4.5	1024	+13.3	1160	+8.2
	%	34		29		25	
Outer city	Number	555	+16.0	644	+40.8	907	+63.4
	%	17		18		20	

Table 7.4 Condition of sites by location (*Source*: Survey, 1989)

Location	Proportion of sites vacant in 1981 but redeveloped by 1989	Proportion of area vacant in 1981 but redeveloped by 1989
Inner city	44.7%	72.1%
Outer city	36.4%	16.0%
North Liverpool	34.4%	15.8%
South Liverpool	51.9%	66.3%

city has better access to rail and motorway networks, airports, more prosperous suburbs and the towns of the Mersey valley, and is, therefore, a more attractive location for many types of investment. Second, differences between the city centre, inner city and outer city might partially be explained by the recent concentration of some central-government and local-government capital-expenditure programmes upon the inner city (i.e. not the city centre or outer city) beginning to have some effect in raising the level of demand for premises in that area. Third, while Liverpool has for many years been faced with two fundamental economic problems (a declining economic base and decentralization of economic activity) our findings are compatible with a view that both of these trends are continuing but that the phenomenon of sub-regional economic decline is increasingly becoming the more dominant and intractable of the two problems. Our argument is that the fairly constant total level of vacancy and the relatively higher amount of redevelopment is consistent with other evidence (e.g. population trends) that is showing a slowing of the rate of urban decentralization, whereas the decline in the use of land and building space in the city centre and the outer city is consistent with the trend of continuing decline in the conurbation's regional role both as a commercial centre and

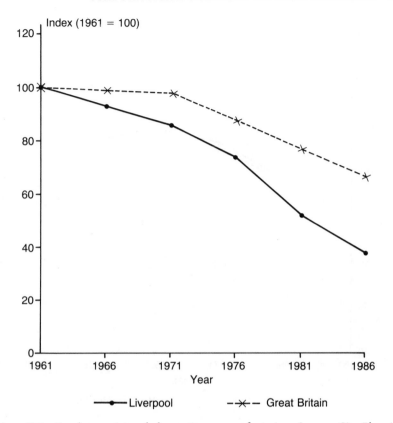

Figure 7.2 Employment trends by sector – manufacturing. Source: City Planning Officer

as a centre of production. Figures 7.2 and 7.3 shows employment decline in these sectors.

Analysis of previous use (from the voids register) in Table 7.5, and use after redevelopment (from our own survey) in Table 7.6, also support this view. Table 7.5 shows the amount of vacancy and the net changes in vacancy over time by use category. The 'best' performance overall, and the only use category to show an improvement in either time period, has been the 'other' category. It is disturbing to note that this is the main category for non-productive uses (recreation, utilities, car parking, etc.) and that all the productive categories of hereditaments are showing considerably more vacancy in 1988 than in 1981. Similarly Table 7.6 shows that of the land that had been redeveloped between 1981 and 1989 50.6% by number of sites and 38.7% by area has been used for residential development while only 3.7% of sites (8.7% of the area) had been used for manufacturing industry. Thus, if economic regeneration policies are working, they are only successful

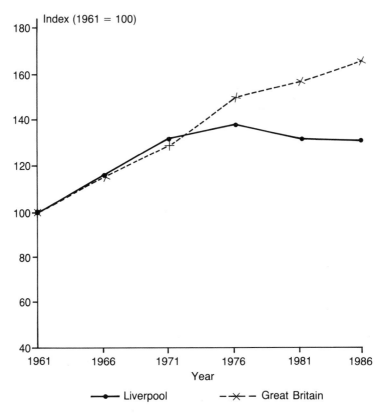

Figure 7.3 Employment trends by sector – white collar services. Source: City Planning Officer

in increasing the amount of land used for consumption purposes and are not reversing the trend of loss of land devoted to production purposes.

A further finding is that there seems to be quite a weak relationship between the re-use and the size of sites. It might have been supposed that the apparent trend towards a larger scale in development projects would lead to less demand for the smaller categories of sites but Table 7.7 shows only a slight tendency for demand to slacken off both at the smaller and larger ends of the site size scale. This may again be related to the predominant tendency to re-use vacant sites for residential development, where developers are quite prepared to build on individual dwelling plots and small infill sites. Further work needs to be done on the average size of different categories of developments before anything further can be said under this heading.

Our final analysis in Table 7.8 shows the rather surprising result that proportionately more publicly owned land has been redeveloped than privately owned land. This goes against the grain of much of the argument

Table 7.5 Total number of void hereditaments by previous use (*Source*: The Void and Vacant Hereditaments Registers for Liverpool, Liverpool Valuation Office)

Previous use		1981	% change 1981–4	1984	% change 1984–8	1988	% change 1981–8
Offices	Number	837	+26.3	1057	+25.6	1328	+58.7
	%	26.4		29.9		29.5	
Shops	Number	813	0.0	813	+22.2	994	+22.2
	%	25.7		23.0		22.0	
Storage	Number	432	+35.9	587	+43.1	840	+94.4
	%	13.6		16.6		18.7	
Workshops	Number	236	+33.4	315	+40.3	442	+87.3
	%	7.5		8.9		9.8	
Factories	Number	66	+22.7	81	+64.2	133	+101.5
	%	2.1		2.3		3.0	
Other	Number	783	−12.9	682	+12.5	767	+2.1
	%	24.7		19.3		17.0	
Total	Number	3167	+11.6	3535	+27.4	4504	42.4
	%	100.0		100.0		100.0	

Table 7.6 Developed sites by current use (*Source*: Survey, 1989)

Current use	Number of sites		Area (Hectares)	
Car park	9	(11.1%)	0.78	(1.3%)
Community use	7	(8.6%)	1.05	(1.7%)
Manufacturing	3	(3.7%)	5.30	(8.7%)
Offices	4	(4.9%)	0.54	(0.9%)
Residential	41	(50.6%)	23.47	(38.7%)
Retail/distribution	11	(13.6%)	2.92	(4.8%)
Storage	2	(2.5%)	0.46	(0.8%)
Other	4	(4.9%)	26.08	(43.0%)
Total	81		60.60	

Table 7.7 Developed sites by size (*Source*: Survey, 1989)

Size category	Number of developed sites within size category	Proportion of sites within size category that have been developed
<0.04 ha	14	33.3%
0.05–0.09 ha	16	51.6%
0.10–0.19 ha	18	43.9%
0.20–0.39 ha	14	37.8%
0.40–0.99 ha	10	40.0%
>1.0 ha	9	33.3%

Table 7.8 Developed sites by ownership (*Source*: Survey 1989)

Ownership in 1981	Number developed		Area developed	
Private	24	(45.0%)	12.01 ha	(34.9%)
Public	52	(38.0%)	41.45 ha	(42.2%)
Other	5	(33.3%)	7.14 ha	(71.5%)
Total	81	(39.5%)	60.60 ha	(42.5%)

emanating from the property industry, particularly during the late 1970s, in which it was suggested that the lack of market discipline within the public sector led to land hoarding and the holding out for 'unrealistic' prices. Here the explanation may lie in: 1. the suitability of land in different ownerships for re-use, i.e. it may be, for example, that more of the privately owned land comprises former industrial land in the north of the city; or 2. the argument that as public authorities find themselves in increasing financial difficulties and as the government has been encouraging and cajoling them into disposals of land, so they have been under increasing pressure to realize their assets.

7.3 CONCLUSIONS

All economic activity requires inputs of land, labour and capital. Under certain conditions a proportion of any of these inputs may remain unused within the market and, therefore, become unemployed. It is normal to categorize labour unemployment in relation to causal factors before proceeding to devise solutions to the problem. For various reasons this approach has not yet been applied commonly in relation to the unemployment of urban land. It has been our contention that important advances could be made in our understanding of the urban dereliction problem if such an approach were to be adopted.

In this paper we have only been able to begin to separate out the frictional unemployment of land in one city (Liverpool) and to make a few empirical observations. According to our assumptions, our findings indicate that perhaps one-third of the vacant hereditaments in Liverpool in 1981 were in that state for frictional reasons and that this proportion had fallen to about one-fifth by 1988. On the one hand this seems to suggest some success for those government policies aimed at 'oiling the wheels' of the market, while on the other hand it implies that there may be a growing proportion of long-term unemployed land which is not being adequately touched by present policies or market trends.

With regard to structural changes in the land market we have only been able to make some tentative observations within one urban area and cannot comment on changes elsewhere or between urban areas. Nevertheless it seems to us that location has played a significant role in determining which sites will be re-used whereas the size and ownership of sites do not seem to have been important. However, we have discussed a number of reasons why the importance of location may have been overstated in our findings and the importance of size has been understated. The principal of these reasons has been the secular decline in demand for any 'productive' uses (factories, offices, etc.) in Liverpool which has distorted the market so that the particular requirements of residential developers show up much more strongly in our analysis than any other category.

During late 1988 and into 1989 Liverpool experienced a miniboom or boomlette as the waves from the national (London-dominated) property boom rippled towards the city. However, the anecdotal evidence is again that Liverpool experienced a smaller and shorter-lived boom even than other northern cities. Relative to other areas the demand for property in Liverpool does still seem to be declining.

PART THREE

DEVELOPMENT PROJECTS

8

EDITORIAL

Solmaz Tavsanoglu
and Patsy Healey

8.1 TRANSFORMING ZONES OF THE CITY

In Chapter 1, it was argued that our thinking about city structure has changed from an emphasis on overall city form and function to a focus on the fragments of cities, such as zones and projects. Public policy has played a critical role in this process of fragmentation by targeting individual elements of cities, such as the designated zones/sites, through providing a package of incentive programmes in the form of land and finance.

New agencies were established to promote and control development activities in several such zones. The power of local authorities in the redevelopment process, therefore, was restricted. The availability of various grant regimes for these zones is also another example of the fragmentation. Hence, it has become increasingly difficult to co-ordinate, integrate and facilitate the initiatives of fragmented agencies and to reduce their adverse effects on each other. This kind of institutional and spatial fragmentation has led, in a way, to the increasing competitiveness of policy initiatives that are designed to tackle the growing urban crisis. Reflecting this fragmented and competitive structure, each agency promoted its own development/flagship project and marketed the image of their territories in order to attract investment from selectively targeted groups.

This section of the book focuses on how development projects and image-improvement initiatives impact on the process of transformation of cities. What are the key actors and patterns of relations through which development projects are realized? How specific is the pattern of relationships to individual urban regions and to the conditions of fragile local economies? What elements of the development process are most significant in getting projects realized? What is the role of urban policy initiatives? What drives and blocks the development process? What are the benefits and costs produced and how are they distributed?

This section presents three case studies, all of which address these questions. Two of them are of development projects. The first one is an area adjacent to Glasgow City Centre which focuses on the relationship between the development industry and the public sector and analyses how this relationship changed over the time. The second one is of a riverside area on the Tyne, focusing on the role of the agencies involved in the process and identifying the pattern of their relations and the driving forces of the process. The third case shifts focus to image-promotion campaigns and compares the place-marketing strategies of various agencies in the Tyne and Wear region.

In Chapter 9, Jones and Patrick examine one of the zones of the city of Glasgow. This zone is characterized by the 18th-century pre-industrial townscape which preserved its original street patterns and infilled with a range of architectural styles. The key task here was to change the qualities of the location. Derelict and unused historical fabric was converted into housing, retailing, leisure and cultural uses by restructuring the interiors of these buildings. Adjacent vacant land was infilled with new buildings. The Merchant City, with specialized shops, cultural activities and new professional class residents, now symbolizes a consumption model of revitalization and provides a tourist attraction centre.

The authors describe how the local authority opened up the development opportunities for private investors through the provision of grant, property leasing and other promotional initiatives. Small local developers, then, were able to carry out the small-scale conversion schemes. The success of these schemes along with the provision of cultural and leisure activities by the local authority attracted the interest of other agencies: the Scottish Development Agency became involved through its development (LEG-UP) and environmental upgrading grants. This opened up the opportunities for large-scale, mixed-use flagship schemes undertaken by national developers.

There was no comprehensive master plan or detailed policy framework for the zone. The new planning criteria were flexible, incremental and pragmatic. Planning/amenity standards were deregulated with respect to the peculiarities of each individual project. Consultants were used to examine the credibility of the proposed scheme. The Merchant City therefore consists of an amalgamation of a series of projects and is hardly integrated within itself and into the other parts of the city.

What made this revitalization scheme successful was the availability of public funds, in particular the LEG-UP development grant by SDA. The success of the project has also led to a number of problems such as an inadequate provision of car parking and conflicting land uses.

In Chapter 10, Healey examines a detailed case study of a transformation from the former heavy industrial complex to a housing, leisure and training complex at Hebburn in Tyne and Wear. She focuses on the process, and analyses the role of the agencies at each stage of the process to identify the patterns of the relations between the agencies and the driving forces of the process.

Hebburn is far from the city centre, on a riverside site within the South Tyneside District. The area has suffered from the collapse of shipyards and an engineering factory which were owned by large, powerful, traditional industrial companies. Land values in parallel to the land and property markets in the area were very depressed in the early 1980s, even though the local council carried out environmental improvement. Hebburn, therefore, was a difficult location to which to attract developer interest.

The major landowners, the local council and a training agency were key actors in the search for development opportunities. The training agency developed ideas for a multipurpose leisure and training complex. Subsequently, a national housebuilder based in the North East was attracted by this imaginative scheme and made proposals for a housing development. A development brief was produced through the amalgamation of these proposals and an informal partnership was formed to implement this scheme.

Healey shows the complexity of the process through a detailed examination of all the agencies involved. A multiplicity of agencies were involved in the process, ranging across all levels of public, private and voluntary organizations. They formed a complex nexus of relations within the region and between regions. However, a small number of these agencies played a critical and major role in the process. The local authority was a key actor in mediating conflicts of interest among agencies and co-ordinating the activities of the development process.

Healey concludes that 'the Hebburn case is best understood as the product of a corporate production nexus where the state had an active role both directly in the production sphere and in assisting production companies to disinvest and realize capital assets'. The process of production and transformation may be explained in terms of the impact of economic restructuring on landowners' interests and local authorities' priorities, and the availability of central government funds through urban policy, under the conditions of very depressed market demand.

8.2 MARKETING THE CITY

Wilkinson's paper shifts focus from the social relations of specific development projects to the use of promotional imagery in Newcastle. She focuses on four principal agencies which were concerned with image promotion. She describes the different approaches adopted by each and examines the spatial and institutional consequences of the marketing strategies. She then discusses the likely future of image promotion and its implication for urban regeneration in Newcastle.

Image-improvement and place-marketing initiatives have become a central element in urban regeneration and economic development strategy in Newcastle. The objective of these initiatives has been to break the spiral of economic decline and to improve internal and external perceptions of the whole city or particular areas within it. Prestigious development projects are often used as symbols of renewed dynamism and confidence in this process. These initiatives are targeted at the key decision-makers, business leaders, financial institutions, opinion-makers, and their highly specialized professional and managerial employees in the South East. Thus, the qualities of locations in terms of environment, lifestyle and business opportunities have become the important components of marketing strategies. The agencies increasingly emphasized the soft infrastructure of the city, such as art, leisure, culture and heritage, as a vital tool in stimulating private investment.

Marketing strategies were developed by the various agencies for their particular areas of the city and the sector of interest. The strategies and images were fragmented, unfocused and also typically transplanted from other UK and North American cities. The agencies have also used large-scale, highly speculative, mixed-use flagship projects as visible symbols of renewal and as powerful place-marketing devices in order to define new niches for the city in the urban market. They represented the continuing fragmentation of the city. Urban regeneration, therefore, has been characterized by a series of entrepreneurial initiatives and speculative projects rather than by an integrated programme.

Image-improvement and place-marketing initiatives manifest a new relationship between the public and private sectors. Urban government has been forced to become more entrepreneurial in order to attract inward investment in the increasing competition between urban regions. However, Wilkinson argues that the entrepreneurial style of urban governance has to some extent been combined with a managerial type of economic development in order to coordinate and integrate various initiatives.

Wilkinson argues that the image-improvement initiatives can be made more effective and suggests that there must be a strong link between image campaigns and urban regeneration strategies and investment programmes. There is also the need for a comprehensive and integrated marketing strategy. She emphasizes that there might be a danger that the promotional agencies may have diverted their resources from the main infrastructure investments to marketing initiatives.

8.3 ACTORS AND RELATIONSHIPS

Who takes the initiative in such projects and strategies? It is traditionally assumed that the private developer assesses market opportunities, initiates development projects and takes the risks. However, developers are prompted by the anticipation of levels of profit. In the case of redevelopment and refurbishment projects (particularly in fragile urban economies and thin land and property markets where high risk, cost and uncertainty are attached to projects) developers need to be persuaded to take risks by the provision of substantial subsidies to fill the gap between the cost and value of the development, by assurances about the economic future of the area through image campaigns, and by the coordinated strategies of public agencies. In this case, it is the public agencies who are the risk-takers.

In these circumstances, is it then the public sector which opens up development opportunities? In the Merchant City, the public sector was the opener through coordinating and diverting its own resources to the zone as well as undertaking a series of promotional initiatives. Subsequently, local developers tested out the viability of the conversion schemes in the market. Then national developers, who tend to seek relatively secure development/ market conditions, became involved in the process in parallel with further subsidy from the SDA. This case shows clearly that the local developers were risk minimizers whilst the national developers were profit maximizers and speculators. In contrast to the Merchant City, a more intricate mix of the institutions put their development proposals together and initiated the redevelopment scheme in Hebburn. In this case, the public and voluntary sectors were the initiators as well as the landowners. Eventually, a national developer became involved with housing development proposals.

Elsewhere, Urban Development Corporations and local growth coalitions were also the openers through the promotion of highly speculative, proposed flagship projects armed with substantial subsidies as well as place-marketing initiatives. In this, they were often assisted by development and planning consultants and by marketing agencies. All these initiatives were targeted at the national developers and financial institutions.

Did the public sector, in this way, crowd out local developers' initiatives, reinforcing dependency on public-sector subsidy? As several chapters in this book demonstrate, the public agencies have targeted the intensive subsidy and place-marketing programmes to attract inward investment to the particular localities in order to restructure their economy from the Fordist production-based relations to the post-Fordist consumption-based ones. Therefore, they have promoted highly commercial, speculative and mixed-used development projects to stimulate outside property and financial interests rather than strengthening the locally based development industry. In their turn, national companies have enhanced their ability to benefit from these initiatives by forming their regionally based urban-renewal subsidiaries and strengthening their local networks. To some extent, national urban policy may have reinforced dependency on the national investors. However, it is also likely that some of the locally based developers might merge with one another to exploit the benefits generated by the public sector. In some cases the national developers may also form partnerships with locally based ones.

In the case of Hebburn, the public-sector facilitated and coordinated the development activities undertaken by the national developer. The small local firms, particularly in the field of construction and consultancy, clustered around the national firms and undertook the activities created by them. In contrast, in the Merchant City, the public sector, initially, strengthened the local developers' initiatives. Subsequently, the local developers were crowded out, except those who reorganized themselves when the national developers became involved in the process in parallel with the further subsidy provision and support by SDA which came forward as a result of the success of the local developers' initiatives. In both the Merchant City and Hebburn cases, the national developers were the regionally-based urban renewal subsidiaries of the major housebuilding companies such as Wimpey, Bellway and Barratt. It could be concluded that local development activities have become dependent on the national development companies and public sector funds as it was before.

8.4   ELEMENTS OF THE DEVELOPMENT PROCESS

Development projects are key components of the transformation of urban environments. The derelict, run down, former industrial areas, in particular, on waterfront locations as well as the declining, neglected historical parts of city centres have been targeted to be transformed to the new patterns of land uses through the development projects, backed by substantial intensive packages. Development schemes are devices to attract inward investment through providing appropriate accommodation and environment for the new sectors of consumption and production activities, such as leisure-retailing complexes, and high-technology industries. Therefore, the new patterns of consumer demand shape development projects which symbolise the quality of life, business and environment.

The development schemes which are so often called flagship projects can be defined as large-scale, self-contained, highly prestigious, consumption-oriented and mixed-use land and property developments. They are powerful marketing tools to help the localities to reposition themselves and to find a new niche in competitive urban markets. These chapters provide much evidence of how the public sector creates market demands through the proposed development schemes. Proposed development projects, therefore, are not only the driving forces of redevelopment activities, they are also shaped by the new patterns of consumer demand.

Development projects represent a new planning notion and practice, individual elements being planned in isolation rather than arising from a comprehensive plan. Therefore, development projects lead to the fragmentation of planning practice and of urban space. The public sector has played a critical role, in particular through the provision of grants and land

and by the creation of partnerships between public and private sector in this process. In both the Merchant City and Hebburn cases, the projects would not have been realized in the absence of the grant regimes, although many still remain as images, rather than completed buildings. Development projects also clearly demonstrate the changes in the institutional relationships between public and private sectors. Urban government has become more innovative and entrepreneurial through promoting speculative development schemes in order to attract inward investment under the circumstances of the competition between urban regions.

8.5   DRIVING FORCES

The development process is driven by a combination of forces which interact with each other. In Chapter 2, Healey suggests a range of possible driving forces for development activity in urban economies (see Table 3.4).

The first driving force is consumer demand. Consumer demand, in many cases, constrains the development process unless real economic growth is achieved. However, in fragile local economies with very depressed property markets, market demand has to be created and maintained. The cases in this section show how the agencies involved in the process struggled to create market demand. They sought for opportunities in different property markets to define projects which could create and attract market demand to sites. Image-promotion and market-positioning initiatives enhanced this process.

In the case of the Merchant City, the local developers' profit as well as the available grant determined the content of schemes. There was a general demand for one or two bedroom flats in the conurbation as a whole. This demand could be supplied in this area. Moreover, further grant provision by SDA along with the national developers' interest diversified and shifted the contents of schemes from housing to retailing, leisure and up-market residential uses. Similarly, in Hebburn, the landowners, the public sector and the residential developer searched for the market opportunities which were, initially, low-cost private housing schemes. There was demand for this type of housing scheme in the conurbation and the local area. In both cases, it could be assumed that locally based public and private agencies identified the type of demand within the conurbation using their knowledge and used this demand as a catalyst for the attraction of further, large-scale, speculative, mixed-use developments with the provision of public funds, as was the case of the Merchant City. However, UDCs and the other urban regeneration agencies struggled to drive new consumer demand, giving less consideration to existing local property market demand. Here, the key task was to restructure the local economy through creating market demand for new economic, social and cultural activities by highly speculative flagship projects with intensive subsidy packages. We could conclude that the agencies were market making and testing.

The second driving force is the pressure from landowners to realize the capital value of their sites. Landowners who are rooted in particular areas are more likely to pursue development opportunities which capture the increasing site values which are attached to new development activities. Place marketing as well as public policy enhanced this process. In the Hebburn case, the landowners sought to realize the maximum exchange value for their disused land holdings. In the case of the Merchant City, the public sector used its landownership power to stimulate development activities.

The third possible driving force was the competition between local, national and international financial and property interests for control over property development and investment opportunities. What seemed to happen in these cases was that local initiatives by the public and private sectors were eventually taken over by national companies.

The fourth possible driving force is economic restructuring and the strategies of the companies to rationalize and reposition themselves in the global economy. The impact of these strategies was critical in generating the development sites at Hebburn.

But, these driving forces were constrained in a number of ways, blocking the development process. These included: uncertainty about planning policies and highway proposals; the topography of an area; the structure of land ownership; and competition with development zones being promoted elsewhere.

8.6 BENEFITS AND COSTS

The distribution of the benefits and costs differs from one case to another. However, landowners and national developers were the main beneficiaries in these cases. The new firms, and professional and managerial classes, have benefited from the revitalization in the Merchant City whilst the local residents have been the beneficiaries through the provision of low-income houses, training and job opportunities in Hebburn. The city as a whole obtained revenue through the activities located in revitalized fabric.

However, the cost of the redevelopment schemes has been very high for the public sector. New developers have also been adversely affected by rising land values. In some cases, locally based developers have suffered from the competition from national firms. Urban regeneration policy thus appears to have made older industrial regions more dependent on national public- and private-sector investment instead of strengthening their indi-genous local economic development.

9

THE MERCHANT CITY AS AN EXAMPLE OF HOUSING-LED URBAN REGENERATION

Colin Jones and Jim Patrick

9.1 INTRODUCTION

The city of Glasgow is today a major provincial city with a population of 725 100 in 1991. But at one time it was the second city of the empire, surpassed only by London. The city's 19th-century growth was based on the marine and locomotive engineering industries which reached their zenith just before World War I. These industries after a long period of stagnation collapsed in the late 1960s and early 1970s. Most of the shipyards and the other major engineering works are now closed or employ only a fraction of their former workforce.

The 1980s have seen Glasgow rediscover its confidence in itself ex-pressed nationally through its hosting of the National Garden Festival in 1988 and the choice of the city as the 1990 European City of Culture. Much of this revival has been based on the physical transformation of its tenemental housing stock and a new-found partnership between the public and private sectors, which has contributed to the enhancement and the development of the commercial role of the city. The Merchant City is a product of this era.

The area of Glasgow city centre known as the Merchant City stretches over 70 acres and derives its name from the 18th-century pre-Industrial Revolution activities of city merchants. By 1980 the area had suffered 15 years of economic decline to the point where approximately 35% of property was vacant or unused. Historical and townscape factors also meant that any renewal solution rested as much with the issue of redundant buildings as with undeveloped vacant land.

This chapter charts the policy initiatives made possible by legislative changes and revisions to strategic planning at the beginning of the 1980s. Its success is based on the creative participation of both the public and private sectors. The public sector has contributed not only financial assistance, but has also released property which it owned and preferred a positive use of its planning powers.

It is estimated that approximately £12m of public money has been attracted into the Merchant City. Much of this capital has been focused on promoting the conversion of buildings to housing for sale. Over 1200 new housing units have been created or are in the process of being built, together with a range of commercial developments. In 1988 the Merchant City Project was awarded the Medal of Honour by the Europa Nostra organization*, the highest accolade they bestow annually to mark 'a distinguished contribution to the conservation and enhancement of Europe's architectural and natural heritage'.

9.2 THE MERCHANT CITY

In 1695, Glasgow was the second largest city in Scotland, a status achieved by its importance as a religious centre, and to a lesser extent, as a port with limited foreign trade links. At that time the city extended from the cathedral to the river crossing. The city's transition from ecclesiastical to commercial centre was signalled by the Act of Union in 1707. The removal of colonial trade barriers, hitherto protecting England, opened new opportunities for Glasgow merchants to form trade links with the Americas, primarily in sugar and tobacco. By 1735 over half of the tobacco trade with the UK was controlled by Glasgow-based merchants.

This growth in the local economy during the early years of the 18th century was mirrored by the expansion of the city westwards along Trongate and Ingram Street. It is this rapid expansion of the city that today is known as the Merchant City. At that time it was a compact arrangement mainly of free-standing residences and some civic buildings contained within an offset or closed grid street plan (Fig. 9.1). The pressures of development led to the release and development of rear gardens to form new streets flanked by town houses. By 1800 the street system was clearly defined as the framework for infill over the following few decades.

---

* Europa Nostra is an international federation of associations for the protection of Europe's cultural and natural heritage.

Figure 9.1 Merchant City

The 19th century saw the basis of wealth transfer from entrepreneurial trade to that of manufacturing. This signalled the move of the fashionable residential areas westwards, which in turn led to the conversion/redevelopment of the Merchant City into warehouses and public buildings. The staggered (short) street plan and imposing civic buildings, however, remain intact today: a city within a city which contrasts sharply with the disciplined and open grid-iron streets established to the west of the Merchant City during Victorian times. Indeed continued building activity over a period of 250 years has created a townscape which is a blend of remnant Georgian townhouses, Victorian splendour and robust inter-war warehouses. Within the area are buildings designed by Robert Adam, David Hamilton, James Salmon and Sir J.J. Burnet.

Lord Esher, in his 1971 conservation study of Glasgow cautioned that, 'the scale of the narrow streets with their axial features and characteristic warehouses will need to be protected' (Esher, 1971). This expression of concern had as much to do with the declining economic fortunes of the Merchant City as with any threat to the townscape heritage. Until the 1960s the area's central and accessible position proved of sufficient economic advantage to attract a wide range of land uses. During this century, warehouse storage and distribution, as well as clothing manufacture, became the dominant activities, and at the peak period some 300 000 square metres of warehouse floorspace were concentrated there. The area had also grown in importance to encompass the regional fruit and vegetable market, a central market hall occupied by stalls and supported by a range of shops trading from adjoining streets.

The decline period of the late 1960s, although sharp, was not unexpected. Certain characteristics of change which were evident generally in the city and regional economy applied equally to the Merchant City. The inability, over time, to compete sufficiently with new world markets seriously affected the viability of the clothing industry which had a significant presence in many warehouse upper floors. More seriously, perhaps, were the changing demands, practices and preferences associated with wholesale distribution, which together with outdated operational facilities and safety standards, progressively highlighted problems of building obsolescence and the inadequacy of the street pattern to cope with increasing traffic. Running concurrently with this, and reflecting the comprehensive nature of renewal planning policies at that time, were two major land-use proposals with significant consequences for the Merchant City. The east flank of the City's inner ring road, if progressed, would cut through and remove the eastern edge of the area and the University of Strathclyde wished to expand its campus south of George Street.

Land-use operational difficulties as well as large-scale demands of this sort ultimately meant the designation of the Merchant City as an Outline Comprehensive Development Area in 1960. The underlying principle of this approach accepted that land acquisition and widespread clearance would be necessary to form the basis for renewal. In 1968, the fruit and vegetable market was relocated to a new site outside the City Centre at once relieving chronic traffic congestion and enabling a programme of land acquisition to be carried out in support of road plans and the University.

Despite this scale of public involvement, the crisis of the Merchant City intensified. The removal of the fruit market created a ripple or domino effect on a range of related uses and caused up to 80 additional businesses to cease trading in the area. In addition, although land acquisition had been undertaken on its behalf, the University was unable to progress expansion plans further. A similar delay in preparing detailed proposals for the east flank of the Inner Ring Road added to the uncertainty about development opportunities and fears about the long-term environmental implications. Thus was set in motion a chain of events common to many UK urban areas: increases in vacant property accelerate the process of decay in the absence of alternative uses leading ultimately to demolition on an extensive scale. In the case of the Merchant City, the old age of many redundant properties intensified the worst effects, causing greater numbers to be declared structurally dangerous than might otherwise have been the case. Because of the negative values which can attach to buildings in this category, it was not unusual for the District Council (GDC) to intervene in a statutory sense to implement demolition orders and by way of recompense, acquire the vacant site.

Default and planned land acquisition therefore meant substantial land and property holdings becoming vested in the District Council. It also implied additional obligations on GDC to promote new uses for these properties, though during the 1970s this proved only marginally successful and certainly formed no basis for economic regeneration. For the most part development initiatives during this time reflected either consolidation of the existing uses that relied on a central location or opportunistic advantage of low property values. By 1980, certain facts about the extent and range of decline in the Merchant City were clear.

1. About a third of all property was vacant.
2. About a third of all property was in GDC ownership including two-thirds of the vacant property.
3. Large-scale redevelopment was unlikely to occur.
4. The east flank motorway proposal was continuing to cause development and investment uncertainty.
5. As a major landlord, GDC was receiving little return on its property resource.
6. The physical fabric and townscape quality were endangered because of underuse and neglect.

9.3   CREATING OPPORTUNITIES

By 1980 the extent of physical and economic difficulty in the Merchant City pointed to key issues which the District Council as planning authority and major landholder was required to face:

1.   How to stimulate new market interest in the area;
2.   How to identify appropriate uses for old buildings and vacant land; and
3.   How to use its own property resources to better effect.

The nature of these issues and the links between them suggested the need for intervention beyond conventional levels. As a planning response, the Merchant City was identified as an area in need of special attention – a Special Project Area – 'where active participation by the public sector was considered a necessary factor towards attracting renewed market interest'. Although defined in this way, no attempt was made to quantify or formalize the manner in which the public sector would take part. Rather, the intention was to signal that, as part of the planning process, a more promotional and enterprising attitude should be adopted towards new uses and their control. Of significance here was the extent of GDC property ownership and the realization that the promotion of new uses would depend upon GDC initiative. Towards the end of the 1970s the development market in Glasgow began to show interest in the prospect of new-build, inner-city housing for sale within clearly defined areas such as GEAR (the Glasgow Eastern Area Renewal project). This interest was in response, for the most part, to policy attitudes within the GDC that sanctioned the release of publicly owned sites (Sim, 1985).

The development of these sites for private housing would help to:

1.   Maintain market interest;
2.   Cause further redevelopment of vacant land;
3.   Reduce population decline in the City; and
4.   Encourage growth in economic activity.

The positive attitudes displayed by GDC did much to reinforce the commitment to active participation. It also suggested, in the case of the Merchant City, that there may be similar opportunities for central city housing and the re-use of redundant buildings, though as yet in the absence of market interest.

Accordingly, in 1980 GDC undertook to examine a selected group of Merchant City buildings in its ownership with a view to determining their feasibility for conversion to residential use. An inter-departmental working group considered the structural, technical and social implications of adapting what were mainly underused, deteriorating and often listed warehouse buildings. The broad conclusion reached was significant on three counts:

1. That restructuring the interiors of such buildings into residential flats would be a practical option; but
2. It would be difficult in many instances to create a standard of amenity based on conventional residential norms; and
3. The likely cost involved in forming housing in this way would be prohibitive in the absence of a clearly defined market demand.

The clear implication to be drawn from these conclusions was that housing as a new use for old buildings would not be viable economically unless the shortfall between costs and likely value could be removed. In 1981, however, certain circumstances changed in a way that proved decisive. The newly approved Strathclyde Structure Plan reduced the status of the east flank motorway proposal to that of expressway and, as one of the consequences, the preferred route became established along a line someway east of High Street and the Merchant City. At the same time, as part of its function to determine the availability and rate of release of housing land, the plan hardened Regional and District Council attitudes over the issue of greenfield versus brownfield development. Policy RES 1 stated, 'Residential development on infill or redevelopment sites within urban areas, excluding zoned open space, in preference to peripheral 'Greenfield' sites, shall accord with the Regional development strategy' (Strathclyde R.C., 1981).

As well as these policy decisions, the Local Government (Miscellaneous Provisions) (Scotland) Act 1981 provided additional opportunities for local authorities to offer financial assistance towards the improvement of the private housing stock. Rules governing the need to repay grants in cases where improved properties were sold within a determined time period were relaxed. This made it possible for local authorities, at their discretion, to aid with grants the conversion of non-residential buildings to houses using existing budgets financed by central government. It should be noted that budget distinctions are made between the Housing Revenue Account which funds the maintenance, repair and management of council-owned housing and the Non-Housing Revenue Account which funds the range of grants available to improve the private housing stock in the City, including housing conversions.

The growing concern for the future of the Merchant City, the changes in housing policy and legislation, the localized planning and GDC's property interests combined to justify resource allocations in support of a housing initiative for the area. As a means of incentive and implementation, GDC was prepared to offer a subsidy package to developers willing to convert redundant buildings to houses. This extended to:

1. The payment of conversion grant at an average rate of £5100 for every house created;
2. The release of suitable buildings in its ownership; and
3. The development of positive planning controls appropriate for city centre housing.

The stance adopted by GDC at this point recognized that whatever mechanisms were involved to achieve improvement and change, there remained a continuing and heavy reliance upon the private individual and corporate initiative and that this would require to be triggered.

It was deemed of no benefit at the outset to stimulate competition in the conventional market sense but rather to promote the belief that public subsidy could bridge the gap between a desirable objective and a profitable opportunity. Although (principally new) inner city housing was being promoted successfully elsewhere in the city, there was little evidence of interest among developers or potential residents to support private sector housing in the city centre. The main obstacles facing GDC were:

1. To establish the feasibility of converting the buildings to housing, in terms both of physical and environmental suitability;
2. To demonstrate, despite the absence of an existing market, that the Merchant City would be viewed as an attractive place to live and to purchase a home; and
3. To provide a subsidy to act as a catalyst to the involvement of private developers.

9.4 THE MARKET-LED PLANNING SOLUTION

Initially, as anticipated, private developers were wary. In the absence of evidence to the contrary the scope for housing in the Merchant City was deemed to be marginal. However, Windex Ltd, a small local development company was prepared to evaluate the viability of the Albion building.

The Albion building at 60 Ingram Street was a four-storey sandstone warehouse built circa 1890. It had become vacant on the upper floors and, owned by GDC, its suitability for housing was confirmed as part of the initial feasibility pilot study. In June 1982, after lengthy discussion and negotiation, Windex were granted planning consent to convert the Albion building into 23 flats for sale, thereby introducing the first new housing to the Merchant City for over 100 years. The most notable feature of the project in terms of its future impact was the level of market response measured by the rapid sale of the houses. This implied strongly that central city living was being viewed as an attractive alternative to other more established locations, and that the GDC financial assistance (noted above), was capable of altering market perception. The conversion of Merchant Court and Blackfriars Court, the two remaining groups of buildings which made up the original feasibility study, followed quickly in the wake of the Albion Building's success. These developments proceeded, as before, in the pattern of a small local developer, clearly defined conversion opportunities and support from GDC in the form of finance and property. This stage also marked the start of the Scottish Development Agency's (SDA) contribution to the renewal process.

Although there were encouraging signs about the potential for housing, no clear view was reached about how wide-reaching this might be or the balance to be struck between residential, city centre or other uses in the Merchant City. Concerns were more basic and tended to consider issues of management and the principles involved in making housing a feasible option. In the conversion of 117 Candleriggs to Merchant Court, for example, the area was declared a Housing Action Area (HAA). HAAs for improvement can be declared where the greater part of the houses in an area lack standard amenities. In this case, while there were no inhabited houses, HAA status permitted higher than normal levels of grant funding. At the same time, GDC retained an equity interest in the six newly formed ground-floor shop units to let. GDC was managing its resources, both property and finance, in a way that promoted and helped achieve broader policy objectives but which did not rely upon the benefit of a master plan or detailed policy framework.

In response the credibility of housing as an attractive new use made viable by public subsidy grew rapidly, drawing the attention of other potential developers and property owners. By 1986 some 300 houses had been developed in conversion projects, a full list of which is given in Table 9.1. Windex had undertaken a further development at Blackfriars Court. A number of developments had been undertaken by local developers. NC Construction, for example, is a local construction/demolition contractor which expanded into this form of development activity. Kantel is a further example; it was set up by two architects in Edinburgh specifically to undertake high-quality refurbishment/conversions. Successful projects had been completed by the national builders – Taylor Woodrow at Mercatgate, Wimpey at Canada Court and Miller at 20 Montrose Street.

1984 saw the beginning of probably the most important development. Kantel's Ingram Square project raised the scale of development potential beyond the conversion of the single building or small group conversion to the complexities of complete streetblock renewal. In all 239 housing units were provided over five years by this comprehensive scheme. It included the first new-build housing in the Merchant City designed to meet the contextual needs of city block infill and to repair gaps in the fabric. The scheme also provided for extensive car parking, a central landscaped courtyard and a number of small shops and offices. The scale of the project also heralded the introduction of the SDA as a major player in this process of urban regeneration.

By 1986 another significant development was underway; Wimpey had bought the disused fire-station on Ingram Street from Strathclyde Regional Council plus the surrounding land and tenements. The 16 tenement flats on the High Street were immediately improved and sold as College View, while

Table 9.1 Housing and mixed-use developments in the Merchant City (*Source*: Glasgow D.C. Planning Departmental Records)

Map key	Development	Developer	Use	Type	Number of housing units	Number of car parking spaces
1	50–70 Bell St	GDC	Tenement Housing	Rehabilitation	21	Nil
2	75–101 High St	GDC	Tenement Housing	Rehabilitation	24	Nil
3	Albion Building	Windex	Housing 1 Retail	Conversion	23	23 Temporary
4	Merchant Court	N.C. Construction	Housing 6 Retail	Conversion	20	Nil
5	Blackfriars Court	Windex	Housing	Conversion	64	6
6	Watson St	Kelvin Homes	Housing	Conversion	14	Nil
7	Wilson Court	Credential Holdings	Housing	Conversion	37	Nil
8	Mercatgate	Taylor Woodrow	Housing	Conversion	47	Nil
9	Canada Court	Wimpey	Housing 2 Commercial	Conversion	69	15
10	20 Montrose St	Miller Urban Renewal	Housing 1 Office 1 Retail	Conversion	30	Nil
11	Ingram Square	Kantel/ Yarmadillo	Housing 11 Retail	Conversion Newbuild	169 70	118
12	Glassford Court	Credential Holdings	Housing 6 Retail	Conversion Newbuild	25 14	

No.	Name	Developer	Use	Type		
13	Macintosh Court	Wimpey	Housing / 4 Retail / 4 Offices	Conversion / Rehabilitation / Newbuild	15 / 16 / 82	81
14	The Stables Bell St	N.C. Construction	Housing	Conversion	29	20
15	College Lands Bell St	Miller Urban Renewal	Housing	Newbuild / Conversion	25 / 158	60
16	Campbell Court	Ainslie Developments	Housing / 1 Retail / 1 Hotel	Conversion	12	Nil
17	Italian Centre	Classical House	10 Retail / Offices / Bar/Café / Restaurant / Housing	Conversion	32	20 offsite
18	Brunswick Court*	Brunswick Developments	Housing / Retail	Conversion/ Newbuild }	117	65
19	Cochrane Square	Kantel	Housing / Offices / 6 Retail	Newbuild/ Conversion }	119	159
20	Virginia Court	Credential Holdings	14 Retail / Offices / Housing	Conversion	56	
21	Glasgow Cross*	Credential/N.C. Construction	Housing / Retail	Newbuild/ Conversion }	70	
22	Hutcheson St*	Unknown		Newbuild/ Conversion }	16	

* Planning consent granted only.

the fire-station was converted into a café style pub and 15 flats. Perhaps more significantly, Wimpey built Mackintosh Court, 89 new-build flats on the surrounding land. This represented the first major new development in the Merchant City.

The conversion of the Bell Street Warehouse by Miller Urban Renewal has had a long gestation period. This six-storey, yellow sandstone warehouse was built in 1881 and is formally listed (Grade B) as a building of special architectural or historical interest. The conversion of this imposing, fortress-like, structure into housing, ranks as the largest single building project of its type in Scotland. Its physical mass and dimension – measuring 147 metres along the street curve – caused numerous problems in producing a scheme to satisfy both building regulations and amenity standards. These problems were difficult to overcome and solving them added three years to the planning and design stages. Now completed it consists of 158 one- and two-bedroom flats and is known as College Lands.

The foregoing illustrates not only the incremental way in which events developed and the initiative evolved but also the nature of the problems it faced. Partly because of these problems and the absence of any tradition of city centre housing alongside other major uses, it was necessary in the practical sense to devise new planning criteria to determine social and environmental suitability. The underlying principle was that of flexibility. Measured against a specifically devised guide of target and mandatory requirements for city centre housing, GDC sought to strike a balance with developers over the circumstances of individual projects. Thus in cases where the physical constraints imposed by the characteristics of an individual building meant, for example, that the preferred level of dedicated car parking could not be achieved then, rather than conclude that housing was an unsuitable use, compensatory and offsetting measures were required such as improved space standards or other amenity advantages.

The introduction of the SDA coincided with the setting up of its property-development division and its move away from the direct provision of industrial property. It had inherited from Scottish Industrial Estates this latter role when it was set up in 1975. Its main remit at that time was to restructure the Scottish economy, but it had gradually switched from an industrial sectoral approach to an area approach. Initially, the SDA considered each project individually but with the realization of a number of schemes in the pipeline it began to consider the area's total potential. At the same time it began to consider its activities not just in terms of needs but also of the opportunities available. The Merchant City was seen as one such opportunity which it could develop and hence enhance the city centre and the city's wider economy. Even so, the SDA never conceived a plan for the area. Instead, they employed DEGW architects urban design consultants to provide credible sketches. With the exception of Macintosh Court it has been involved in all the major projects, e.g. site assembly, and with financial support.

In parallel with the housing initiative, other efforts, often involving property leasing and grant assistance, have been directed towards encouraging new city centre activities. In 1980 an 18th-century church was converted into the Tron Theatre. This was the first of the vacant GDC-owned buildings in the Merchant City to find a new use. It was followed in 1984 by the restoration of a ruined Georgian town house and its re-use as a hotel. In the following year work commenced on converting another church into the 'John Street Jam' bar and restaurant. Much of this work was funded by the public sector but the creation of these social amenities attracted people to visit the Merchant City and reinforced the character of the area.

The original conversion projects often incorporated shops as a matter of convenience on the ground floor where housing was deemed inappropriate. The success of the area's housing renewal and its trendy image has spawned a range of small fashion and furniture shops within these units. The commercial possibilities of the area have also been influenced by its location adjacent to the regional shopping centre. This in turn is being upgraded and redefined with the creation of Princes Square (a speciality shopping centre), the opening of a major new centre (the St Enoch Centre) and the construction of the Buchanan Centre. All these developments have helped to move the centre of gravity of the city's principal shopping centre east toward the Merchant City. However, the Merchant City remains very much a secondary location for shops.

A number of large-scale multi-use projects currently under construction extend the role of retailing and other commercial activities in the Merchant City. The Italian Centre, which incorporates flats, shops, offices, restaurant, café bar, etc., around a central courtyard, has developed this fashion theme. The commercial element of this scheme represents approximately two-thirds of its value with housing filling a secondary role. Two developments, Virginia Court and Cochrane Square, started in the spring of 1990 contain significant amount of office space.

This later generation of schemes also incorporates more up-market housing units. The Italian Centre has sold the first phase of 12 flats for prices ranging from £75 000 to £125 000. Cochrane Square's 110 flats will have access to a gymnasium and a pool, and the provision of a porterage service. They are expected to be marketed at prices around £120 000 and above.

Proposals waiting to go ahead include the conversion by Merlin International of the Sheriff Courthouse into a Fashion Centre. This will be totally commercial although it will include a fashion museum as well as design studios/workspaces, retail outlets and support facilities. This will represent the development of a complete street block and the pedestrianization of some of the adjoining streets.

In terms of retail growth, both GDC and the SDA have encouraged new forms of shopping based on trends towards specialist and leisure themes and on the growing tourist attraction of the City Centre. As a contrast to developments like the St Enoch Centre, which aims to re-focus the primary role of Buchanan Street, new retail forms in the adjacent area would serve to complement the mainstream provision and expand the range of choice. Prince's Square is a good example of this relationship and the way it is reinforcing the attraction of the city centre. The extent to which retail forms like this can be developed depends on market response and the scope for real growth in the city centre.

This broadening of the public sector's development strategy also raises questions about land use and amenity conflicts when viewed in the context of a growing residential population. There are important considerations regarding the nature of Merchant City living. It is recognized that the mixed-use environment of the city centre means that it cannot be a suitable place for all to live. However, the combination of housing opportunity with the benefit and attraction of city centre facilities is unique within the regional housing catchment area and is especially important to the relatively modest numbers of people who seek the lifestyle that such an arrangement offers.

Despite the assumption that people live in the Merchant City because they choose to, there is increasing pressure on the authorities to tackle some of the perceived drawbacks, principally shortages of dedicated car parking and the quality of the environment. The cumulative effect of restricted car parking built up over a range of developments is emerging as a constraint to fuller residential amenity. Alternatives, such as controlled and selective on-street parking are being restricted because of the over-intrusive and dangerously high levels of traffic. In essence, the Merchant City is unable to cope adequately with all the traffic demands placed on it, the consequence being that the proper functioning of the area is being compromised. An unwelcome level of non-essential through traffic, i.e. having no origin or destination there, is attracted as a means of avoiding the more congested routes. As well as this, demand for car parking from shoppers and residents is not matched by supply, so contributing to high concentrations of illegal on-street parking. Traffic abuse to this degree affects the ability of essential on-street servicing to operate successfully and causes street congestion. It is a danger to pedestrian movement, creates noise pollution, and undermines the residential initiative and commercial viability.

The relationship of all these factors – retail change, land-use conflicts, and concerns about parking and the environment – supports the need to resolve issues as well as promote new opportunities. Because of public-sector intervention, some of this is beginning to happen. Each of the new retail projects, for example, is being subsidized by the public sector to incorporate adjacent street pedestrianization and other environmental benefits. Two new multi-storey car parks, one of which is under construction, will not only ease parking congestion but will also contain additional spaces for dedicated use by residents. The increasingly complex nature of the

Table 9.2   Socio-economic structure of house purchasers in the city centre (*Source:* Glasgow University (1986) and Glasgow D.C. (1987))

Socio-economic group	Ingram-Square (%)	Central Glasgow (%)
Professionals managers	49.1	54.5
Intermediate junior non-manual	29.1	20.0
Skilled manual	9.0	9.5
Semi-skilled and unskilled	7.3	5.1
Armed forces	–	2.1
Other	5.5	8.5
Sample size	58	50

Merchant City is such that there is now a need to consider what other measures might be necessary and where priorities lie.

9.5   DEMAND FOR MERCHANT CITY HOUSING

An indication of the nature of demand is given by two surveys of flat buyers in the city centre. One survey undertaken by Glasgow University (1986) sampled buyers generally in the Merchant City and the other by GDC (1987) was of purchasers of flats in the first phases of Ingram Square. The majority of flat buyers in both surveys were young, indeed 16% of the Ingram Square buyers were under 25 and 70% under 29 years. The more general Merchant City survey found a slightly older age profile and also a high proportion (17%) of buyers aged over 60 years. These age structures are reflected in the marital status of the two samples. The Ingram Square sample is predominantly single while the more general survey is evenly split between married and single owners with divorced/separated householders in both cases representing less than 5%.

House buyers were predominantly drawn from the non-manual occupational groups as Table 9.2 indicates. Overall about three-quarters of these home buyers were drawn from white-collar jobs. More than half of these buyers had been attracted into the city centre from outside the district council boundary. Migration patterns, however, differed depending on the former tenure of the purchaser. 58% of Ingram Square buyers were owner-occupiers in their former residence, and two-thirds of these were migrants into the city. In contrast, 25% of these buyers who were formerly living in privately rented accommodation were principally local residents.

For Ingram Square respondents the attractions of living in the city centre derived principally from its central location (40%), the closeness to place of employment (33%) and the local amenities (18%). Despite these reasons for purchasing there was still a high incidence (56%) of car ownership among heads of households. The overriding impression these surveys imbue is that the demand predominantly stems from young professionals on relatively high incomes. Many were owner-occupiers moving into the city, or local first-time purchasers formerly in the private rented sector. These households are attracted to the Merchant City by a combination of its convenience for work and social amenities.

9.6   THE ROLE OF PUBLIC FINANCE

At the beginning of the 1980s GDC committed itself to providing financial assistance to ensure the regeneration of the area. Initially this took the form, as we have seen, of a £5100 per housing unit (currently £6300) conversion grant. Where housing had formerly existed at some time in the past this figure could be raised by use of improvement grants and Housing Action status as occurred in the Merchant Court project.

However, these sums provided by GDC soon proved inadequate for the more complex conversions and the SDA's help was requested. The agency is responsible for the administration of LEG-UP, which is broadly equivalent to the former Urban Development Grant in England and Wales. Any public support through this means is provided on the basis that it is 'the minimum which is required to make the project happen'. Besides LEG-UP the SDA can also provide a grant toward environmental work, although it is subject to a clawback.

The SDA's involvement, initially simply in the form of grant provision, has subsequently become more complex, as indeed has GDCs. This was first necessitated in the Ingram Square development by both the scale of the project and the size of the public contribution. A subsidiary, Yarmadillo, of Kantel, the developers, was set up to administer the project and a development agreement was drawn up between Yarmadillo, the SDA and GDC in 1984.

GDC contributed properties in its ownership to the project which were valued at £410 000. However Yarmadillo paid only a 10% deposit and the remainder was not paid until completion, December 1989. In addition it provided a conversion grant of £1 344 600. The SDA also contributed an environmental grant of £208 000 which was subject to a clawback, together with an interest-free loan of £1 069 000 (paid back in December, 1989).

The development agreement entitles Yarmadillo to 10% of the residential income, and any profits to be split three ways, the developer receiving 50% and the SDA and GDC 25% each. With the project nearing completion the SDA is likely to receive £100 000 under its clawback agreement with just under £400 000 to be divided by the participants.

The Italian Centre is a further example of the complex financial partnerships between the public and private sectors. The 32 flats in the development received £352 000 conversion grant, following Scottish Development Department approval, while the SDA provided £220 000 of LEG-UP and £290 000 environmental work grants. GDC also owned the original buildings valued at £200 000 prior to the beginning of the project. These properties will be paid for at the completion of the project and hence represent a form of interest-free loan. GDC also issued a loan guarantee to the British Linen Bank enabling the developer, Classical House, to receive finance at a beneficial rate. The development agreement sets out a management fee to Classical House and any profits to be split equally between the developers, GDC and the SDA. It is estimated that the SDA clawback on this scheme will be £300 000.

The increasingly complex nature of these financial arrangements with the use of equity sharing loans, the retention of equity interests, etc., makes it difficult to assess the precise contribution of the public sector. Indeed, in the Virginia Court project, the SDA has taken a minority equity interest of £500 000. The picture is further complicated by the lack of published information on out-turn financial appraisal. In this analysis we are confined to the use of approval stage appraisals shown in Table 9.3 which probably predate construction by 18 months. As such the analysis will tend to over-estimate the role of the public sector in this respect. Further, with the successful marketing of the houses at prices above those originally envisaged, there has been the increasing use of clawback by the SDA.

In the first conversion project the public-sector contribution amounted to 30% of the development cost although GDC retained an equity interest in the ground-floor shop. This figure rises to 40% for the next developments; Merchant Court (it retained interest in six shops) and Blackfriars Court. Since, then, although the picture has become more blurred the vast majority of the schemes appear to have at least a 30% contribution, i.e. a private- to public-sector investment ratio of 2.3:1. This is the average ratio found in an evaluation of urban development grant for housing projects by Public Sector Management Research (1988). This latter study was based on out-turn costs and includes newbuild projects and is therefore not directly comparable.

Seen from the perspective of costs per housing unit a broadly equivalent pattern emerges with unit costs in two developments of more than £12 000. The scale of public expenditure on these individual projects mirrors the relative difficulty of the schemes and to some extent the public sector's view of their importance. The figures presented in Table 9.3 compare with the UDG study above, which found an average cost of £7800 per unit in 1985–6. More recent figures published by the National Audit Office (1990) have found an average unit cost of £5500 (no precise date) but that these costs ranged from £3553 to £14 900. The variable nature of Merchant City unit costs therefore is not abnormal and within the bounds to be found elsewhere.

The analysis so far has focused on the public-sector contribution and its cost. However, the logic of this financial assistance is partly at least that of

Table 9.3 Public-sector contributions to developments (in £). The public sector contributions to Canada Court and 20 Montrose Street which received interest-free loans were based on 25% of their value. In the case of Ingram Square, given the length of the development period, interest-free loans were treated for these calculations as 100% grant. (*Source:* Glasgow D.C. and S.D.A. Records)

Development	Type	GDC	SDA	Public-sector contribution (% of development costs)	Public-sector† contribution (per housing unit)	SDA clawback
Albion Building	Conversion	117 300		30	5 100	
Merchant Court	Conversion	186 346		40	9 317	
Blackfriars Court	Conversion	321 300	219 000	41	8 576	8 000
Watson Street	Conversion	–	–	Nil	Nil	
Wilson Court	Conversion	240 500	–	N/A	6 500	
Mercatgate	Conversion	229 500	–	N/A	4 883	
Canada Court	Conversion	443 200	400 000*	21	7 872	
20 Montrose St	Conversion	240 525	200 000*	26	9 684	
Ingram Square	Conversion/Newbuild	(See text)		37	12 513	100 000
Glassford Court	Conversion/Newbuild	198 900	342 000	31	13 869	To be determined
Macintosh Court	Rehab/Newbuild/Conversion	–	–	Nil	Nil	
The Stables Bell St	Conversion/Newbuild	–	Ph. 1 210 000 Ph. 2 98 000	27	6 563	30 000 107 000
College Lands Bell St	Conversion	831 300	300 000	35	7 160	266 467
Campbell Court	Conversion	–	–	Nil	Nil	300 000
Italian Centre	Conversion	(See text)		N/A	N/A	
Virginia Court	Conversion	900 000	1 282 000			To be determined

* Interest-free loan.
† Public-sector contribution at approval stage.

pump priming the market from which the public-sector support will eventually be withdrawn. While the level of clawback has increased comparison of Tables 9.1 and 9.3 reveals that there are two small schemes (one mixed use) that have received no public assistance and only one large scheme, Macintosh Court in 1986–7 in this position. This scheme was described earlier; it encompasses 82 newbuild flats out of a total scheme of 113 units. This suggests that newbuild is viable in the Merchant City, but as yet this 'success' has yet to be replicated.

Despite the establishment of a thriving housing market there are no major conversion schemes which have come forth without public assistance. Part of the reason can be traced back to how the initiative began with the structurally easier projects. Later schemes have faced more difficult design problems and undoubtedly the planning authority has set higher standards, particularly in regard to local environmental work and car parking. For example, if it is feasible for car parking to be physically located in the cellar its provision will be a condition of the grant of planning permission.

Furthermore the availability of public finance has perhaps inevitably influenced land values. Potential assistance has been built into many site valuations with the result that land prices have been bid up. This is illustrated by the following example. A public body some years ago marketed a site in the Merchant City and received a number of offers. The highest bid was three times the lowest, but while the lowest presumed no subsequent grants the highest was conditional on a range of public assistance. The success of the initiative has therefore raised land prices: whereas at the beginning of the 1980s the price of land was virtually zero, a one-acre commercial/housing site has recently been assembled at a cost of £1.2 million.

The form of public-sector assistance has also tended to distort development in the area. The availability of conversion grants on a unit basis has resulted in a high proportion of small flats to take maximum advantage of this. In addition, the fact that this GDC grant is only available for conversions has biased development projects away from gap sites. There has, however, been some cross-subsidization within mixed conversion/newbuild and mixed residential/commercial projects if GDC was convinced of its necessity. A further interesting distortion is created by the tax system which zero rates for VAT purposes the conversion of listed buildings. This has led to a number of redesignations.

9.7   CONCLUSION

The Merchant City is a microcosm of Glasgow's continuing efforts in urban renewal. GDC since the late 1970s has sought partnership with the private sector to effect the revival of the city. This is very evident in the Merchant

City where the policy emphasis has been one of facilitating and supporting the private sector. The scale of the initiative, however, would not have been possible without SDA support and LEGUP.

In many ways the Merchant City is not a typical example of housing-led urban regeneration. The developments have principally been aimed at the young middle classes and increasingly at high-income groups. The spinoff retail services have not necessarily been aimed at meeting the needs of this group but rather have latched on to the image of the area. More recent commercial developments are building on this through the provision of specialist shopping in off city centre locations. Yet the promotion of housing has not only found a solution to the redundant and decaying warehouses of the 1970s but has also demonstrated a new role for an area which had lost its comparative advantage as a distribution centre.

The success of the project has brought with it a number of new problems in the form of conflicting uses, traffic and car-parking issues. It is also important to remember that the revitalization of the Merchant City is incomplete. Furthermore, despite its success, it is still dependent on public funds and therefore its future relies on these monies continuing. It would be very difficult for the public sector to withdraw its support without the painful acceptance that the current momentum would fall by the wayside. The conundrum of rising land values and the ongoing need for public assistance is therefore likely to continue. Perhaps the public sector can comfort itself with the knowledge that financial support enables a degree of quality control over private-sector development.

10

FROM SHIPYARD TO HOUSING ESTATE: THE TRANSFORMATION OF THE URBAN FABRIC

Patsy Healey

10.1 INTRODUCTION

This case study is an example of the process of transforming waterfront sites which were formerly used for heavy industrial production into environments primarily for consumption. It is intrinsically of interest since it is a substantial site, within an industrial conurbation but far from downtown/city centre. It represents a difficult location to transform in a conurbation full of difficult waterfront sites. It was not in an area specifically targeted for government attention other than via the Urban Programme, until 1987 when it was absorbed into the Tyne and Wear Development Cor-poration's area. It attracted from central government the largest Urban Development Grant in the country for a housing project. One of the most significant agents in the transformation process, and arguably the most significant, has been the local authority, South Tyneside Metropolitan Borough Council.

The aim of this case study is:

1. To describe the processes involved in the transformation of the environment in this instance;

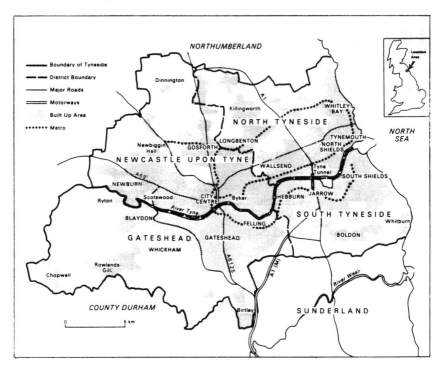

Figure 10.1   Hebburn in Tyneside. Robinson (1989b)

2.   To identify the actors and agencies involved in the process and their relationships with the local, national and global economy; and

3.   To assess the main driving forces structuring the strategies of the actors, the patterns of relationships between them and the nature of the transformation achieved.

10.2   CONTEXT

The case focuses on shipyards and land adjacent to them on the riverside at Hebburn. Hebburn is within the Tyne and Wear conurbation in the North-East of England, the central focus of which is Newcastle City Centre (Fig. 10.1). The conurbation and its development opportunities have already been described in Chapter 5. The shipyards are located on the south bank of the Tyne halfway between Newcastle and the rivermouth. Shipyards were established here (by Andrew Leslie and others) in the middle of last century, and through mergers became known as the Hawthorn Leslie and Palmers (Hebburn) Yards (Fig. 10.2). These faced a collection of shipyards on the opposite bank at Walker and Wallsend (Fig. 10.3). The yards were bordered

Figure 10.2 Andrew Leslie's shipyard. Photograph of original print, with permission from AMARC

on the east by a colliery and on the west by open land used as a dumping ground for ships' ballast. Rail lines crisscrossed the yards themselves, and crossed the southern boundary road (Wagonway), providing access in the past both from the sites to the main rail network and to the riverside for firms on the level land above. To the south-west and south were terrace housing, council housing and workshops on the edge of Hebburn itself, which, until 1974, had been a municipal urban district.

By the 1970s the yard had been absorbed on nationalization into the Swan Hunter complex, which owned yards on both sides of the Tyne, as part of British Shipbuilders. During the 1980s, British Shipbuilders were re-privatized, and Swan Hunters re-emerged with a management buyout. By this time, the fortunes of British Shipbuilding had tumbled dramatically. British Shipbuilders decided to close the Hawthorn Leslie Yard, apart from its Training Agency. (The latter, which on privatization became an independent charity, AMARC, was originally the Swan Hunter Training Section.) The neighbouring Palmers (or Hebburn) Yard was 'mothballed', held in reserve in case of a future upturn in the industry's fortunes (and also to avoid competitors getting access to a valuable large dry dock). Production was concentrated on the north bank, with over 2000 jobs lost in the Hawthorn Leslie and Hebburn Yards in the early 1980s. Meanwhile, the southern

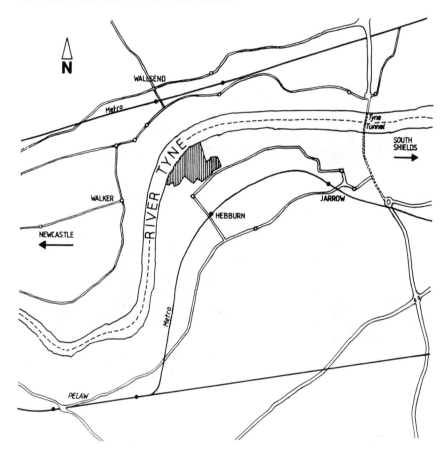

Figure 10.3   The Hebburn Riverside. Drawn by Peter Sanderson

part of the site was in the ownership of Vickers Engineering Limited, a major company based in the conurbation. This company, too, was rationalizing production from the late 1970s. It closed its premises in Hebburn in the early 1980s.

The local authority, South Tyneside Metropolitan Borough Council, was created through local government reorganization in 1974, merging the Urban Districts of Hebburn, Jarrow and South Shields. Incoming Councillors and Officers were able to shape the new authority into one dedicated to environmental improvement and local economic development as well as carrying out a council's normal service delivery and regulatory roles. The Planning Department had a strong economic development team within it. It also had responsibility for co-ordinating Urban Programme activity. Given the poverty in the area, South Tyneside became an Urban Programme authority under the 1978 Inner Urban Areas Act. Urban Programme funds

Figure 10.4   The Hebburn area in 1986

provided a budget which could be focused on social, economic and environmental development objectives (although this spending flow had to be approved annually by the regional office of the Department of the Environment). In the late 1970s, the council put considerable effort into environmental improvement along the Hebburn riverside, to open up a riverside walkway and to landscape derelict sites. In the 1980s, they also refurbished St Andrew's Church and Centre, converting it to small workshops. Council housing (four-storey walk-ups) adjacent to the Vickers' properties was also gradually demolished in the 1980s. But the council's major involvement in this area in the 1980s was in the transformation of the shipyard complex to a housing estate and a leisure and training complex (Fig. 10.4).

In this effort, they negotiated with the main landowners (Vickers, and particularly British Shipbuilders), and by the mid-1980s, formed what was in effect a partnership with the Training Agency (AMARC) and with Bellway Urban Renewals Limited, although no formal partnership agreement was ever entered into. This North-East-based housebuilding firm had arrived in the area in 1985, and was quickly attracted to the idea of a major housing scheme. By the end of the 1980s, the first stage of this scheme was occupied by the purchasers of houses built by Bellway.

By this time, the economic prospects of the conurbation were considered by many to have improved substantially. However, at the time it was thought that shipbuilding was unlikely to recover and, with a glut of riverside locations, the industrial potential at Hebburn appeared extremely limited. The Council, Bellway and AMARC hoped to develop the riverside itself for a leisure complex with a shipbuilding museum. This would provide work opportunities for the training agency and create an attractive market for the top-of-the-market housing Bellway hope to develop on the western part of the area, previously landscaped by the District Council.

But, by the late 1980s, the institutional context had changed. Until 1988, South Tyneside MBC had responsibility for planning and Urban Programme funds for all its area. It had decided to concentrate its economic regeneration efforts on the riverside, including Hebburn. South Tyneside did not have the benefit of an inner city partnership which would have brought more resources, nor were they able to benefit from Enterprise Zone status in their area. But they overcame these potential financial limitations by maximizing the co-ordination and targeting of the resources they could largely control (Urban Programme funds, local authority discretionary spending) or attract (European Regional Development Funds, Derelict Land Grant, Urban Development Grant). However, in 1987, the Hebburn riverside was included in the territory of the new Tyne and Wear Development Corporation. This meant that the Council lost both its planning control powers and, by 1989, its control over Urban Programme funds and Derelict Land Grant. From 1989, the local authority role in bidding for Urban Development Grant was cut, with applicants negotiating directly with the DoE for the new City Grant. As a result, the local authority's stakes in the development process were drastically reduced. The Tyne and Wear Development Corporation, which has its own budget and can promote City Grant schemes, targeted resources more strongly to Newcastle, Sunderland and the Port of Tyne project in North Tyneside. In this context, major questions hang over the completion of the transformation of the Hebburn area as envisioned by the main participants in the mid-1980s.

Transformation of the urban fabric takes time. This case study covers the period 1979–89. Work was already underway on riverside landscaping prior to this, while a substantial amount of development remains in project for the 1990s. The 10-year period of the study can thus only be an episode in the transformation process. It does, however, cover the major change, when production activities were largely closed down, and schemes for the consumption revival developed.

As Yin (1989) notes, writing up a case study is a difficult task. A simple chronological account would have the merit of presenting evidence in detail before analytical emphases were imposed in interpretation. However, this would require a lengthy document. It is also misleading to suggest that a case story can be told neutrally. All research of this nature is filtered and

Table 10.1 The elements of the development process: a descriptive model

---

Roles in consumption (of land/property)

End user ⟨ for consumption activities ——— goods / services
for production activities ——— goods / services

Landlord of end user
Financier of end user
Financier of landlord of end user ——————— consumption / production

Advisers to/promoters of end uses

Factors of production	*Events in the development process*	
Land	Identification of development opportunities	
Labour	Land assembly	
Capital	Project development	Products
	Site clearance	and
	Acquisition of finance	impact
	Organization of construction	
	Organization of infrastructure	
	Marketing/managing the end product	

Roles in production
Land owner
Developer
Land clearance company
Financier for development
Controller of use/development rights
Builder
Building materials supplier
Infrastructure agency   *re* production processes
Professional advisers   *re* consumption markets

Marketing

---

biased in some way towards the questions the researcher is concerned with. The solution adopted has therefore been to provide first a summary of the facts of the case followed by an account of the processes through which the site was transformed.

The account is focused by a descriptive model of the elements of the development process through which sites are transformed from one built form, set of uses and set of land rights to another (Table 10.1). This has been developed from a review of models of the development process (Drewett, 1973; Barrett *et al.*, 1978; Bryant *et al.*, 1982; Goodchild and Munton, 1985; Healey *et al.*, 1988, Chap. 7; Ambrose, 1986; Harvey, 1985).

It presents factors of production which are transformed into development outputs by the performance of a number of acts or events. To activate these transformations, agents perform a number of roles. The model makes no assumptions about either the sequence of events or the way roles may be associated in the activities of any particular agent. It does, however, demand an analytical breakdown of roles into those involved in the production of sites and properties and those involved in their consumption. In reality, such a separation is not always easy to sustain. A developer will need to assess the end-user market for property, and a financier for development may be an intending end-user, or the financier of an end-user. The separation is maintained however for analytical purposes, in order to assist in assessing the balance of power in the process between supply-side and production factors, and demand-side or consumption factors. A further distinction has been made with respect to the consumption side. Development is produced for consumption, but this consumption could either be for economic production purposes or consumption purposes. To the extent that our interest is in the contribution of the development process to the local economy, it is necessary not only to examine how the processes of production of sites and buildings use labour and capital in production and the effects of this on the local economy, but to assess the way the product of the process supplies sites and buildings as inputs to production and consumption activities locally.

10.3   HEBBURN RIVERSIDE IN 1979 AND 1989

Figure 10.5 summarizes the activities in the area at the start of the study period. The two shipyards were still in use, though employment levels were much reduced from levels of 10 years previously. Both were part of the nationalized Swan Hunter/British Shipbuilders enterprise, but the centre of activities in Tyneside was across the river at Wallsend (Fig. 10.5). Behind the shipyards and fronting on to Wagonway was the Vickers plant. This was a galvanizing works, said to have the largest galvanizing bath in the country, with associated steel-fabrication works. The west part of their site was leased to British Shipbuilders, and their whole site was crisscrossed with rail lines, over which Carr Ellison estates had rights of way. To the west of Ellison Street was a former ballast hill, which had been cleared by South Tyneside MBC which was in the process of laying it down to grass as temporary landscaping. Beside the river were two buildings used by HMS Kelly Sea Cadets. To the south, the Council was renovating the landscape to provide a riverside park, in which was also a group of small factory units, built in the 1970s. To the south of Ann Street were terraces of small Tyneside flats, renovated internally and with external street improvements. St Andrew's Church and Centre commanded the site from the top of the hill. Opposite

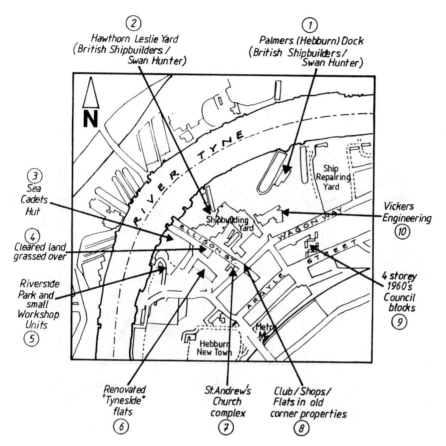

Figure 10.5 Hebburn in 1979. Drawn by Peter Sanderson

it, on a small corner plot on the edge of land in Vickers ownership was a group of decaying old properties with a club/pub and shop premises. South of Lyon Street were older workshops and houses on the edge of Hebburn Centre, and to the south of Wagonway was an estate of 1960s four-storey walk-up council houses.

This landscape of 1979 was not so different to that in 1959 or 1969. It was dominated by production activity and particularly the shipyards, represented by large powerful industrial companies. The main changes in physical terms were the renovation of some housing, some housing clearance (and industrial clearance) and in the 1970s attempts to tidy up the landscape and open up abandoned areas, particularly by the riverside, for use as parkland for local people. But in terms of activity, investment and environmental quality, the picture in 1979 was very different from that in 1959. Then, large numbers worked in the shipyards and at Vickers, and the area was dominated by the flow of people and freight and the noise, fumes and dust of industrial activity.

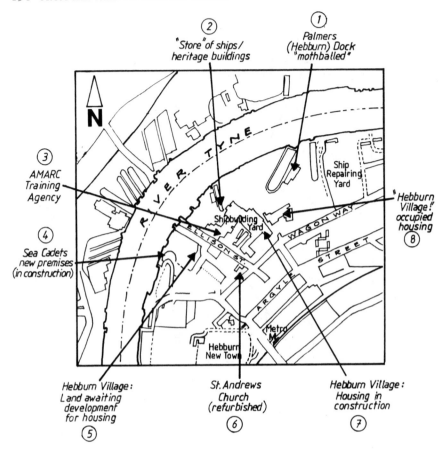

Figure 10.6   Hebburn in 1989. Drawn by Peter Sanderson

Faced with the collapse of production activity in the area, the vision of the local council and of the Tyne and Wear County Council as embodied in the Structure Plan was nevertheless for a renewal of industrial activity, accompanied by environmental improvement, a humanized production environment. It was not until the mid-1980s that the council reluctantly accepted that this vision might not be achievable.

By 1989 parts of the Hawthorn Leslie Shipyard and all of the Vickers plant were cleared. Work was underway on the road framework for the housing scheme. To the south-west, refurbished buildings stand in a landscape of grass, with trees marking the area dedicated to the Riverside Park. The Hawthorn Leslie Shipyard remained in 1989 merely as structures, providing a distinctive landscape for a 1980s private housing estate, buildings for a Training Agency, and a store of heritage buildings and ships for an envis-aged future as a shipbuilding museum and leisure complex (Fig. 10.6). The new activities are nearly all concerned with consumption. The only remaining connections with production are the small factory units (5 in Fig. 10.5) and those provided in the St Andrew's Church renovation, as well as AMARC's training role. However, this new landscape is quite unlike the waterfront redevelopments of the international 'urban renaissance' literature (Fig. 10.7). Although the intended shipbuilding museum is aimed to attract a national and international visitor market, the environment so far created shows little sign of the consumerist lifestyle symbols which typify the international image of regenerated docklands. So far, the landscape is provided for local people and the housing is being sold into a low-cost local market.

But this is still some way from the vision of the area as conceived by the Borough Council, the AMARC Training Agency and Bellway Urban Renewals Limited. This is summarized in the development proposals in Fig. 10.8. The project, according to STMB, is 'without doubt one of the most ambitious schemes ever tackled by South Tyneside'. It involved:

1. The expansion of AMARC's activities into the adjoining fabrication sheds, conversion of the clock-tower building into Enterprise Workshops, and the development of a yacht haven (part completed; clock tower now expected to be exhibition space only);
2. The establishment of a shipbuilding exhibition area and centre on the rest of the former Hebburn Yard, to further 'exploit the tourism potential of the Borough' (awaiting funding); and
3. Housing construction on the former shipyard land and adjacent sites (part completed).

As for Spring 1992, major uncertainties hung over the funding of the Shipbuilding Exhibition Centre. This raises two questions. First, how interrelated were the elements of these projects? Did Bellway need an attractive leisure facility to redefine the area in market terms to allow building the more expensive properties which would ensure the profitability of the scheme? Or is the future of the housing as a local estate increasing the stock of low-cost private housing in the area? If the vision is eventually achieved, how comfortably will the various elements coexist? Local people and businesses are used to a close association between work, leisure and living space, which is what the scheme offers in its mix of housing, leisure and training. Does this mixture fit in with the lifestyle imagery of new generations who may live in the area? The council shifted its strategy from 'humanizing production' to 'fostering consumption'. The transformed environment is intended as both an asset for local people and to attract new investment, in the short term in building and refurbishment work, and in the long term, in the form of leisure spending by people outside the area which will filter through to local people. How realistic and how valuable these benefits will be for local people remain a matter of debate.

Figure 10.7 Housing landscapes in 1989/90. Photography by Dr Ali Madani

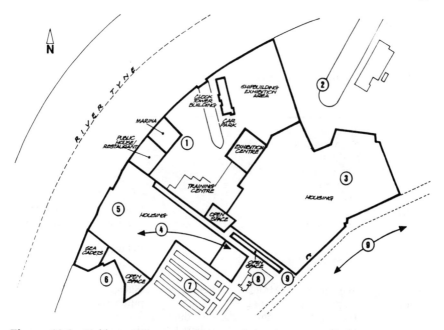

Figure 10.8   Hebburn Village and associated development proposals

10.4   CHRONOLOGY AND LAND OWNERSHIP

To condense the story, activity during the decade fell into three phases:

1. 1979–84   Environmental improvements and the dawning realization of the implications of closures of Vickers plant and the shipyard.
2. 1985–7   The era of partnership between STMB, Bellway and AMARC in promoting a new 'consumption' vision for the area.
3. 1987–9   Transfer of responsibilities to the Tyne and Wear Urban Development Corporation, and the consequent change in powers and resources to implement the new strategy.

Urban redevelopment typically involves the reorganization of land parcels in terms of configuration and ownership as well as physical structures and uses. Table 10.2 shows how sites have been reallocated among owners. The major owners in 1979 were South Tyneside, Vickers and British Shipbuilders. By 1989, the area was still dominated by large owners, although parts had been broken down into housing plots and sold off to individual owners, a process that will increase as housing development proceeds. Ownership of the site in 1989 was concentrated in the hands of AMARC, South Tyneside and Bellway. But both South Tyneside and Bellway had acted as developers, taking over land, reparcelling and leasing or selling sites. Bellway will terminate its ownership role in the area during the 1990s unless their plans are

Table 10.2 Land ownership transfers 1979 to 1989

| 1979 | 1989 | | | | |
	STMB	AMARC	Bellway	Individual Home Owners	Individual Firms
STMB	Riverside Park St. Andrew's Church Sea Cadets (moved site)				
Vickers	(Bought site and sold to Bellway)			(Sites purchased from Bellway)	(Artec Ltd. purchased part of site in mid-1980s but went bankrupt.
British Ship-builders/ Swan Hunter	Site for Ship-building Museum;	AMARC Training Centre	Remainder of Site, including ballast hill	(Sites purchased from Bellway)	
Individual Home Owners				Some Tyneside flats; Corner Site	
Individual Firms					Corner Site

seriously delayed. South Tyneside at one point in 1987–8 owned virtually the whole area, buying out British Shipbuilders' and Vickers' interests. But it immediately transferred much of the land purchased to Bellway. In the long term, it expects to be left with some open spaces, a landowner interest with respect to St Andrew's Church and some Tyneside flats, and an ownership role with respect to the Shipbuilding Museum. (Note: No STMBC land at Hebburn was vested in 1987 in the Tyne and Wear Development Corporation, although the Borough did lose ownership of sites elsewhere through vesting.)

10.5   THE MAIN AGENTS OF CHANGE

A small number of agencies have played the major role in the transformation at Hebburn. Yet documentary material shows a vast array of agencies involved. Some were directly involved, as landowners, end-users, financiers, regulators, builders, etc. Other agencies appear in the records because they were approached to be involved, or because they sought to be involved. Some were there as political representatives, the area being visited during the 1980s by MPs (Norman Lamont, David Trippier, Kenneth Baker and Neil McFarlane, representing DoE and DTI interest) and by an EEC Commissioner.

Table 10.3 lists the major and other significant agencies involved in built-environment transformation at Hebburn. Even here there are eight major agencies and 15 other significant ones, spanning all types of agencies, all levels of government, private firms ranging from local consultants to national companies, and voluntary groups from St Anthony of Padua Community Association to the CBI. A hypothesis which should be explored in other projects is whether such a pattern of agency involvement is normal for transformed industrial sites in the 1980s, and whether there are distinctive patterns which link to types of outcomes.

Detailed examination of all the agencies involved shows some other interesting features of the pattern of agency involvement. First, there was a large number of smaller firms involved. These tended to be in the building contracting field, or were consultants (including solicitors, needed for the land deals). Such firms tended to cluster around the main actors. Second, these clusters of smaller firms were not necessarily local. Bellway used contractors from the conurbation, and also from the Northern Region as a whole. South Tyneside's range of contacts spanned all spatial scales, from very small firms in Jarrow and South Shields, to the office of the EC in Brussels. Third, a number of firms sought to purchase sites in the area before the consumption-based development framework was agreed upon. These were all in the production sphere. Only one such firm, Artec Structures Limited, obtained a site from Vickers Properties, with a business development loan from South Tyneside Council. But this firm went bankrupt after a year or so, leaving South Tyneside with a possessory title to the site. It was then incorporated in the sale to Bellway. It is possible that all the other firms were similarly unlikely to succeed, and were therefore not really viable end-users. British Shipbuilders received a firm offer from one company for part of the site, but to accept this would have impaired the opportunities for the rest of the site. South Tyneside Council persuaded them not to accept this offer in the interests of the development of the wider area. It is possible that this strategy had the effect of forcing out production companies, so that South Tyneside's original production-based vision for the area could not be implemented.

10.6   THE DEVELOPMENT PROCESS

How did the transformation in physical environment and social relations at Hebburn take place? What were the key factors which drove the process?

Table 10.3 The main agents of change

Agency	Sector	Type of interest
Major		
Bellway Urban Renewals Ltd	Private	Developer
AMARC	Charity	End user: production training
British Shipbuilders/Swan Hunter	Nationalized/privatized industry	Landowner (formerly end-user production)
Bowey Construction (for Bellway)	Private	Builder
Vickers Properties Ltd	Private	Landowner (formerly end-user production)
South Tyneside MBC (solicitors, planning and economic development)	Local authority	Controller of development/use rights Landowner Developer Financier of development via rates and UP funds Financier of end-user End user: consumption (open space) Promoter of end-users Landlord of end-users
Tyne Wear Development Corporation	Central government agency	Controller of Development/user rights Financier of development via UP funds
Department of the Environment	Central government	Financier of development (via UP, UDG, DLG) Political representation
Significant		
Browne, Smith and Parker (architects for Bellway)	Private	Consultants to developer
Blacketts (land clearance for Bellway)	Private	Land clearance company
Coopers Lybrand (consultants for Shipbuilding Museum project)	Private	Consultants to developers and end-use promoters
Sanderson Townend & Gilbert (property consultants)	Private	Consultants to development producers
Storey Sons & Parker (property consultants)	Private	Consultants to development producers
Norwest Holst Soil Engineering	Private	Consultants to developers and landowners (*re* ground conditions)

Table 10.3 (Continued)

Agency	Sector	Type of interest
Artec Structures Ltd	Private	End-user (production)
South Tyneside MBC (Engineers, Chief Executive's Department Councillors)	Local authority	Controller of development standards (road layout) Promoter of end-users Political representation
Department of Trade and Industry (MSC/C Programme)	Central government and agencies	Finance for labour for development Finance for end-user: production (AMARC)
Tyne Wear Museums Service	Local authority agency	End user: consumption
TED Co.	Local authority agency	Promoter of end-users: production
HMS Kelly Sea Cadets	Voluntary agency	End user: consumption
St Anthony of Padua Community Association	Community association	End user: consumption (promoter of)
Tudor Trust	Charitable trust	Finance for development (AMARC) refurbishment
CBI (promotion of private sector community programme)	National pressure group	Promoters of finance for labour for development (private sector-led community programme)

What were the opportunities exploited and constraints encountered? This is explored by summarizing the actors and events which achieved the various stages in the development process indicated in Table 10.1. It is stressed that these stages were not necessarily sequential. Problems of land assembly, for example, were not fully resolved until building on the Hebburn Village Housing Scheme was just about to start.

10.6.1 Identification of a development opportunity

The key players here were British Shipbuilders, Bellway Urban Renewal Limited, and South Tyneside Metropolitan Borough Council. In the 1970s, as already noted, South Tyneside's concern was to improve the local environment and open up the riverside for local people. They then became concerned about the threatened closure of first the Vickers plant and then the Hawthorn Leslie Yard. The training agency AMARC was also concerned to develop a strategy for the area. They promoted to British Shipbuilders the idea of a feasibility study of opportunities for re-use. This helped in the process of identifying the possibility of waterfront leisure after-uses. British

Shipbuilders sought finally to dispose of the site as a whole, as did the Council. To assist in this, a planning concept and development strategy were needed, to indicate future development opportunities. Bellway appeared on the scene in 1985, initially attracted by the waterfront leisure-related opportunities. Their ideas for a housing scheme then provided the momentum for subsequent development activity. At this stage, therefore, two large national companies defined the opportunity with respect to disposal and re-use. The local authority meanwhile actively mediated to reduce the costs and increase the benefits for the area and its people.

10.6.2 Land assembly

Given that the interests in the transformation of the area were (including Vickers) three large companies and the local council, land assembly should have been relatively straightforward. In practice, it took three years to negotiate the deals to transfer ownerships from British Shipbuilders and Vickers to Bellway and South Tyneside Metropolitan Borough Council. The problems related initially to establishing price. This was partly related to calculations about the scrap value of the sheds and equipment (e.g. cranes) in BSB's yard, which was considerable. South Tyneside, and the Training Agency AMARC, wished to retain some sheds and equipment for training purposes, and as assets for the proposed Shipbuilding Museum. BSB had originally expected to demolish everything and clear the site. A second delay arose from the privatization of BSB which became Swan Hunter in 1986. The deal was to be struck with Swan Hunter. A complication was that the deal became a purchase and sale contract, with South Tyneside Council as the intermediary. BSB and Vickers sold to the Council, who then sold most of the site on to Bellway. The terms of the sale deal were formalized in negotiations with the DoE for the substantial Urban Development Grant awarded to Bellway. Expectations about land value also fluctuated, falling in the early 1980s as depression in the industrial sector deepened, but rising again when Bellway showed interest in the site. Values were more or less confirmed by early 1987. Both BSB and Vickers probably benefited from the delay allowing them to dispose of their land with some housing value attached, rather than selling into a depressed industrial property market. However, exchange of contracts was delayed by a whole series of difficulties in the title to land. South Tyneside solicitors spent a great deal of time checking out the ownership of parts of the Vickers site and ensuring that various rights of access and use had been extinguished. Such problems indicate the advantage to BSB, Vickers and Bellway of transferring ownership of the site through South Tyneside Council. Bellway needed a 'clean' title, free of outstanding claims and without pollution or subsidence threats, to pass on to home purchasers and their mortgagors.

10.6.3 Project development

In some redevelopment schemes, a proposed after-use is the driving force. In this case, the issue was to **imagine** a possible after-use and get sufficient organizational commitment and resources to bring this to fruition. In these conditions, ideas about after-use evolved in parallel with land deals and related negotiations.

The original idea was a continuation of industrial and port-related activity in the shipyards and the Vickers sites. In 1982, South Tyneside actively explored the industrial potential of both sites, although one of Vickers' reasons for withdrawing from the site was lack of Enterprise Zone status. They preferred to consolidate on their holdings further up the Tyne in the Tyneside Enterprise Zone. In 1983, ideas for small workshop units were being discussed. A site-investigation study was undertaken to check ground conditions. However, by 1984, the Council approached both BSB and Vickers.

'In view of the lack of progress in terms of obtaining new industrial use for the land and the considerable amount of industrial land/ buildings in the area (the Council) gave consideration to alternative uses.' Housing might be considered, but this would be 'totally conditional upon there being no possibility of industrial development on any of this land.'

(File record STMBC 1989)

BSB nevertheless continued to prefer industrial after-use until early 1985. They had been approached by several companies interested in a part of their site. But for reasons which are unclear, no progress was made with these.

Meanwhile, the training agency AMARC developed ideas not only for workshops using part of the shipyard site, but saw potential in a riverside marina development. AMARC's interest was in the potential training opportunities such activity might provide. In collaboration with South Tyneside, a feasibility study was undertaken into the potential for multipurpose workshops, a marina and an Enterprise Centre for training. Sponsored by TEDCo (Training and Enterprise Development Company), this study, which reported in late 1985, supported the Enterprise Centre idea, but urged caution about both the workshops and the marina. The issues raised here related to market demand. Such schemes were by now popping up all over the North East.

By this time, Bellway had arrived on the scene. Originally contacting AMARC in connection with the marina proposal, Bellway had by late 1985 made proposals for housing development. By January 1986, South Tyneside's Town Development Committee, responsible for planning matters, agreed the proposals for a housing-led strategy for the area, through a partnership between Bellway, AMARC and South Tyneside. A development brief was to be produced jointly by Bellway and the Planning Department, and the Chair of Town Development Committee was given delegated powers to fast-track project negotiations. The brief was agreed by February 1986 and Bellway declared themselves 'excited' by the project and 'delighted' with progress (File record STMBC 1986). They nevertheless remained cautious about the housing market until well into 1987. The scheme involved smaller, lower-cost housing to the south, with 'executive' housing along the waterfront. The first phases were low-cost units to the south. Nevertheless, Bellway was concerned about people's ability to pay. They therefore sought a high level of subsidy from the DoE in negotiations over the Urban Development Grant. The DoE however, required renegotiation to increase the numbers of dwellings, and the proposed selling prices (thus increasing the calculated leverage ratio for the UDG from 1:1.9 to 1:2.5). They also explored relationships with housing associations (The Bradford and Northern) and with providers for specialist housing needs. None of these were successful, and in the end, the booming housing market of 1988–9 averted the need for such measures.

As the housing proposals became increasingly defined, uncertainty remained with respect to the waterfront sites around AMARC, the core of the old Hawthorn Leslie Yard. With questions raised about a marina, AMARC nevertheless believed that a tourist facility was essential to change the character of the area and bring in enough income to support some of the training work. Bellway also considered that a leisure scheme along the riverside was important for revaluing the location to allow its more expensive housing to become viable. The only reservations were from the council solicitors, who wondered if home owners might complain about the noise and intrusion from leisure uses and sue the Council for allowing these to proceed. In early 1986, the leisure idea the participants had been waiting for appeared in the proposals for a Shipbuilding Heritage Centre on the Tyne. This idea had been around in the conurbation for some time. On this occasion, the St Anthony of Padua Community Association at Walker, on the other side of the river, took the initiative in promoting the idea. It was attractive both for its job-generating potential and as a national exhibition facility which would also celebrate a very important aspect of the conurbation's cultural and industrial heritage. But the problem was first to determine which of several competing locations was the best site, and second to determine how such a project could be financed. This led to another consultancy study (by Coopers Lybrand). Meanwhile, South Tyneside energetically took up the idea, and began collecting items for the Museum, including *HMS Cavalier*, which they bought from Brighton. The consultancy study confirmed that Hebburn was the most appropriate site and that the Shipbuilding Museum project was an exciting idea. But they also noted that it could never be self-financing. From 1987, the future of the project was in the hands of the Tyne and Wear Development Corporation. The Corporation was set up with a brief to attract private investment to take responsibility for urban redevelopment in their area. The Shipbuilding Museum project hardly fitted this remit. Nevertheless, the Corporation continued to explore possibilities, commissioning further consultancy studies, particularly from L & R (Leisure) Consultants (1988–9) and Conran Roche Planning (1990).

Three points arise from the way the various ingredients of the transformation project have been developed. First, although finally collected into the North Hebburn Development Proposals in late 1986 (Fig. 10.8), these proposals are hardly an integrated development and design brief. The brief has rather grown as an amalgam of proposals. A critical issue for the future of the area is how integrated they really are. Second, extensive use was made of feasibility studies and consultancies to test out the ideas as they arose. Consultancies here were being used to evaluate and filter project ideas rather than generating them. There is an interesting contrast here between this approach and that used by the Tyne and Wear Development Corporation when it commissioned consultancy studies to develop planning frameworks for the various parts of its territory. Here, the consultants were briefed to generate ideas, and certainly did so in North Tyneside and Sunderland (Davoudi and Healey, 1990). Third, the proposals were effectively fast tracked through planning procedures and building regulations. Only the Engineers Department in South Tyneside raised significant objections, particularly about the design of estate roads and of the access roundabout.

10.6.4 Site clearance

All sites of this nature involve complex clearance as a result of the structures on them, underneath them and the potential past pollution of sites. Site clearance work also creates contracts for companies and hence jobs. Norwest Holst Engineering were commissioned early on (1983) to check on ground conditions and found little to cause concern. After this, site clearance issues focused on:

1. What should be demolished and who should do it (see above under land assembly);
2. Getting access to sites to check on conditions prior to purchase (Bellway naturally wanted to do this); and
3. Finding out about unexpected underground pipework as construction started. This required Bellway to check ownership, use and potential hazards with the various infrastructure agencies. No one appeared to have an accurate record of what was under the site. Bellway encountered much more substantial clearance problems on the site than they expected, with poor ground, and pickling baths which took time and cost to break up.

10.6.5 Acquisition of development finance

Table 10.4 summarizes the flows of finance involved in the development activity at Hebburn as far as these can be established. Clearly, the major contributors were Bellway (nearly £10 million, net of the UDG), and the Department of the Environment (£4.5 million in the form of a UDG, and considerable sums via Urban Programme funding to South Tyneside). Other significant contributors were South Tyneside (from its own funds; indirectly from its ratepayers), and the MSC's Community Programme (as a subsidy to labour costs). In these circumstances, it is difficult to calculate the relative contribution of public and private finance. The official agreed proportions for the UDG granted for Hebburn Village assumed a ratio of 1:2.5. However, this left out necessary road access works, which were funded by South Tyneside and the DoE through Urban Programme funds, with Bellway undertaking the design work. At a rough estimate, the total public-sector contribution is unlikely to be less than £5 million, while Bellway's net contribution has been probably in the order of £10.5 million. This would produce a leverage ratio overall of around 1:2 public: private contribution. Even this estimate is probably on the high side, although Bellway's costs rose as a result of unexpectedly expensive ground-clearance work.

What have these funds so far produced and where have they ended up? The finance has been spent primarily on clearing the site, building houses, refurbishing some of the fabrication sheds and the clock tower of the shipyard, buying *HMS Cavalier*, sorting out access problems, and landscaping. Bellway has recouped its investment through sales, and up to the end of 1989 had experienced no problems in this respect. (By late 1990, the executive housing element by the riverside was being reviewed in the light of the market downturn.) A considerable number of people have received training on the refurbishment work. *HMS Cavalier* is a potential tourist asset. Swan Hunter (former British Shipbuilders) and Vickers have been able to realize capital from the land deals.

However the product of the development so far may be valued, the financial flows have nevertheless been from the public purse (DoE and South Tyneside) into the hands of Swan Hunter, Vickers and Bellway. From Bellway, funds have then flowed to the firms involved in construction, notably Bowey Construction. Bellway has in turn been reimbursed by sales, with house purchases financed by mortgage companies. None of this would have happened without public money. This stage of the process has thus been driven by the resources available through urban policy, and by developers' capital, Bellway using their own internal capital. The key agents in this stage were thus the DoE and Bellway, with STMBC playing a critical role as broker.

10.6.6   The building process and infrastructure provision

Bellway and South Tyneside Metropolitan Borough Council were the critical actors in organizing the building process. Bellway and South Tyneside also had a major role in dealing with the infrastructure agencies, though there were few real difficulties here. What is of particular interest is that both Bellway and South Tyneside acted as developers and project managers, perhaps unusual roles for a local authority. Bellway is a residential company, and subcontracted construction work to Bowey, a North East construction firm. To sustain progress, given the complex negotiations over land ownership and the concern to deal rapidly with difficulties, Bellway, South Tyneside and AMARC formed an informal project management partnership team which met monthly in 1987 and 1988 to maintain progress. South Tyneside was not only a very active member of this team, troubleshooting and progress-chasing for Bellway: they also acted as project managers for the refurbishment work on the fabrication sheds for AMARC, as they had also done for the riverside landscaping and conversion work on St Andrew's Church. There can be little doubt that both Bellway and AMARC considered the council to be most effective partners in this respect.

10.6.7   Marketing and managing the end product

This stage was the least problematic for the housing scheme. Bellway accepted a responsibility for maintaining the landscaping for five years after completion of each development phase. Otherwise, the maintenance responsibility was passed on to owner-occupiers and normal council services. As regards marketing, Bellway did not advertise the scheme widely, as in the first phases they were able to tap a highly local and responsive market. Running costs were on the other hand a critical problem with the shipbuilding proposal. No calculations suggested that running costs could realistically be met out of income, and a continuing subsidy was expected. Meanwhile, South Tyneside faced problems of caring for the site intended for the museum in its present state. Guards and dogs were needed to protect the site from vandals. Whatever the outcome, South Tyneside and AMARC, along with Hebburn Village residents, will have a continuing acute interest in the future management of the area. Bellway will also remain involved until all their land is developed or otherwise disposed of. This new configuration of interests in the area thus acts as a significant constraint on future plans for the area.

10.7   CONCLUSIONS

10.7.1   Production versus consumption

The Hebburn riverside area 20 years ago was dominated by large-scale mechanical production activities, shipbuilding and heavy engineering. Now

Table 10.4 Financial flows in the transformation of Hebburn

Organization	Paid out	Received	Financial backing for investment
British Shipbuilders/ Swan Hunter		From ST Council for shipyards	
Vickers		From ST Council for industrial site	National taxation
Department of the Environment	*Urban programme:* (a) For AMARC for refurbishment of fabrication sheds (b) For Hebburn Village road access		
Manpower Services Commission, Department of Employment	For Stage 1 of AMARC refurbishment programme; authorization for Community Programme works		National taxation
AMARC	Community Programme Labour for: Fabrication sheds Sea Cadets new building *HMS Cavalier* refurbishment Riverside landscaping	(a) From MSC (b) From Bellway for Fabrication Shed Refurbishment (proposed) (c) From Urban Programme for Refurbishment Fund (see under South Tyneside)	(a) From a Trust for refurbishment (b) National taxation

South Tyneside Council	(a) For BSB/SH (b) For Vickers (c) For riverside landscaping (d) To buy, move and renovate *HMS Cavalier* (e) For Shipbuilding Museum feasibility study (f) For road access for Hebburn Village	(a) From AMARC refurbishment (b) From DoE (UP funds) (c) From Bellway for site	ST Ratepayers and Urban Programme
Bellway	(a) For AMARC fabrication shed (b) For construction of Hebburn Village (c) For STMB for site design costs for road access	(a) From DoE in UDG (b) Profits on house sales (financed by personal savings/mortgage companies)	(a) Internal capital (b) Share capital

these activities are only a memory on this side of the mid-Tyne, kept alive by the structures of a shipyard and the active shipyards on the opposite bank. They have been replaced by a large housing estate, a training agency and the prospect of an active lesiure facility in the preserved part of the old Hawthorn Leslie yard. This consumption transformation remains only partially achieved until funds should come forward to subsidize the imaginative proposal for the Shipbuilding Museum. It is also a rather uneasy mix of modestly priced private housing aimed at a local market, a training agency, and a leisure complex designed to draw consumption spending from a national and international market. The intention of the museum complex is to attract consumer spending from outside the area into the local economy, thus supporting jobs directly and indirectly through increased local wealth. Some jobs, training and business opportunities have also been generated through the process of transformation, particularly in the use of Community Programme labour in refurbishment work and more generally in the jobs in construction. These cannot of course replace in levels of pay or skill those lost in the shipyards and galvanizing works. Nevertheless, the environment and housing created appears so far to be primarily a local resource, with little sign of 'invasion' by newcomers from outside the area or gentrification. It remains to be seen whether the Shipyard Museum complex would alter this.

However, if locals have retained a strong interest in the new consumption landscape, financially the flow of benefits has been from the public purse to major national companies. BSB/Swan Hunter received a useful return on their land at the time of privatization in 1986. Vickers were able to walk away from a potentially difficult-to-sell site. Bellway has so far made a good return on investment, their initial worries about the market disappearing in the North East's housing boom of the late 1980s.

Viewed in the longer time, however, questions may be asked about whether the consumption vision was the only alternative, and, if so, was it pursued in the most effective way. There is evidence of production activities looking for sites in the mid-1980s. Their interests at Hebburn were effectively closed off by the arrival of Bellway. From the perspective of 1990, however, with a shortage of industrial sites in the conurbation and specifically in South Tyneside, and with something of a revival in shipbuilding, perhaps there was a real alternative to reorganize this stretch of the riverside for modern industrial production activities. However, this would have required a long-term perspective, a coherent approach to the emerging character of the area, and some certainty of resource flows, particularly in the form of public subsidies. The institutional context of the public sector in the 1980s was deliberately set against any of these things. The result, a partially achieved, fractured consumption landscape is perhaps an apt reflection of this context.

10.7.2   The relationships of transformation

This case illustrates the complexity of links which can build up between agencies in such situations. Public and private sectors are interlinked intimately in these relationships. South Tyneside Metropolitan Borough Council's role was critical throughout, with an energetic involvement in most stages of the development process. Specifically, it was a key actor in the three-way informal partnership with Bellway and AMARC. The object of this partnership was to progress the development of the area. South Tyneside could until 1987 offer contacts, expertise, a land-transfer capacity, political and bureaucratic influence, a mediating role and a channel to DoE resources. In return, they achieved some form of physical transformation and assisted the leverage of private investment into the area. But the case also illustrates first the complexity of negotiating changes of the kind occurring in Hebburn in a highly pluralist institutional context, especially from the point of view of the conurbation as a whole. Second, the nexus of links spanned national space, as well as connecting to some very local firms. It could be that this is a long-standing characteristic of the North East, with small local firms clustering around major companies whose fortunes are dependent on national decision-making about international markets. It could also be that institutional conditions and specific urban policy initiatives in the 1980s have further opened up opportunities in South Tyneside to companies from outside the area.

10.7.3   The driving forces of transformation

How then can we explain the process and product of transformation in this case? Chapter 2 suggests a range of possible driving forces for development activity in urban economies in older industrial areas. The first is consumer demand. In the Hebburn case, the agencies involved struggled to create demand, rather than simply responding to it. Property market conditions in almost all sectors were very depressed in this area until the late 1980s. Landowners, the local council and residential developers searched for opportunities in different property markets to define projects which would create and attract demand to the sites in question. Limitations on demand – with respect to marinas, workshop units, industrial sites and, initially, low-cost private housing, all had to be faced. The agencies were in effect market making and testing, rather than market-led. Had they followed the market, would the sites now be available for industrial production and shipbuilding expansion?

The second driving force was pressure from landowners to realize site value. There can be no doubt that this was a powerful factor in this case.

British Shipbuilders in particular pressed to realize the maximum exchange value for their land in a relatively short time period. Their interests were no doubt coloured by the process of privatization.

The third possible driving force identified was the competition between local and external interests with respect to finance and property. Financial institutions have had little involvement in this case, Bellway providing its own capital, and the rest coming from the public sector. Passed on to BSB/ Swan Hunter and Vickers Armstrong, the capital has stayed in the production sphere. Bellway recouped its investment through purchasers' savings and mortgages. In contrast to many of the urban regeneration projects occurring in Britain in the 1980s, which illustrate a nexus between property companies and financial institutions of various kinds, the Hebburn case is perhaps best understood as a corporate production nexus, in which the state has had an active role both directly in the production sphere (via support of various kinds to BSB and Vickers) and in assisting production companies to disinvest and realize capital assets in doing so. This kind of nexus is long-established in the economy of the North East. The beneficiary was then a housing production enterprise.

The fourth possible driving force is economic restructuring and the strategies of companies to rationalize and reposition themselves in the global marketplace. The Hebburn case is clearly driven by the strategies of both the major companies and central government towards restructuring. South Tyneside's approach has also been directed by its concerns over the consequent job losses and environmental dereliction.

Bellway's involvement has to be explained by something else, however. They would not have been involved without the possibility of an Urban Development Grant. Along with other large residential development companies, they set up a special Urban Renewal Section to exploit the opportunities created by government policy. Much else required the availability of Urban Programme finance. It could be argued that the implicit purpose of these funds has been to buy out the land assets of major production companies to soften the blows of economic restructuring. The above analysis suggests this has been a significant consequence in the Hebburn case. But urban policy has in part had a life of its own, linked to a perceived political challenge to be seen to achieve urban transformation by private-sector property initiatives. Bellway has been a beneficiary of this driving force, which offered gap finance to make the Hebburn opportunity a realistic challenge. Meanwhile, Urban Programme funds gave South Tyneside Council some flexibility to provide support to the initiatives of other agencies. But the detailed story of agency activities and relationships with respect to Hebburn illustrates all too clearly the constant changes in the priorities and funding of public agencies, the appearance of new agencies and the reduction in powers and abolition of other agencies. Economic restructuring has thus been parallelled here by institutional restructuring, culminating in the transfer of regulatory and promotional power from South Tyneside to the Development Corporation. In this context, a coherent long-term realizable programme for transformation has been difficult to sustain.

To conclude, the process and product of transformation at Hebburn may be explained in terms of the impact of economic restructuring on landowners' interests and South Tyneside Council's priorities, and the availability of central government funds through urban policy, in conditions of very depressed market demand. But the manner of the transformation also reflects the institutional context not only of urban policy but more generally the role of the state in local economic development and environmental management.

10.8   NOTES

The primary source material for the study are files held by officers in South Tyneside Metropolitan District's Planning Department. A single officer (Cliff Ayton) was in charge of planning and development matters in this area since 1979, and played a major personal role in the transformation process. The files record all transactions in which he or colleagues were involved, from informal memos of meetings and telephone calls, to correspondence, reports and contracts for grant receipt and land sales. Detailed notes were taken of file items from January 1980 to December 1987, with less intensive recording after this. This material has been supplemented by discussions with some of the key agents involved, and knowledge gained as part of the general research exercise. This case study is thus based on documentary research supplemented by interview evidence. As with any such work, the researcher has to be systematically cautious in drawing conclusions about events and relationships, seeking out multiple sources of evidence as the basis for judgements as to what happened. To assist in the process of validating the findings, participants in the case, particularly South Tyneside Planning staff, have reviewed this interpretation and challenged or confirmed findings from their point of view.

Comments from Cliff Ayton are gratefully acknowledged.

The case is described in more detail in Healey (1991) with the supporting evidence cited.

11

TOWARDS A NEW CITY? A CASE STUDY OF IMAGE-IMPROVEMENT INITIATIVES IN NEWCASTLE UPON TYNE

Sue Wilkinson

11.1 CONTEXT

The marketing of places is increasingly being acknowledged as a central element in local economic development and urban-regeneration strategies by public- and private-sector agencies. This chapter aims to identify more precisely the nature and significance of place-marketing initiatives in the present period of economic and social transformation using a case study of current image-improvement campaigns in Newcastle upon Tyne in England. The paper will seek to address a number of questions. For example, why has image become such an important element in urban regeneration and local economic development strategies since the late 1980s? Who are the image creators, what strategies are they employing, and what types of images are they projecting? Who are the target groups for image campaigns? What are the implications of a marketing-orientated approach to economic development? What do image initiatives reveal about the style of and approach to urban regeneration in the late 1980s and early 1990s?

Traditionally, place marketing in the UK has been the province of development agencies and the private sector. During the 1970s and early 1980s, agencies such as New Town Development Corporations, English Industrial

Estates and regional development bodies were actively involved in the marketing of specific localities. Their work focused primarily on industrial promotion, although a number of agencies did undertake major image campaigns, largely with the aim of creating a specific identity for a new development area or a greenfield location, as in the case of Milton Keynes Development Corporation. However, the late 1980s and early 1990s have been marked by a change in the style of, and approach to, place marketing. Image initiatives have become a more central element of urban regeneration and economic development work, particularly in older industrial northern cities such as Liverpool, Bradford and Newcastle. This shift has resulted in a series of city-based place-marketing initiatives, exemplified by campaigns such as 'Bradford Bounces Back', 'Glasgow's Miles Better' and Birmingham's 'Highbury Initiative'. In comparison with the 1970s and early 1980s, there are currently a much wider range of agencies involved in these high-profile image campaigns including local authorities, urban-development corporations and public-private sector coalitions (Fig. 11.1). Many of these agencies are also increasingly turning to marketing consultants to assist them in repackaging and selling a city's image. This has resulted in a marketing-led approach to city promotion, embracing techniques and strategies adapted from the world of product marketing. Rather than merely promoting a location, the new wave of image campaigns are characterized by complex marketing strategies based on an audit of a city's strengths, weaknesses, opportunities and competitors, linked into a comprehensive economic development programme.

Why then has image become an important element in urban regeneration and economic development agendas in the late 1980s and 1990s? Harvey has argued that urban governments are having to become more innovative and entrepreneurial in exploring new avenues through which to alleviate their distressed condition (Harvey, 1989b).

As a result, during the present period of restructuring the economy of older industrial cities, there has been an increasing emphasis on new forms of crisis management and new local economic development strategies. According to Mayer, this has resulted in a growing trend towards exploiting local resources and to a more entrepreneurial type of urban politics (Mayer, 1989). This has led to cities placing an increasing emphasis on developing a competitive edge. In the face of fierce competition between cities for new inward investment and development opportunities, image has become increasingly important. As a result, many older industrial cities have become more conscious of the need to improve their image both internally (to the local business community and residents) and externally (to inward investors and decision makers elsewhere in the UK and abroad). Many have been strongly influenced by the US model of place marketing with which they share a number of similarities in the style of approach and the marketing strategies adopted.

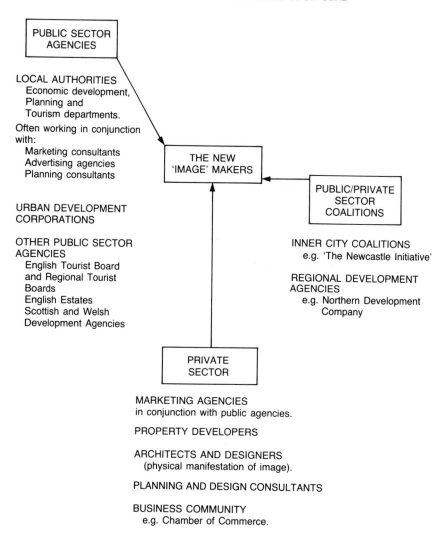

Figure 11.1 Major agencies and organizations involved in image-marketing initiatives in Great Britain

This new entrepreneurial style of local economic development has been parallelled by an increasingly consumerist style of urbanization in older UK cities, involving their physical and spatial remodelling. This has largely been the consequence of the continuing process of deindustrialization in older industrial cities which has resulted in a shift from production-orientated to consumer-orientated activities. In physical terms, this has manifested itself in new consumer attractions, an emphasis on the soft infrastructure of cities and the quality of life, the production of new lifestyles (reflected in urban revitalization schemes), and the gentrification of older, run-down areas. It reflects a shift from the Fordist to the post-Fordist city involving a move from modernist to post-modernist forms of architecture, design, culture, leisure activities and lifestyles. As Featherstone points out, 'the postmodern city is much more image-conscious and culturally self-conscious, it is both a centre of cultural consumption and general consumption (Featherstone, 1989). In terms of physical development, the post-modern city is characterized by a shift away from comprehensive redevelopment projects, characteristic of the 1960s and 1970s towards the planning of urban fragments, evidenced in the mosaic effect created by the development of new urban villages, flag-ship schemes, self-contained waterfront developments and cultural quarters. These 'islands of renewal' also act as highly visible symbols of urban regeneration and, as such, they are regarded by public- and private-sector agencies as vital ingredients in the place-marketing process.

The following section of this chapter aims to provide an early and tentative analysis of place-marketing initiatives in an older northern industrial area, using the city of Newcastle upon Tyne as a case study. It should be stressed that image-improvement initiatives in Newcastle are still at an early stage of development and they will require further analysis and monitoring over a period of time. The following analysis therefore aims to provide an evaluation of work in progress, and to indicate the likely future trajectory of image work and its implications for urban regeneration in Newcastle.

11.2   IMAGE INITIATIVES IN NEWCASTLE UPON TYNE

Over the last three years, the question of image has become an important feature on the local economic development and urban regeneration agendas of public- and private-sector agencies in Newcastle. Image-improvement strategies have become as important as more traditional economic development interventionist measures such as the provision of infrastructure and financial incentives. In the face of fierce competition between localities for inward investment, image has become a key factor in Newcastle's economic development strategy. It has become clear that the city must reposition itself in a more competitive marketplace in order to gain a competitive edge. It is within this context that public sector and public–private sector coalitions in Newcastle have become increasingly concerned with the question of image. The local economic development agenda has expanded to include not only hard-edged initiatives (e.g. the provision of sites and buildings) but also a concern with less tangible issues such as place image and marketing. There has been an increased emphasis on the provision of what has been termed the soft infrastructure of the city – leisure, the arts, tourism and the quality of life – as a vital tool in stimulating local private capital accumulation and attracting investment, labour and tourists (Harvey, 1989b).

However, it would be extremely inaccurate to imply that the concern with image is a new phenomenon. Rather, it can be argued that there has been a strong element of continuity in the way Newcastle's image has been managed and manipulated in recent decades. For example, during the 1960s, T. Dan Smith and Wilfred Burns (the City Council's Leader and City Planning Officer, respectively) were extremely proactive in projecting a vision of Newcastle as 'the New Brasilia', a progressive and vibrant regional capital with a bright and prosperous future. It was a vision that sought to build on the best of the past (such as Dobson's Victorian City), to articulate the 19th-century traditions of Newcastle with a visionary, modernist future. Newcastle was to be re-born out of the ashes of economic decline to become 'the Milan of the North'. As T. Dan Smith points out in his autobiography:

> In Newcastle, I wanted to see the creation of a 20th-century equiva-
> lent of Dobson's masterpiece, and its integration into the historic
> framework of the city. If this could be achieved, I felt that our regional
> capital would become the outstanding provincial city in the country.
>
> (Smith, 1970, p. 46)

In common with the present period, this vision was strongly linked with the drive for urban regeneration. The rhetoric was backed up by a major £200 million redevelopment plan for Newcastle City Centre and a £50 million slum-clearance programme for the city's inner areas. The aim was to create a revitalized city 'equal to the demands of the 21st Century' (Smith, 1960) which would rank alongside Venice, Milan and Stockholm as 'one of Europe's most advanced cities' (Burns, 1967).

This approach reveals a number of similarities with the current wave of image initiatives in Newcastle. However it also exhibits several important differences. The projection of Newcastle's image in the 1960s as a 'progressive, beautiful and free' city (Smith, 1960, p. 9) was reflected in a series of large-scale, high-profile, comprehensive development schemes rather than in any coherent marketing strategy or promotional package for the city. The T. Dan Smith era was concerned primarily with civic pride, and a Utopian vision of the city as an urban machine fit for living in. It was essentially a modernist vision with a strong social welfare component, managed by the public sector on Keynesian functional principles. However, the civic boosterism and comprehensive planning projects of the 1960s have given way to a more fragmented, marketing-orientated approach to the image question in the post-modern city of the 1980s, and this has manifested itself in the relatively new process of image projection which involves the encoding of new identities for places via image and media campaigns.

11.3   THE MANUFACTURED CITY

The explicit marketing and promotion of Newcastle as a locality for inward investment and new development has become an important area of activity for public sector agencies and public/private sector coalitions over the last three years. This section seeks to provide an overview of existing image management initiatives being undertaken in the city. It considers the work of the four principal agencies concerned with image promotion in Newcastle and it examines the different approaches adopted by each.

11.3.1   Marketing the city: Newcastle City Council

Newcastle City Council has adopted a marketing-orientated approach to the question of image and local economic development. The City Council recently engaged J. Walter Thompson, a leading advertising agency, to undertake a marketing campaign for the City with the aim of repackaging and repositioning Newcastle in the urban market place. The campaign will be concerned with neutralizing unfavourable images, creating new images and reinforcing existing positive images of the city. The methodology being employed by J. Walter Thompson is clearly derived from the world of product marketing and forms part of the trend towards an increasingly consumerist style of economic development and urban regeneration. It aims to create a strong, positive image for the city, principally in London and the South East of England, and to remove any negative perceptions of Newcastle. It also hopes to create a unique selling point for Newcastle together with a corporate image which is both strong and positive, and which can be applied locally, nationally and internationally. In addition, it will seek to raise local awareness and generate civic pride. J. Walter. Thompson aims to achieve this through a centrally co-ordinated marketing programme using a range of marketing techniques, including promotional literature; television, raido and press advertising; exhibitions; press and public relations work; and corporate image work.

The starting point for J. Walter. Thompson's work was a review of the strengths and weaknesses of Newcastle together with an analysis of the gap between perceived attitudes about the city and reality. J. Walter Thompson's approach has adopted a **SWOT** style analysis of the city in a similar way to that used for a consumer product. The campaign, which is primarily targeted at key decision-makers (business leaders, the financial institutions and opinion-formers in the South East) will cover a three-year period at a cost of £300 000 per annum (Fig. 11.2). This represents a substantial diversion of resources from the City Council's relatively small and constrained economic development budget. However, the City Council believe that the marketing strategy being developed by J. Walter Thompson will provide an effective

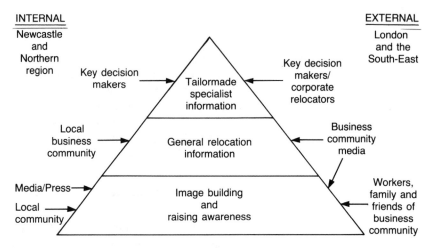

Figure 11.2 Target groups and marketing strategies for the Newcastle City Council image campaign. Source: J. Walter Thompson Image Campaign

corporate overview which was previously lacking when promotional work was diffused through different departments of the council.

The first stage of J. Walter Thompson's image campaign for Newcastle City Council was launched in Autumn 1990 with an advertising feature in the national quality press (Fig. 11.3). This phase of the campaign was designed to concentrate initially on image building and raising the awareness of Newcastle as a product with the aim of 'repairing the perception gap' and 'getting Newcastle on the serious relocation shortlist' (Thompson, verbal interview with Simon Burridge; J. Walter Thompson, 1990). The campaign sets out to sell Newcastle as a brand name with a definable brand personality. As Bernadette Knox (1990) from J. Walter Thompson points out:

> We see it very much as selling Newcastle to potential inward investors. It is therefore very much like handling any other of the brands that I deal with – like Persil or Andrex. What you have got to do is to find a means of making Newcastle the most potent brand that investors can buy. So we need to think about Newcastle as a brand. In some ways, Newcastle faces many of the problems any brand would face. . . . Unless you create the right emotional climate, all the rational advantages which Newcastle offers will not come into play because other places can offer just the same rational advantages.

As a result of the need to stress Newcastle's emotional appeal as an investment location, J. Walter Thompson has embarked on a campaign which relies heavily on the marketing technique of brand personality and product positioning. The emphasis in the advertising campaign is on the

A CITY MADE FROM COAL AND STEEL. A PEOPLE MADE OF STRONGER STUFF.

Nobody could deny that Newcastle has a proud industrial past.

Wherever you look you can see the results of our endeavours. Britain's greatest ships were built in Newcastle. The first steam turbine was made in Newcastle. The light bulb was invented in Newcastle. And a brewer on the Tyne gave us the finest bottled beer in the world.

But the city's success story doesn't end in the past.

New companies are succeeding here today. Companies like British Airways, Dunlop, Findus and AA Insurance Services have all come to Newcastle in the last few years.

And they're succeeding because they've found a workforce of people with the kind of qualities others don't have.

Qualities you can probably recognise in people you can probably recognise. Like perseverance and strength for example. The perseverance to see a job through from start to finish. The kind that Bruce Oldfield displayed in his struggle from a Dr Barnardo's home to his own exclusive fashion house. The strength to keep going no matter how tough the going gets. The kind that enabled Steve Cram to keep on running until he was the fastest man in the world to run the mile.

They've found people with foresight. But that's hardly surprising. We've never been backward in looking forward in Newcastle. (Remember it was here that George and Robert Stephenson developed the railways over 150 years ago.)

They've also found people with incredible versatility and creativity. The versatility to take on any job, no matter how challenging. Just as Rowan Atkinson has, throughout his career. The creativity that's personified in Sting, formerly a secondary school teacher in Newcastle.

And, above all, they've found a workforce with an unparalleled sense of humour. The legendary Geordie sense of humour that has made Viz Britain's best selling comic.

But new companies aren't just finding miracle workers in Newcastle. They're finding it easy to get here as well.

By road, we're on the intersection of the A1 and the A69. By rail, we're bang in the middle of the East Coast line, two hours from Edinburgh and less than three from London.

By air, we're within easy reach of every European capital from Newcastle International Airport.

While in the city itself there's the Metro, the best Rapid Transit System in Europe, linking everything together.

In addition, there is Europe's largest indoor shopping centre, quality city centre shopping, and some of the best theatres and galleries outside London. And, on top of all that, we're surrounded by miles of beautiful countryside.

So, if you're thinking about moving your company, think about moving it to Newcastle.

You couldn't find a better place to be in business. Because you couldn't find better people to be in business with.

For more details call Phil Payne on 091 261 7392, or you can write to him at: The Economic Development Unit, Newcastle City Council, The Civic Centre, Newcastle upon Tyne NE1 8QN.

NEW ERA. NEW ATTITUDE. NEWCASTLE.

Figure 11.3 J. Walter Thompson's image campaign for Newcastle City Council – advertising in the quality press. Courtesy of Newcastle City Council.

'new face of Newcastle', the idea of 'a prosperous Newcastle at the heart of a regenerated region'.

> The brand positioning we suggested for the city is very much about the city with a proud past looking to the future. . . . The campaign is actually saying that 'the past has made Newcastle what it is, now how can we take that forward? A very important thread that runs through it all is the people – they are the best motivation for moving to the North East. In terms of advertising, the aim is to change people's attitudes, firstly by showing them the new face of Newcastle with all the resources and confidence to look to the future, and then to actively do that in such a way to create positive perceptions about the city.
>
> (Bernadette Knox, J. Walter Thompson, 1990)

The advertising campaign is deliberately designed to reassure potential relocators that Newcastle possesses 'a people made of stronger stuff' particularly in terms of the quality of its workforce. In the words of the advertisement 'you couldn't find better people to be in business with'. The campaign's focus is strongly people-centred with the aim of conveying positive images of Newcastle as a city in which to live and work. In particular, it presents reassuring messages to investors about the quality of the workforce with a multiplicity of references to its 'versatility', 'strength', 'pragmatism' and 'perseverance'. It also places emphasis on qualities such as creativity and foresight, reinforcing the message that Newcastle is a city of status and innovation, with internationally acclaimed exports and expatriots such as fashion designer Bruce Oldfield and rock star Sting. There is also an emphasis on Newcastle as a friendly city with references to *Viz* and the Geordie sense of humour, designed to reinforce the idea that Newcastle is a good place to live in. Finally, the campaign presents messages about the quality of life on Tyneside, referring to 'quality city centre retailing', 'the best rapid transit system in Europe', 'beautiful countryside' and the area's wealth of cultural resources. The campaign aims to reposition Newcastle in a national context, stressing its proximity to major British cities. However, there is surprisingly little reference to Newcastle's positioning in a European and international context compared with image-marketing campaigns in other UK cities such as Glasgow, Birmingham and Manchester.

It is interesting to note that it was originally J. Walter Thompson's intention to use an alternative campaign based on the archetypal North Eastern cartoon character, Andy Capp. The character is famous for his lazy, irresponsible, scruffy, beer-drinking and crude personality. The original marketing concept proposed turning this stereotypical image on its head by transforming and updating Andy Capp, giving him a suit and tie, and showing him throwing away his working-class cap. The campaign was intended to

Figure 11.4   Andy Capp campaign – critical reaction in the local media, May 1990.
Source: *Evening Chronicle*, 22 May, 1990

indicate a new era and new attitude in Newcastle in a similar fashion to the current advertising strategy for the city. The drawing's caption drew attention to the fact that no city had changed as much as Newcastle in the last 30 years. The early leaking of the campaign to the press ensured a public outcry that effectively killed off the marketing executives' idea of using the 'reformed' Andy Capp figure as a symbol of the resurgence of Newcastle (Fig. 11.4). However, it is interesting to consider the implications of the original proposal for image-improvement work in Newcastle. The use of the Andy Capp figure by a London-based advertising agency is in itself revealing, illustrating how firmly the cartoon stereotype is embedded in the minds of Southerners. One potential reading of the Andy Capp campaign could have been that the cartoon character had not become transformed, rather he had become 'yuppiefied' on the outside but had remained his old self beneath the veneer. The use of Andy Capp as a symbol of Newcastle's re-birth may have been counterproductive, reinforcing the stereotypical image of Northerners to target audiences in the South East of England, whilst at the same time being patronising and offensive to North-Easterners. The new Andy Capp would have confirmed rather than opposed traditional stereotypes. The selection of Andy Capp as a symbol for change also reveals the tension between enterprise and tradition in image-improvement initiatives, and illustrates how the new spirit of urbanism and enterprise wants to destroy Andy Capp in an attempt to re-image the Tyneside area. It reflects the problem of how Newcastle articulates its past heritage with its post-modern future in an international marketplace.

This marketing-orientated approach to selling Newcastle as an inward-investment location raises a number of important questions. What are the long-term ramifications of adopting a marketing-directed approach to local economic development? Who will benefit from the image-improvement campaign in the short and longer terms? What are the implications of packaging a city in a similar way to any other product using marketing techniques? It is the view of Alan Clarke, Head of Economic Development at Newcastle City Council that there are important differences between marketing a place and a product.

> It is much more difficult and complex to market a city compared with a Kit-Kat or tin of soup. But I do believe that the same sort of principles that you apply to a product can be applied to a city – the same logical rational steps, e.g. what do people think of your city at the moment; what would you like people to think of your city in the future; what steps do you need to take to narrow the gap between perception and reality? It's not as scientific as it can be for a product, but if you use people with an understanding of and a feel for the city (and they are not at the same time doing a similar job for 10 other cities), I think that a job can be done.
>
> (Clarke, 1990)

However, to keep abreast of the inter-urban competition game, Newcastle will need, like other cities periodically to update its marketing strategy. Rather like a consumer product, the packaged images of cities seem to have increasingly short lifespans, indicating the need for continuous product innovation to gain a competitive edge over other localities. As Alan Clarke points out 'people just get bored with the same old story'. Also, cities must keep abreast of their competitor's product development not only to better position their own product, but also to appreciate what they have to match or surpass in the competitive marketplace. There is then a leapfrogging logic: once an agency becomes part of the image game, it must constantly run harder just to stand still (Hirsch, 1977). Can this then be regarded as a cost-effective approach to local economic development in the longer term, and does it represent a diversion of resources from economic development budgets which could be targeted more effectively elsewhere?

11.3.2   A vision for the future? Tyne and Wear Development Corporation

> Marketing is at the very hub of the wheel of our regeneration efforts
> . . . . Perceptions of the North will continue to be a major factor in
> determining the success and prosperity of investment to the region.
> (Tyne and Wear Development Corporation, 1986)

Tyne and Wear Development Corporation was established by central
government in 1987 with the aim of regenerating the waterfront areas of the
Rivers Tyne and Wear. The Development Corporation's concern with image
can be divided into two interrelated areas – the institutional image of the
Corporation and the image of the locality which the Corporation covers.
The Development Corporation's concern with projecting a positive self image
to the local community and to the business sector stems from a number of
factors. The Development Corporation has a relatively short lifespan and its
main remit is to accelerate change in the urban regeneration process. As
an agency of change, it is also an imposition of central government in a
potentially hostile region; as Linda Conlon, Public Relations Officer for the
Corporation points out.

> We don't want to come in like Thatcher's stormtroopers and destroy
> everything. We want to open up the riverside so people will be able
> to work there and to live there.
> (Interview with Linda Conlon, 1990)

As a result, the Development Corporation must create 'a climate of confidence and optimism' (verbal interview with Robson Brown, Marketing
Executives, 1990) within the region. Its own image as an institution must be
seen as action-orientated, sensitive to local needs, dynamic, proactive and
responsive to development opportunities. Conlon notes:

> We are here to accelerate change. People do not like change. They
> like change to come about slowly and surely; we aren't really here to
> do that. . . . On a local level, image is important to reassure people
> that what we are trying to do is for the good of the area and we will
> try as far as possible to accommodate their wishes.
> (Interview with Linda Conlon, 1990)

The approach is reflected in the Development Corporation's logo. The
early image of high-rise tower blocks on the waterfront was quickly dropped
as being too strident, unsympathetic and authoritarian in style, and was
replaced by a more subtle abstract logo with an upward tilt suggestive of
optimism (Fig. 11.5) and the regional quandrant symbolic of a rising sun.
The action-orientated image which the Development Corporation wishes to

Figure 11.5 Tyne and Wear Development Corporation logos: (a) the original Development Corporation logo was quickly dropped to make way for a less authoritarian and harsh image; (b) the second TWC logo emphasized the integration of old and new; and (c) the current Development Corporation logo is more abstract. The upward-tilting curves represent the Rivers Tyne and Wear but they are also suggestive of optimism and the wealth-generating curves of sales graphs

cultivate is also reflected in its use of assertive rhetoric which marries the language of evangelism ('a mission', 'a vision') with the terminology of Mrs Thatcher's enterprise culture ('a window of opportunity', 'skill, courage and ambition', 'pride, confidence and commitment'). In its promotional campaigns, the Development Corporation has been keen to stress that its approach is bold, imaginative, proactive and forward looking.

> Our Mission. . . . We think the unthinkable. With our programme of flagship projects we introduce wholly new uses in sufficient scale and imaginative quality to change the character of the riverside areas dramatically. Within the 'goldenglow', others follow naturally.
>
> (Tyne and Wear Development Corporation, 1989b, p. 3)

A further area of the Development Corporation's image work has focused specifically on place-marketing initiatives. This work can be divided broadly into two main stages. The first phase was targeted at the local community with the aim of 'informing people of a new product' and 'changing the mood of people to appreciate that things are changing on the waterfront and there is a growing mood of optimism'. The early marketing work took a number of forms encompassing intensive public relations work, a Development Corporation display and presence at the National Garden Festival and the 'Brightside Campaign' (verbal interview with Robson Brown, Marketing Executives, 1990). According to Robson Brown, a marketing agency working with the Development Corporation, the basic theme of the early Brightside Campaign was confidence boosting through the projection of optimistic images and the use of aggressive marketing techniques to suggest that the Development Corporation's schemes are in the process of becoming a tangible reality and that action is going to take place on the ground in the short to medium term. Indeed, the Brightside Campaign exemplifies a spirit of urban renaissance in both its rhetoric ('Ritchie and Doug are looking on the brightside . . . helping us create a new riverside') and its visual imagery (Fig. 11.6). The sunglasses branding device is used to create an image of optimism, confidence and brightness designed to counteract negative perceptions of the riverside as a dreary, depressing and colourless locality, a view reminiscent of T. Dan Smith's concern with sunshine cities such as Milan, Venice and Brasilia.

Although the early stages of the Development Corporation's place-marketing work were targeted primarily at the local population, a number of smaller-scale marketing efforts were also directed at the national and regional business community. For example, Robson Brown's 'Inward Investment' and 'Hod Carrier' campaigns (Figs. 11.7 and 11.8) were targeted primarily at the national and regional business marketplace. The image of a bricklayer (building a base for success) with £50 notes was used to connote a sense of the generation of new wealth, a new spirit of enterprise and attractive investment opportunities. It also attempted to reposition Newcastle in a European context with an emphasis on 'the most attractive financial packages available in Europe'. Both of these campaigns used powerful, bold, single-minded images and arguments to signal the coming revival of the waterfront.

...HELPING US CREATE A NEW RIVERSIDE.

RICHIE AND DOUG ARE LOOKING ON THE BRIGHT SIDE...

Figure 11.6 Tyne and Wear Development Corporation's Brightside campaign

THANKS TO MASSIVE INVESTMENT RICHARD WON'T FORGET WHAT HIS DAD LOOKS LIKE.

Richard's dad is bricklayer, Richie Ward. Until recently Richie had to leave home to go to London and West Germany to find a job to support his family. The fact that he's now employed by Barratt Newcastle in his native Tyneside is a result of the £250 million investment already attracted to the area by Tyne and Wear Development Corporation.

The effort the public and private sectors have put in is at last paying tangible dividends. Major companies such as Liebherr, British Telecom Marine, Mitsumi and Goldstar have moved to the riversides. Exciting new housing schemes and leisure facilities are rising out of what was derelict land. Above all, thousands of jobs are being created.

For Richard's generation the future looks bright. But for the moment he's just glad he's seeing more of his dad.

TYNE

WEAR
DEVELOPMENT
CORPORATION

CREATING A BRIGHT
NEW RIVERSIDE

Tyne and Wear Development Corporation, Hadrian House, Higham Place, Newcastle upon Tyne NE1 8AF. Also at Bridge House, Bridge Street, Sunderland SR1 1TE. Tel: (091) 222 1222.

Figure 11.7 Tyne and Wear Development Corporation's Inward Investment campaign

WE'RE MAKING MASSIVE INVESTMENT WORK.

Dramatic changes are taking place along the banks of the Tyne and the Wear. We've already attracted £250 million worth of investment and we're pulling in a further £250 million. The development of 27 miles of riverside is well under way.

By the end of the year 300,000 square feet of the £60 million Newcastle Business Park will have been taken up. AA Insurance Services have just announced the establishment of their Northern Headquarters at the Park. Very close to the city centre, the Park's rents are around a third of those in the South East – and it still benefits from Enterprise Zone status. In addition, some 400,000 square feet of office, business and industrial space is being created in Sunderland, much of it at the prestigious Hylton Riverside Business Park.

And one of the largest mixed developments ever seen in the UK, Royal Quays on the Tyne, will become a 200 acre mini-town, the size of the City of London, at the cost of over £200 million. The provision of office, business and industrial space will be substantial.

Profitable property opportunities are opening up all the time, especially combined with some of the most attractive financial packages available in Europe. Which makes it worth your while calling Tom Fenton or Mike Robinson on (091) 222 1222 or contacting the address below for further details. Then you too will have a chance to make your (or your clients') investment work.

TYNE

WEAR
DEVELOPMENT
CORPORATION

Tyne and Wear Development Corporation, Hadrian House, Higham Place, Newcastle upon Tyne NE1 8AF. Tel: (091) 222 1222.

Figure 11.8 Tyne and Wear Development Corporation's Hod Carrier campaign

Table 11.1   Regional image comparison – a comparison of current perceptions of the region held by persons based in the North East and South East (*Source:* National Garden Festival, 1989)

Attitude statements about NE region	% of agreement		% difference between SE and NE
	Perception of NE sample	Perception of SE sample	
1 Good area for country living	91	64	−27
2 Culturally rich area	64	41	−23
3 Warm/friendly people	95	78	−17
4 Many *beautiful* places to visit	99	78	−21
5 Many *interesting* places to visit	99	73	−26
6 Offers high quality of life for people like me	75	40	−35
7 Good residential areas within easy access of work	92	42	−50
8 Good place for a holiday	73	55	−18
9 Shops are very good	94	37	−57
10 People enjoy *working* there	79	41	−38
11 People enjoy *living* there	90	61	−29
12 Has excellent schools	75	22	−32
13 Business and commerce are very vibrant	62	19	−43
14 Appeals to people who like sports and recreational activities	87	48	−39

The Development Corporation is currently building on these groundwork campaigns with the launch of a national advertising campaign linked to a comprehensive marketing strategy. It is believed that the campaign, which will take place over an 18-month period, will cost in the region of £1.5 million. It will be targeted at a national marketplace, particularly the media, decision-makers, opinion-formers, the financial community, property developers, and business leaders in London and the South East. It will seek to close the difference between reality and perceptions of the region held by those based in the South East of England (see Table 11.1 for a comparison of attitudes held about the region). The main theme of the campaign is 'The New North East', with an emphasis on quality of life, lifestyle and enterprise culture images (Fig. 11.9):

Out of the foundations of a proud and prosperous past a new North East is rising up. A New North East – confident and ready to take up its rightful place as a leading European centre of trade and commerce.

Figure 11.9 'The New North East' campaign launched by Tyne and Wear Development Corporation in September 1990. This national advertising campaign takes the form of a montage of quality of life and lifestyle images, including imagery of new development schemes, leisure facilities, high-quality retailing, educational opportunities, 'the new age man' and news references to the North East's Japanese links in industry and its higher standard of living. Compared with earlier Development Corporation campaigns, it is characterized by a more subtle approach in the context of the 'new mood of the nineties'. Source: Tyne and Wear Development Corporation

A New North East already welcoming companies of the calibre of Nissan, British Airways and Cellnet. A New North East that will be more than a match for its proud past. Have no doubt. This is just the beginning.

(Tyne and Wear Development Corporation
'Welcome To The New North East' Campaign, 1990)

The campaign will be complemented by ongoing public relations work, editorial and marketing in the quality press, direct mailing and other activities such as relocation seminars in London. This work will be aimed at 'creating the right perceptual infrastructure for attracting inward investment' and establishing Tyne and Wear on 'the business relocation circuit' (Interview with Alistair Dalziel, 1990). This approach to marketing the waterfront areas is more subtle and softer in style than the Development Corporation's earlier aggressive marketing work evidenced in the Brightside and Gold Bars campaigns.

The Development Corporation's campaign is being packaged as a piece of quality advertising featuring montages of quality images and 'well-researched editorial marketing in the quality press'. In common with Glasgow's earlier Miles Better campaign, the Development Corporation aims to attract what it calls 'innovators' or business executives who can identify up-and-coming investment locations in advance of their competitors. To this end, the campaign emphasizes the region's Japanese links and the potential for Tyne and Wear to become a leading European centre of trade and commerce.

On a more local level, it is likely that the Development Corporation's Brightside Campaign will be discontinued, having achieved its initial objectives. Future place-marketing work aimed at the local community will focus on more subtle marketing techniques including intensive public relations, posters, advertising, community development work, and local flagship-scheme monitoring panels involving members of local communities. It represents a shift to a more people-centred approach to promoting the image and regeneration of the Development Corporation's area, perhaps reflecting the need to diffuse local tension and opposition to a number of high profile development schemes such as Royal Quays in North Shields and East Quayside in Newcastle.

The Development Corporation has been instrumental in promoting lifestyle images as part of its image improvement work in order to change perceptions of the waterfront area amongst the local population and business community, and to counteract the negative perceptions which many South-Easterners continue to hold of the region. This approach is characteristic of the consumption model of urban regeneration which has now become so prevalent. In terms of spatial development, it involves the reshaping and restructuring of urban space to include new nominally mixed-use areas (e.g. the proposed East Quayside scheme), retailing (e.g. proposed festival shopping on the Quayside), urban spectacles and consumer attractions (e.g. the Tall Ships Race, 1992), and the gentrification of older inner areas (e.g. the transformation of the run-down Ouseburn area into an urban village). It involves a concept of city living in which urban space is increasingly segregated socially and differentiated culturally into different lifestyles which cross the traditional pattern of single zoning, replacing it with an alternative lifestyle-zoning principle. It has also resulted in the post-modern predilection for the planning and design of urban fragments as evidenced in the Development Corporation's flagship projects and their notion of urban villages along the riverside area. The new urban imagery promotes a prosperous cosy lifestyle with all the glamour of the reborn city. It is an image which is expected to appeal most strongly to the consumption power of high-income groups attracted by the quality of life and the glamorous urban infrastructure (in the form of waterfront leisure, cultural attractions and consumer attractions). But does the power of the imagery create a psychological barrier to lower income groups who are likely to feel excluded form this new lifestyle? This potential problem is likely to be reinforced by the relatively high cost of the new lifestyles which the Development Corporation is promoting. Although the Development Corporation has been working hard to create an image of affordable lifestyles in the riverside area, early indications suggest that the emphasis has been on high-profile development schemes with a strong appeal to the more affluent sections of society (e.g. Blue Anchor Scheme, Newcastle Quayside).

11.3.3 The Newcastle Initiative

The Newcastle Initiative (TNI) was launched in June 1988 as a result of the CBI National Task Force study into the role that business could play in urban regeneration. It was formed to pursue the revitalization of Newcastle and to act as a test-bed for a new type of public/private sector partnership. TNI provides a model of a multi-agency approach to urban regeneration and to questions of image and civic identity. It is essentially a growth coalition which exhibits a strong consensus image of the City. Its approach to place marketing in Newcastle can be described as a model of corporate responsibility. TNI illustrates an amalgamation of both the entrepreneurial and the managerial style of promoting the city which draws heavily on the rhetoric of the marketplace and on notions of an enterprise culture. However, its lack of resources and effecive policy-making powers have resulted in this entrepreneurial style being married to a more managerial approach which stems from TNI's facilitating and co-ordinating role. Although TNI does not possess a marketing strategy, it aims to play a pivotal role in levering in other people's efforts and working in partnership with a variety of agencies to promote a new vision of a great city (Fig. 11.10). TNI has also

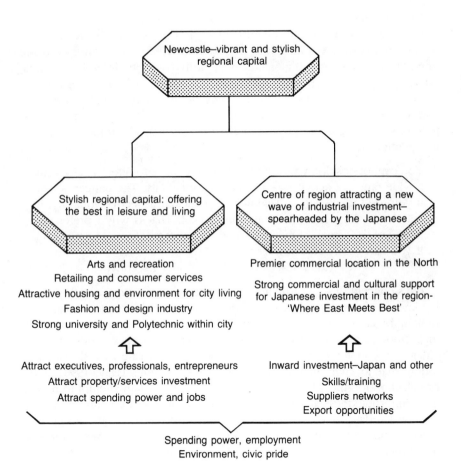

Figure 11.10   TNI's Vision for Newcastle. Source: The Newcastle Initiative TNI, 1988

been instrumental in identifying a number of flagship projects which are intended to 'symbolise Newcastle's regeneration in tangible form and attract commercial support from the private sector' (TNI, 1988). These flagships symbolize TNI's approach to recreating the city in a spirit of urban renaissance: in the words of the TNI, they 'embody the dramatic change of outlook for the future' and 'fit logically with the overall thrust of TNI's vision' (TNI, 1988).

TNI's vision of Newcastle as 'a strong, vibrant and stylish Regional Capital' (TNI, 1988) is superficially reminiscent of T. Dan Smith's 1960s vision of 'a city progressive, beautiful and free' (Smith, 1960). Both emphasize the importance of a strong Regional Capital, 'a liveable city' in which the arts, education and leisure flourish. However, TNI's approach illustrates how, in the present period, cities are increasingly being commodified as products and are being sold in the marketplace to potential investors. This is illustrated by TNI's desire to position Newcastle distinctively in the inter-urban competition game.

> You cannot position yourself narrowly. You have to offer the city with a wide range of activities – a multi-functional city. The danger is that if you are too specific in selling one particular aspect of your city, it may be to the detriment of another aspect. That is why I prefer the notion of the 'liveable city'. . . . You can market that for a longer period if you can subtly shift it over time.
>
> (Interview with Bill Hay Chief Executive, TNI, 1990)

TNI's concept of Newcastle as a liveable city is synonymous with projecting images of new lifestyles, a good quality of life and an attractive forward-looking business environment. Images of lifestyle are seen to be important in promoting a new scenario of urban living based on a series of urban villages to counteract negative perceptions of Newcastle as 'a threatening, tough, macho environment with high levels of crime' (Hay, 1990). TNI's predilection for 'the village in the city' can be seen as an attempt to restore meaning, routedness and humanizing qualities to the city in an era dominated by standardization and depersonalization. It represents the struggle for place in the wake of modernism and reflects a renewed interest in the 'soft infrastructure' of the city – its sense of community, its quality of life and its ambience. It is an attempt to construct a new urbanity, a post-modern city with a sense of community, identity and animation. It is a vision which looks back to the past and forward to the future. TNI's promotional literature (Fig. 11.11) illustrates the inherent contradictions in its view of the past and future city. For example, 'a great heritage' is seen to embrace both the Victorian architecture of Grey Street and 'the most advanced telecommunications systems' whilst 'a great future' somewhat perversely takes in 'fine refurbished buildings' and a 'unique cultural identity' as well as 'superb opportunities for new commercial, development'.

A GREAT Vision for a great city

A new programme of regeneration in the thriving commercial heart of Newcastle is now underway. Public and private sectors are working together under the umbrella of the Newcastle Initiative to stimulate new interest and investment in the historical capital of the great North.

● A GREAT HERITAGE

Behind the elegant facade of Grey Street lies the opportunity to create a modern office environment serviced with the full range of the most advanced telecommunications systems.

Classic Georgian style meeting the needs of the 21st century.

● A GREAT FUTURE

Superb opportunities exist in the Theatre Village for new commercial development alongside fine refurbished buildings, drawing on the strengths of the unique cultural identity of this part of the city centre

Theatre Village, a new community of leisure, entertainment and housing.

Join us in our GREAT vision

Contact: Bill Hay, Chief Executive, The Newcastle Initiative, Tyne Brewery, Gallowgate, Newcastle upon Tyne, NE99 1RA. Telephone (091) 222 0939

Figure 11.11 TNI's publicity material

TNI's approach to promoting Newcastle as one of Europe's great regional capitals and a liveable city places considerable emphasis upon a taskforce approach to urban regeneration based on partnership, coordinated teamwork and a consensus vision of the city. It is essentially a managerial approach to regeneration and place marketing which has been influenced strongly by Japanese styles of management with their emphasis on quality circles and teamwork. As Bill Hay points out, TNI is pivotal in promoting 'a consensus image' of the city: it is 'the only formal structure whereby the City Council, the Development Corporation, NDC, quasi-public sector agencies and the private sector come together resulting in a commonality of approach' (Hay, 1990). The Japanese influence is also evident in TNI's Japan Links Taskforce (again with an emphasis on consensus and teamwork) and in its promotional material for Newcastle which boasts a new vision of the city as 'Where East meets Best'. A recent TNI promotional supplement in the local media pointed up the Newcastle–Japan links further with its slogan 'For Newcastle Upon Tyne, read Tokyo on Tyne' (Borrell, 1988).

An entrepreneurial approach drawn from the business community also permeates TNI's style of operation. This is reflected in TNI's emphasis on leadership, new forms of public/private partnership and a marketing-directed approach to selling 'A Great Vision For A Great City'. TNI's specific brand of urban entrepreneurialism is well illustrated in its brochure which states 'Leadership can release the energy and commitment needed to develop and pursue a common vision for the city' (TNI, 1988). This vision based on a public/private partnership is rooted in the Thatcherite enterprise culture notion of 'initiatives beyond charity' and an emphasis on creating a climate of confidence and optimism.

11.3.4 The Northern Development Company – selling the great North

The Northern Development Company (NDC) is England's largest regional development agency – it is essentially an enabling body which coordinates the efforts of local government, public sector agencies, regional employers and trade unions into what it calls 'a unified drive for the regeneration of the North' (NDC, 1989). It is primarily concerned with securing inward investment from overseas and promoting the Northern Region to the rest of the UK, particularly the South East, as a centre for relocation. NDC is different from the other agencies analysed in that its remit is regional rather than purely metropolitan. Over the last two years, NDC has mounted a carefully targeted image improvement campaign with the aim of improving business perceptions of the North both within and outside of the region. The main target audiences for the campaign are opinion-formers and decision-makers within and outside the region, potential inward investors and corporate relocators, the media, politicians and policy makers. It aims to 'destroy old myths and prejudices' and to persuade potential investors that the North possess quality of life advantages over the South as well as a range of resources and skills. Much of NDC's work is targeted at opinion formers such as the media in order to remove misconceptions and to reinforce the regions' strengths. As David Williams, NDC's Director of Marketing, points out:

> Misguided perceptions of the North persist in the South generally, and in London in particular, and this is certainly a media-sustained image. The region is still seen by many as a cold and distant place, living in the shadow of depression, and those myths are sustained by cliche-ridden media profiles written by whistle-stop journalists in too much of a hurry to explore beyond the boundaries of their own prejudices.
> (Williams, 1989)

The campaign is also aimed at the general public within the region with the aim of promoting self-confidence and a spirit of optimism. This inwardly directed element of the campaign is targeted at the local community, the business sector, educational institutions and chambers of commerce.

One of the main strands of NDC's image-improvement work has been the Great North Campaign which is now nearly two years old. It is essentially a public relations and promotional campaign focusing on a series of events and activities. It differs from the image campaigns undertaken by other agencies in Newcastle in that it had tended to be events-led, focusing on activities such as The Great North Media Conference and The Great North Festival of Sport. This approach has enabled NDC to use such events as focal points for coordinating efforts to promote the region. For example, NDC's Great North 2000 Tower, a series of promotional displays and videos at the National Garden Festival, was sponsored by a range of public-sector agencies and business organizations including Durham County Council, English Estates, Cameron Hall Development, Tyne Tees Television, and Derwent Valley Foods, all of whom have a shared interest in the regeneration and promotion of the Northern Region. According to David Williams, the Great North Campaign was not so much designed to promote an identified or defined image of the region but it rather aimed to 'act as a vehicle for coordinated efforts' (Williams, 1989). The main objective was to present an image of 'a coordinated and responsive region'.

The designation of the region as 'The Great North' is particularly interesting in place-marketing terms. The title is designed very much as a piece of regional boosterism, having been selected to suggest a new spirit of dynamism and optimism. This is further reinforced by the campaign's logo of balloons (Fig. 11.12) which are synonymous with images of uplift and exuberance. As David Williams of NDC points out:

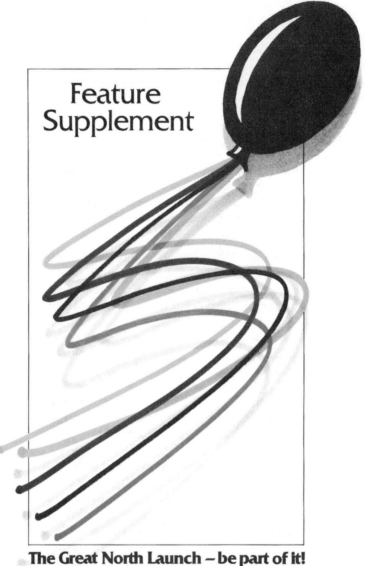

Figure 11.12   Northern Development Company's 'Great North' balloon logo

Why 'The Great North'? The word 'Great' is at once friendly and dynamic, carrying a range of appropriate meanings and associations – big, powerful, and yet it is easy to use casually. It's great in the North, it's great to be here, etc. Visually what we try to do is to give the phrase real bounce and colour, a bright and confident image to counteract the depressed image of the Southern myth.

(Williams, 1989)

However, the 'Great North' campaign illustrates some of the potential problems inherent in image-marketing initiatives. For example, this type of promotional campaign cannot provide a panacea for encouraging inward investment into the region, it can merely supply what NDC calls 'a banner for uniting the region's strengths, aimed at the better use of economic resources' (NDC, 1990). A further potential problem is that a regional image campaign can overpromise and underdeliver unless it is backed up by more substantive measures to promote regional development. NDC have been keen to stress that their promotional campaigns are supported by other activities aimed at stimulating economic growth and providing substance to their public-relations orientated work. However, their activities in a more substantive capacity are constrained by a lack of financial resources and by the relatively narrow confines of the organization's remit. As a result, NDC must target their image-marketing strategy at the business community with the aim of encouraging investment and adding value to their budget by levering in support for their campaigns.

The next phase of the regional image campaign is concentrating on what NDC considers to be more substantive measures. It will aim to promote the North East as a quality region, characterized by quality of production, quality of people and quality of life. NDC believe that the 'quality' theme will add substance to its promotional efforts. One major plan of the strategy is to persuade Northern companies to make more positive efforts to improve the quality and efficiency of their processes and services, partly by aiming for BS5750 or comparable certifications, which, it is hoped, will increase their competitiveness in the growing European markets. The first stage of the campaign will be 'to win the hearts and minds of the bosses' and to encourage the ownership of the quality theme' (NDC, 1989). The 'Think Quality' ethic could be said to reflect a Japanese approach to managing and selling the region's image. Indeed, the Northern Development Company is proposing a number of specific initiatives with a Japanese-style feel, notably the idea of a quality club of companies and the notion of quality circles (based on what NDC calls 'the Komatsu model'). The Japanese model of teamwork and consensus also permeates NDC's style of image management which places a strong emphasis on regional coordination and co-operation.

NDC's notion of the quality region incorporates the theme of the quality of life which has been an important element in other image campaigns in the region. NDC has been promoting the concept of the Great North with its emphasis on the region as a great place in which to live and work by presenting a more diverse range of lifestyle images than the traditional working class Andy Capp stereotype. It is NDC's view that the images presented in its promotional campaigns portray 'a truer picture of the North today than the traditional images'. These images aim to illustrate the region's cultural variety, its strengths in new industries such as fashion and offshore technology, and its range of high-quality retailing and leisure facilities. However, the Great North campaign also illustrates some of the contradictions inherent in the image-engineering process. On the one hand, its quality of life arguments play down traditional working-class images of the North. However, the Geordie accent and traditional identity can also be sold as positive features of the region because of their warm and affective character which emphasizes the quality of people. A further dualism in selling quality of life in the region relates to urban and rural images and values. For example, NDC is keen to promote the idea of the region as 'a big village', emphasizing its cosiness and community cohesiveness. However, at the same time it has been instrumental in promoting a new urbanity – a vibrant and exciting urban lifestyle. NDC sees no inherent tension, urbanity and rural values in the North. Rather, it regards the urban–rural images as being complementary, being illustrative of the region's topographical and cultural identity.

The NDC style of intervention in the image-management process could be described as a regional consensus model combining an entrepreneurial, managerial approach. It is essentially a long-term approach which could find itself in conflict with shorter-term marketing campaigns being undertaken by other agencies over the coming 18 months. There is a danger that a series of fragmented, shorter-term campaigns may pose a real threat to NDC's more focused and coordinated approach to promoting the region and its image.

11.4   LOCAL CORPORATISM AND A LOSS OF DYNAMISM

It is evident from the foregoing analysis that a plethora of public- and private-sector agencies have become involved in image-management initiatives in Newcastle over the last three years. Although place-marketing initiatives have taken a number of different forms, each has been characterized by a similarity of approach resulting from local corporatism and inter-agency consensus. The corporate consensus model, however, can be criticized for being essentially stale, unimaginative and lacking in real substance or dynamism. Furthermore, many of the techniques being used to reimage Newcastle have been transplanted from other cities in the UK and North America with little attempt to question the validity or suitability of this image-marketing approach to local economic development.

The consensus model has also resulted in attempts by public- and private-sector agencies to develop a planned urbanity, to create and mould an image of the city reborn. As a consequence, the city is now rediscovered as a focal point for urban living with a sense of vibrancy, excitement and animation. This trend could perhaps be described as the re-enchantment of the city. However, we would argue that attempts to plan and manage urban re-animation represent a blind alley for urban regeneration. They represent an attempt to superimpose a manufactured image on the city rather than encouraging an urban renaissance to develop from within. It is our view that the use of the consensus model will lead to a lack of any real urban vibrancy or *frisson* in the longer term. More disconcertingly, the application of standardized image-improvement strategies is likely to result in the serial reproduction of certain types of urban development – the marinas, cultural quarters, Chinatowns and 'villages in the city', all designed to boost city image and profile but ultimately superficial and undistinctive (Harvey, 1989b). The unquestioning use of the consumption model of urban regeneration is likely to render any competitive advantage marginal in terms of inter-urban competition for inward investment. It is essentially a short-term vision which succumbs to the temptation to copy rather than to innovate.

The consensus view of the re-imagined city is also characterized by a strong similarity between the various agencies' images of the past and future city (Table 11.2). The past city is perceived in fairly negative terms, being regarded as somewhat bleak, impersonal, insular, harsh, threatening and lacking a strong sense of community. It was also felt to lack a distinctive identity and to suffer from a somewhat flat image in the way it was perceived by outsiders. This past image of Newcastle is essentially a view of the modernist city which is seen to be synonymous with a sense of anomy and disillusionment. It is interesting that all of the agencies stressed the city's past heritage and its stock of find historic buildings as a strength, reflecting a desire to recreate a sense of identity and distinctiveness in the future city and also illustrating the post-modern emphasis on style and look. Indeed, the heritage theme is carried forward into the agencies' image of the future city which is seen to be stylish, architecturally elegant and a place of tradition. The future city is also perceived as being a vibrant place, with an enterprising business environment, a high quality of living, a strong sense of community, and a diversity of lifestyles. Several of the agencies are keen to redefine Newcastle as a big village with its connotations of cosiness, community and humanizing qualities. However, we would contend that the similarity of the approach by the various agencies involved in image-improvement work in Newcastle is leading to a lack of dynamism in promoting a future vision of the city. Rather than being distinctive and unique, the consensus model has resulted in a series of future images of the city which are stale and unimaginative. It is a future vision which could be transplanted to any number of older industrial cities. As a result, the hoped-for competitive advantage afforded by these new visions may well be rendered null and void.

Table 11.2   Comparison of image initiatives in Newcastle upon Tyne

Agency	Style of approach	Geographical focus	Main promotional strategies
Newcastle City Council	Marketing-orientated approach Place-specific campaign	Newcastle	High-profile image-improvement strategy and campaign
Tyne and Wear Development Corporation	Marketing-led approach to urban regeneration A dual focus on 'institutional' image and the image of the locality	Waterfront areas of the Rivers Tyne and Wear	Marketing and advertising campaign to 'inform people of a new product' and to raise confidence in the regeneration of the waterfront areas
The Newcastle Initiative	Business-orientated, entrepreneurial style of promoting the city married to a managerial approach A series of place-specific campaigns	Specific areas of Newcastle	No overall campaign but a series of promotional efforts working in partnership with a variety of agencies to promote a new 'vision' of the city
Northern Development Company (NDC)	Marketing-orientated approach Place-specific campaigns based on the region Strong focus on a coordinated, multi-agency approach	Northern Region	Image-improvement strategy comprising: 1. The Great North (an events-led campaign) 2. The Quality Region campaign

Target audience	Past image of the city	Future image of the city	Key words and phrases
Key decision makers, business leaders, financial institutions and opinion-formers in London and the South East	A city with a proud past confidently looking to the future Aims to remove negative images of the city as bleak, depressed, derelict remote and lacking a vibrant economy	A vibrant and strong regional capital with a high quality of living and sustainable inward investment 'A service economy with a healthy slimmed-down manufacturing sector'. A European business centre of excellence and quality	New Era, New Attitude, Newcastle Regional capital Inward investment Quality of life
Initially targeted largely within the region. Major advertising campaign, launched 1990, aimed at national business community and opinion formers	'A proud and properous past' resulting in a new North East rising up Aims to remove images of physical decay by positive action, and to capitalize on the city's heritage	New lifestyles New riverside communities A new spirit of business enterprise 'A leading European centre of trade and commerce'	'The New North East' Mission Vision Lifestyle Confidence Quality of life Optimism
Primarily the business community and opinion formers within and outside the region. Also the general public	'A great heritage' but also aims to remove images of the city as the blackest of black holes' (a tough, threatening, depressing and decaying place with a poor quality of life)	A vision of 'a great city', a strong and vibrant regional capital with a good quality life and a healthy forward-looking business economy. A dynamic and stylish city based around a series of urban 'villages'	Vision Partnership Consensus Liveability 'Village living'
The 'informers' and decision makers within and outside the region notably inward investors, corporate relocators, opinion formers and the media. Also the general public, the financial community, commerce and the education sector locally.	A history of innovation in industrial development Aims to remove the low opinion by the South of the North's quality, and to counter images of the region as stark, desolate, insular and remote	The city as a strong regional capital within a 'quality region' Diversity of lifestyles The region seen as 'a big village' with a strong sense of community and a high quality of life	Quality – 'the quality region' The great north Regional coordination Consensus A new culture – 'a culture of regeneration'

11.5 FRAGMENTS OF A NEW CITY

The problem of corporate consensus and a loss of dynamism is exacerbated by the fragmentations of agencies and image initiatives in Newcastle. One major problem is that each public sector or coalition agency holds a different view of what constitutes 'the local' which it is actively engaged in marketing. For Newcastle City Council, it is Newcastle; in the case of the Development Corporation, it is the waterfront; for TNI it is a series of flagship projects in different city centres and inner area localities; and for NDC, it is the region, the Great North with Newcastle as its regional capital. This has resulted in each agency selling a different spatial territory with the effect that initiatives aimed at creating a new Newcastle have become fragmented and unfocused despite attempts to promote inter-agency coordination. This problem is likely to be exacerbated further by Tyne and Wear Development Corporation's recent 'Welcome to the North East' campaign. The campaign's spatial coverage is broader than previous Development Corporation place-marketing initiatives which focused specifically on the Tyne and Wear waterfront. The new campaign extends its focus to take in yet another spatially defined territory, the North East, as opposed to the even wider Northern Region being promoted by NDC. A direct result of the campaign is likely to be a further reinforcement of the fragmentation of place, time, space and agency in image-improvement initiatives in Newcastle.

Many of the agencies involved in image-improvement and place-marketing initiatives in Newcastle have come to place an increasing emphasis on flagship projects in their urban regeneration efforts. The growing importance of these mega-projects is further evidence of the fragmentation of the urban regeneration process in the present period. In one sense, flagship projects can be regarded as high-profile schemes which help to focus attention, gain the interest of local people, and highlight progress on the ground. They are being used increasingly in Newcastle as visible symbols of renewal, as an aid to confidence building and in an attempt to define new niches for the city in the urban market place. However, flagships can also be seen to reflect an obsession with urban fragments, the planning of individual elements rather than comprehensive and integrated urban systems. We would argue that as part of the image-management process, flagship projects represent the continuing fragmentation of the locality which has been a characteristic feature of urban regeneration efforts in the 1990s. They can be seen as isolated growth nodes within larger areas of decay, often dislocated in spatial and temporal terms from the localities which surround them. We would argue that flagships represent a marketing tool, a form of 'branding' device aimed at boosting a city's image but in reality creating urban fragments which are floating free from the rest of the distressed urban area. It is an approach concerned with superimposing fragments on the city rather than with the comprehensive planning of urban areas.

A further theme in the fragmentation of the city is the notion of 'the urban village'. For many of Newcastle's public- and private-sector agencies, the city of the next decade will be fragmented into a series of self-contained but interlinked urban villages. In Newcastle, public-sector agencies appear to be moving towards a consensus view that the new city should exhibit the atmosphere and cosiness of a village mixed with the excitement and vibrancy of urban life. On the one hand, this represents a reassertion of the urbanity of the city and the glamour of urban living. However, on the other hand, it harks back to rural values, to an idyllic, unthreatening and idealized village lifestyle with a sense of community and identity. It is a vision of a rejuvenated city in which the problems of urban alienation, poverty and deprivation are hidden from view. These disaggregated 'village' communities will, it is hoped, enable people to identify more readily with a fragmented but more legible city. It is a theme which permeates the image-improvement work of all agencies in Newcastle ranging from the Development Corporation's penchant for urban villages through to NDC's concept of 'the region as a big village' and TNI's notion of a 'necklace' of village communities:

> The underlying challenge to Newcastle is one of rebuilding the 'Inner Cities' as a Community. The strategy of creating a ring of 'Villages' from the Theatre Village to Byker might be one long-term strategy.
> (Interview with Hay, TNI, 1990)

It is clear that urban villages are regarded by the public- and private-sector agencies as fulfilling a valuable symbolic function in reconstructing the city's image. However, it is questionable whether this planning of fragments represents an effective strategy for tackling the problems of urban regeneration. It perhaps reflects a crisis in city planning and a lack of confidence in the validity of a single, all-embracing vision of the city. Unlike the modernist city, conceived of as a whole and with its emphasis on comprehensive planning, the post-modernist city is being re-imaged as a series of fragments. In the case of Newcastle, these urban fragments can be seen eddying around a central point – the City Centre. The result is a splintering effect in the urban regeneration process characterized by a series of entrepreneurial initiatives and speculative projects rather than by integrated programmes. As a result current initiatives have a tendency to focus on the lifestyle and business images of individual fragments of the city. It leaves us with the question of 'what sort of city' should we be aiming to provide for the 21st century and how do we attempt to fashion a new urbanity?

11.6   MANAGERIALISM AND ENTREPRENEURIALISM

The current wave of image-improvement initiatives in Newcastle reflects a new relationship between the entrepreneurial and management approaches to local economic development. We would challenge Harvey's contention 'that "the managerial" approach so typical of the 1960s has steadily given way to initiatory and "entrepreneurial" forms of action in the 1970s and 1980s' (Harvey, 1989b, p. 4). Whilst urban governance has become more entrepreneurial, there has always been a strong element of management in its approach to economic development. We would argue that urban managerialism in the present period involves what Hesse has described as 'the organisation of interaction processes with the goal of arriving at consensus and gaining acceptance, as well as the organisation of providing resources and competences in order to materially allow for common action' (Hesse, quoted in Mayer, 1989). It places a new emphasis on local authorities and other public-sector agencies as crisis-managers, coordinators and facilitators. At the same time, inter-regional and inter-urban competition has forced cities such as Newcastle to become more entrepreneurial in exploring new ways in which to reposition themselves in the emerging post-Fordist era. We would suggest that this new entrepreneurial approach to economic development has its roots in US models of urban regeneration whilst the revamped managerial style of local authorities has been influenced strongly by Japanese approaches to business management.

In terms of urban entrepreneurialism, it is possible to discern a trend towards an 'Americanization' of local economic development in the approaches to place marketing adopted by public sector agencies in Newcastle. The concept of place marketing has long been an important component of economic development and urban regeneration strategies in US cities starting with New York's 'I Love New York' campaign in the 1970s, and continuing with image-improvement campaigns in cities such as Pittsburgh (branded as 'The Liveable City'), Minneapolis (with its 'We like it here' advertising campaign) and Detroit (recast as 'Renaissance City'). Figure 11.13 illustrates the approach to place marketing recommended by the US National Council for Urban Economic Development. The emphasis is upon a SWOT style of marketing analysis which is not dissimilar from the current approach to image being adopted by Newcastle City Council. The US style of entrepreneurialism is also characterized by civic boosterism and the marketing of quality of life. This marketing directed approach is extremely similar in conception and practice to the work of The Newcastle Initiative with its emphasis on talking up Newcastle.

This entrepreneurial approach has been married to a managerial style of economic development which draws on the Japanese model of management. It is evident in place-marketing initiatives in Newcastle, particularly in the work of NDC, the Development Corporation and TNI. All of these agencies place considerable emphasis on the quality ethic, on teamwork, and on collective loyalty. The Japanese ethic has also exerted an influence on images of new lifestyles in Newcastle. For example, Tyne and Wear Development Corporation's recent Brightside Campaign leans heavily on

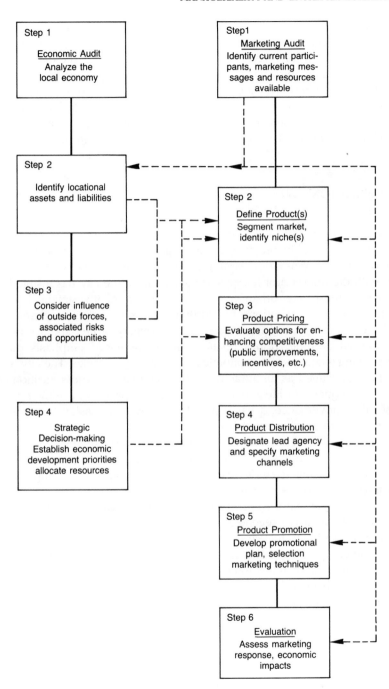

Figure 11.13 Developing an area marketing programme: methodology suggested by the US National Council for Urban Economic Development. Source: Haider, 1989

the Japanese model of worker-employee relations. This Japanization of the workforce is evident in the Brightside advertisements (Fig. 11.6) in which Ritchie and Doug, the bricklayer (equals the 'doer') and the site-manager (the action-orientated thinker), are portrayed as equal partners working together to create 'a new riverside' in a spirit of teamwork and partnership. The new Tyneside worker has swopped his cloth cap and lackadaisical *Auf Wiedersehen Pet* image for a construction helmet and a major role in the urban regeneration team, finally laying to rest the ghost of Andy Capp.

11.7 CONCLUSION

It is clear that image-improvement initiatives have become an important area of activity for public-sector agencies engaged in economic development and urban regeneration strategies in Newcastle. The increasing concern with the question of image and packaging of the city has resulted largely from intense inter-urban competition for inward investment. It is also a response to perceptions of Northern cities as localities characterized by decline, a lack of innovation, a poor quality of life, and a non-entrepreneurial attitude. It has resulted in an increased emphasis on place-marketing techniques in economic development strategies. The city is now to be repackaged as an attractive and progressive business location, boasting a high quality of life and a progressive, entrepreneurial attitude. In terms of urban governance, it has resulted in a new relationship between entrepreneurialism and managerialism, and an emphasis on consumption-led strategies in urban regeneration. It is reflected in the changing nature of local corporatism which has led to the public-sector actively engaging in the marketplace and assuming a more marketing-orientated approach compared with its traditional role as regulator and policy maker.

However, do image-improvement campaigns and initiatives really represent a panacea for urban regeneration and local economic development agencies? Is it possible to recreate or re-image the city in the present period or are we merely grasping in the dark for fragmented solutions? One of the potential problems of image-marketing initiatives is the danger of a city or region overpromising and underdelivering. If image campaigns are to reposition older industrial cities effectively in the urban marketplace, they will need to relate more successfully image-marketing strategies to urban regeneration strategies and investment programmes. In addition, if image campaigns are to result in sustainable and sharable benefits, they must be both credible and backed up by substance. This may suggest the need for a greater range of more integrated strategies than those being employed at present. In addition, there is also a further potential danger that image-marketing campaigns can foreclose options by focusing on a particular theme or locality, they can divert resources from mainstream economic development work and they have a tendency to be partial and selective. However, the real crisis is perhaps one of 'how do we recreate a city fit for the 21st-century?'. There is no easy solution.

PART FOUR _____

FORMS OF
PARTNERSHIP

_____

12

EDITORIAL

Mo O'Toole and David Usher

The concept of partnership, and the rhetoric surrounding the term, ascended meteoric heights with the dawning of a new decade of urban regeneration in the 1980s. The diversity of partnership arrangements in the UK, their varying degrees of success and cohesion and the apparent dissimilarity between the role ascribed to them in government hyperbole and that which they actually played on the local stage of economic development, have ensured the centrality of their position in debates on UK urban policy and property development amongst academics and policy practitioners alike.

This section of the book addresses the questions that partnership formation raised in the 1980s which seem even more pertinent in the 1990s. The role of partnership in the postwar period, the nature of the new partnerships, and their changing participants, the contribution which they make to city rebuilding and the lessons to be drawn from their application to urban policy are covered in these four chapters which examine a wide variety of institutional arrangements that constitute themselves under the banner of partnership.

Harding is concerned to assess the applicability to the UK of the US growth coalition model advanced by Molotch and Logan. Through an assessment of 11 partnerships in Scotland and England, he weaves an analysis of the role of property in setting the agenda for bodies as diverse as the Birmingham Heartlands and the Sheffield Urban Regeneration Committee. He concludes that there is certainly evidence to suggest that the notion of growth coalition politics is of increasing importance in the UK. There are significant differences from the US, however, such as the position which local authorities occupy as **rentiers** (landowners and dealers) and the disassociation between political parties and business interests at a local level which precludes the wholesale application of the model in the UK.

In this, Harding concurs with Lloyd, who suggests that a variant of the growth coalition model operates in Scotland. Lloyd examines four projects, two of which function in a fairly traditional manner and two more recent examples that are distinctly entrepreneurial. He ties the four together by looking at the crucial role which the SDA has played in maintaining the multiplicity of partnerships which straddle Scotland's efforts in urban and economic regeneration. He then focuses on the changes that have taken place within the agency, propelling it towards a more enterprising approach to local economic development.

Flagship projects, and the part that they now play in re-imaging cities, preoccupy Bianchini *et al.* Their chapter illustrates how flagships have been both a catalyst in the creation of partnership and a result of partnership actions. In determining the relationship of flagships to urban policy and property development, the chapter evolves a means of measuring the success of a flagship, utilizing a critique based essentially on a social equity model, as referred to by Harding. This provides the reader with an important means of evaluating the merits of flagships, but significantly also assists in determining the merits of new partnership arrangements.

Finally, Whitney and Haughton survey five local-authority districts in West Yorkshire. Despite their close proximity, the districts have thrown up a vast array of partnerships. Their overlapping programmes, conflicting objectives and organizational jealousies present a chaotic but not entirely unsuccessful catalogue of achievement in a small geographical arena.

12.1 THE NEW ROLE FOR PARTNERSHIP

Partnership in the 1980s has witnessed a redrawing of the boundaries of public and private provision, involving the private sector in a more proactive and extensive role in the process of urban rebuilding. But a precise definition of the role accorded to the private sector is more difficult to suggest. Harding in particular points to the difficulty in clarifying the role of the private sector from his research across 11 cities. That there has been a reformulation of the positions adopted by various actors is not in doubt. The primary thrust of this change has catapulted the private sector into a position of pre-eminence on the public stage. Its role has been emphasized above all others, while the rhetoric of modernization minimized an ongoing role for the public sector in urban land-use planning and change. The scope of this transformation was dramatic and coincided with the limitation, through statutory and resource measures, of public-sector involvement in land-use change. A greater emphasis was placed upon entrepreneurial activity which was initiated and overseen by the private sector, governed by the assessment of market forces and by commercial viability.

It is this characteristic in particular that differentiates the new partnerships. The numerous partnerships that have operated in the field of land-use planning since 1947 were based on a synergetic relationship between public and private interests. The system itself, as Lloyd suggests in his chapter, was predisposed towards this type of arrangement. The extensive redevelopment programmes of the 1950s and the 1960s, during which high-rise flats transformed the urban landscape of most UK cities, represented publicly funded development carried out by private construction firms. Indeed, seven construction firms accounted for 75% of all industrialized high-rise approvals during the period 1963–73 (Dunleavy, 1981).

In the new context, however, the private sector has become a legitimate provider of public policy initiatives. This has been developed in a variety of forms: joint ventures, Training and Enterprise Councils and Urban Development Corporations to name but a few. As Whitney and Haughton point out, the public sector provides a strategic framework, information systems and in many instances, land or access to land. The private sector then boosts this with entrepreneurial, managerial and project operation skills, and gives access to much needed finance. This final facility was previously a public sector and primarily a local authority domain.

Implicit in all the contributions is the conviction that the private sector bestows on partnerships a credibility in the development industry that the public sector simply does not have. But whilst the role enjoyed by the private sector in public provision is new, the participants are not. Many of the construction firms involved in British Urban Development (BUD) and Phoenix in the late 1980s were developers in high-rise construction in the 1960s. The development industry has consistently made strong representations to the Conservative Party but the powerful lobby of BUD and Phoenix has co-opted and enabled these interests to have direct control over the rebuilding of cities and thus dictate the pace and scope of development. It must be emphasized, however, that much of the market-led property activity of the 1980s was underwritten substantially by public subsidy and that this has been perhaps more accurately labelled a public subsidization of speculative development (Gibson, 1986).

The question underpinning the chapters in this section concerns the role that the new institutional arrangements now operating in the public policy arena play in city rebuilding. It is apparent from these chapters that partnerships have not had a consistent role in either urban policy or city redevelopment. In many locations, partnership has galvanized private and propertied interests in physical developments, exemplified by Glasgow Action or the Leeds City Development Company. In other areas the partnership has provided the necessary impetus with which to rebuild the image of declining cities wishing to compete in a new world marketplace; the Bradford is Bouncing Back campaign typifies this approach. But perhaps most potently, partnerships have in themselves represented a flagship, a symbol of a new era of urban governance, with whom outsiders and some insiders can do business.

Of course all the partnerships have been a combination of some or all of these. The emphasis has varied according to the vicissitudes of the locality, and the whims of both central government and international capital. It appears, however, that as the decade progressed, arrangements were characterized by a pragmatic use of complimentary resources in an era of fiscal contraction. Local deal-making was perhaps the inevitable outcome of national government policy.

The post-war property market in the UK has been subject to the ebb and flow of political influences, moving from private to public sector and back again. For the 1980s, it seemed at first glance as if the tide was out for the public sector. New initiatives changed the institutional arrangements through which government subsidy was delivered to the urban regions. But as Harding makes clear, the demise of the public sector in city rebuilding is far from upon us.

For a variety of reasons the public sector, and local authorities in particular, have been key actors in initiating and maintaining the momentum of partnership. As Bianchini *et al.* illustrate from cases in Glasgow and Birmingham the creation of flagship projects could not have happened without the sponsorship of the respective local authorities.

12.2   ENTREPRENEURIALISM VERSUS MANAGERIALISM

Partnerships are associated with an entrepreneurial approach to urban policy and the redevelopment of the built environment (Harvey, 1989b). The task allotted to the private sector at the beginning of the 1980s was to deliver a centrally prescribed entrepreneurial shot in the arm to the rather slow-moving and cumbersome bureaucratic practices that were perceived to be the vice of the public sector. At the end of the decade we are faced with a number of questions regarding the validity of entrepreneurialism as an approach to economic development, and indeed the applicability of the term itself to the processes observed.

The practices of the public sector in relation to city rebuilding have undergone a transformation in the last 10 years. Undoubtedly city governments have become more selective, opportunistic and have oriented their strategies towards projects aimed at profit and revenue maximization. But it is questionable that it has been the private sector which, by example or in joint working, has engineered this change. It is clear from the case studies in these chapters that to a great extent private-sector manoeuvrability is dependent on public-sector finance, especially in areas of high risk. The Scottish and West Yorkshire examples are perhaps the most illuminating in this respect.

As Lloyd points out, public agencies have responded to government pressures to become more entrepreneurial. The SDA provides a good example of this in the policy changes that have attended its 15-year history, from initially interventionist stances towards industry in the late 1970s to the market modified stance of the late 1980s, where concerns with employment retention and creation have been superseded by an interest in property development and housing.

In practice, however, the UK government has remained highly interventionist. This interventionism was precipitated at the beginning of the decade by extensive urban unrest in a number of UK cities. In the aftermath of the Brixton and Toxteth riots of 1981, Michael Heseltine visited Liverpool and invited Tom Baron, the Chairman of Christian Salverson (Properties) Limited to prepare a scheme for the renewal of Cantril Farm, a 1960s housing estate. Baron had been Michael Heseltine's housing adviser in 1979–80. He was an outspoken advocate of a wider role for the public sector in housing renewal (Brindley, Stoker and Rydin, 1989). Their visit announced the Government's intention to abandon old-style corporatist policies in city renewal.

Private-led partnership of the 1980s variety is underpinned by an exposition of the virtues of intervention, through aid to the private sector. Paradoxically the drive to open the way for a renewed involvement of the private sector in the regeneration of cities by encouraging private-sector investment and an enterprise culture would not have been possible without massive state intervention. Not only has central government remained highly active in promoting and sustaining partnership, but local government, the original object of exclusion, has become increasingly entrepreneurial as it has fought to maintain its position in the public policy arena of economic development.

12.3 MEASUREMENTS OF SUCCESS

In parallel with the institutional changes marking the 1980s has been the neo-liberals' obsessive search for efficiency and performance assessment in public expenditure. Throughout the 1980s a range of evaluation measures were introduced to appraise the effectiveness of enhanced urban programmes. Leverage planning became the fashionable designation by which the level of private investment secured in relation to the public money necessary to pump-prime activity was gauged. Other measures included the amount of derelict or unused land brought back into use, the amount of new development floorspace produced and the number of jobs created, either during or after project completion. The range of indicators was applied uniformly across the UK, irrespective of local property market conditions. The maxim in the case of gearing or leaverage ratios was the higher the level of private investment procured the better the project. Attempts to achieve high gearing in land and buildings were not surprisingly most successful in areas like London's Docklands, while older urban regions were left to defend large-scale commercial projects against charges of poor value for money. The suspicion is growing, and is echoed in Lloyd's chapter, that private-sector led regeneration is confined to areas with clear commercial potential for development (Boyle, 1988a; Robson, 1988).

This suspicion has been intensified by the set of standard measures of success which the Government has sought to apply to urban policies of economic development and regeneration. Dissatisfaction with these measures has grown as property-led initiatives have failed to deliver a widely dispersed regeneration in the inner city and indeed have failed to show any sign of promoting long-term stable economic renewal. Bianchini *et al.* elucidate the limitations in government criteria for evaluating partnership policy and success. They offer alternative criteria for the measurement of success of flagships, and suggest a critique of partnership that might well be valuable in questioning the thrust of the policy of the 1980s. Testing flagships against redistribution and access rightly begs the validity of the concept of **trickle down**, which Harding also questions. Trickle down has become a contentious issue in urban policy. Private-sector investment has increased the prosperity of some zones in urban regions, but produced dual cities composed of islands of regeneration surrounded by seas of accentuated poverty (Harvey, 1985). It is also true that, with few exceptions, and these tend to be enterprise-led coalitions such as in Ferguslie Park in Strathclyde or the BIC project in Calderdale, that partnerships inevitably reinforce the existing polarization between the city centre and parts of the periphery.

The criticism which Bianchini *et al.* lay at the door of flagships, namely their ability to skew public spending, the secrecy that surrounds their decision-making structure and the proliferation of initiatives leading to an overcrowding in the market place, are equally well applied to the institutional regimes with which they are associated.

Crucially a question mark hangs over the ability of the private sector to secure broadly based regeneration. This is in part to do with its inability to act strategically but also because of the contradictions between corporate role in profit maximization and the now popular notion of corporate responsibility involving community benefit. This notion of community benefit transcends traditional notions of planning gain suggesting a conscious effort on the part of the private sector to meet social needs in the absence of the traditional structures of public sector provision. But the evidence suggests, and this is further reinforced if one uses evaluative criteria such as those proposed by Bianchini *et al.* that community benefit has occupied a low priority in many partnerships, being brought into play only when community opposition forces the issue, or when local authorities seek to secure those gains, as in the West Yorkshire district of Kirklees, or when the property market slumps into one of its periodic declines. It appears that the new management offered is more apparent than real and that the new purpose does nothing to solve the old problems.

12.4   THE SEMIOTICS OF GROWTH

A consensus began to emerge in the 1980s, well-illustrated in these chapters, that a city without a flagship did not have a regeneration strategy and a city without a partnership lacked the key component in attracting new investment and thus the means of regeneration. To lack a partnership, it seemed, equalled outworn, outmoded and ineffective public-sector strategies. These concerned themselves with the non-physical processes of regeneration, were preoccupied with outdated considerations of social improvement and failed to get to grips with the importance of land and property in spearheading a city's regeneration. So the partnership itself became a vital tool in the marketing of the city. It was not just a vehicle of policy formulation and implementation but a symbol of the changes that had been brought to bear in the locality. It in itself became a saleable item, a technique of the advertising programme that increasingly accompanied the physical revitalization programme (Chapter 9).

12.5   LESSONS OF THE PARTNERSHIPS OF THE 1980s

The lessons of partnership are only just beginning to emerge from the euphoria of the mid-1980s property boom and the obfuscation of the consequences implicit in that. Two dominant problems have underpinned business-led initiatives. First, the role of the private sector within them and, second, the institutional capacity of the initiatives to effect significant change. Apart from the blaze of promotional hype which surrounded the launch of partnerships such as The Newcastle Initiative, forays into social projects have met with limited success. Amidst attempts to introduce a business compact for residents on a housing estate in one of the most deprived wards in the Northern Region, it transpired that local business lacked specific knowledge of dealing with social problems. It is difficult to suggest that any of TNI's flagship projects have achieved progress, reflecting the low level of financial resources available to the organization. Effectively, TNI had no statutory powers of its own, relying instead upon the ability of its directors to influence business to become more proactive in the regional economy.

Additionally, the sheer number of initiatives operating in any one region leads to lack of strategic vision, duplication of services and development projects and jealous abuse of resources as Whitney and Haughton demonstrate in West Yorkshire. The large number of actors, property developers in addition to the business community, who targeted the inner cities on the back of the property boom, and who were offered generous strategic planning frameworks and subsidies by the second- and third-generation Urban Development Corporations, converged to propose numerous developments.

Harding points out that these interests were further fuelled by organizations such as BUD. Ultimately, many of these developments were to become unsustainable and BUD, which was established in 1987, was being wound down by 1990 due to the state of the national property market. The property-led agenda set by the development industry was dealt a mortal blow by the property slump, itself a product of national fiscal policies. This reinforces Harding's view that the coincidence of interests between central government and the property industry was no more than a brief encounter.

The authors of these chapters record some benefits accruing to the inner city from partnership initiatives, for example the positive contribution which flagships have made to the development of cultural industries, particularly in the growth of tertiary and subsidiary activities based on the media. However, the failure of the new partnerships to produce a wider economic regeneration and the frailty of their policies in the face of local and national political and economic pressures, unite the contributors in a critique of the long-term utility of the partnership-mode of policy making. Indeed, there is a growing consensus that partnerships as they are presently constituted will result in the further degradation of many of the urban regions through a fragmentation of the planning system, the selective distribution of revenue benefits and a burgeoning facadism that obscures the increasing polarization of wealth and poverty in cities.

Significantly, no one model of partnership has emerged, perhaps reflecting the uneven development of the city regions and the unequal interests which exercise power in them. But Harding proposes the model that generated some of the early partnerships, and which now stands as a polar opposite to the dominant 1980s model of economic development. The Social Equity movement advanced in largely Labour metropolitan authorities in the late 1970s and early 1980s, was rooted in the idea that economic development could be used to secure advances for labour. Training agreements, contract compliance and equal-opportunity policies massed to symbolize the re-distributive potential of local authority intervention in the economic sphere. The new property-led partnerships can clearly be seen to stand as an alternative to the type of gain negotiated in the heady days of the advancement of municipal socialist policy. But what, in the present unfriendly climate, do they stand for?

The form of future involvement by the property industry may be based in the future upon a different range of considerations, relating to attempts to introduce more revenue expenditure and community benefit into the development process. The exact form of these alternative arrangements remains imprecise, though it is certain that the dominant thrust of property development in its current form will remain undermined and may not recover in the foreseeable future. In these terms the emphasis of partnership and government support may be shifted within the new institutional arrangements to cover a wider range of issues than merely property development.

13

PROPERTY INTERESTS AND URBAN GROWTH COALITIONS IN THE UK: A BRIEF ENCOUNTER

Alan Harding

This chapter examines a major feature of recent attempts to regenerate the UK's urban areas – the formation of alliances between public and private sector interests and actors on the basis of a common economic growth agenda – with reference to a concept first developed in the USA: the growth coalition or growth machine (Molotch, 1976; Logan and Molotch, 1987). Other terms are used to describe similar phenomena, for example public-private partnership (Fosler and Berger, 1982), local corporatism (Cawson, 1985; King, 1985; Saunders, 1985; Simmie, 1981, 1985), and local governance (Harvey, 1989b). The growth coalition literature is examined because it provides a comprehensive account of the mechanics of local coalition building and, especially interesting here, argues that property interests are central to the process. The chapter first examines the notion of growth coalitions as applied in the USA and comments on its applicability in the UK. Next, it identifies key factors which have contributed to the recent development of UK variants of the growth coalition. It then assesses the part which property interests have played, and the strategic weight which is attached to property development, in a number of growth-coalition like bodies now operating in the urban UK. Finally, it examines some implications for the process and impact of urban change.

13.1   GROWTH COALITIONS

In *Urban Fortunes*, Logan and Molotch (1987) argue from a voluntarist perspective – 'the activism of entrepreneurs is, and always has been, a critical force in shaping the urban system' (Logan and Molotch, 1987, p. 52) – that a coalition of local interests, acting out of narrow, partisan motivations but espousing an ideology of **value-free development**, can become the dominant force in urban redevelopment. The coalitions' critical players are said to be the most place-bound elements of capital: rentiers (property owners) who rely on an intensification of land use for enhanced profits. Joining rentiers are other key players in the property business who stand to benefit from the intensification process itself, and those for whose products demand will increase as a result of any economic (income and/or population) growth. Pre-eminent among the latter are local media and utility companies.

Auxiliary players allegedly include universities, cultural institutions, professional sports clubs, labour unions, the self-employed and small retailers. Corporate capital, normally disinterested in local issues, plays a role only when pro-growth movements lose momentum and groups representing use values as opposed to exchange values mount a significant political challenge. Corporate interventions can quickly remobilize and restore the dominance of the growth machine, however, as the case of Cleveland, involving the business-induced downfall of a populist mayor who was not backed by the corporations (Swanstrom, 1985), is said to show. Local government, for politico-administrative reasons, is fully supportive of growth coalitions and 'primarily concerned with increasing growth' (Logan and Molotch, 1987, p. 63).

There is no question that many of the factors which implicitly underlie the formation of growth coalitions are more apposite to the USA than to the UK. Higher levels of centralization in corporate and financial capital mean that most UK cities outside London lack local control over the resources for regeneration enjoyed by many of their US counterparts. Partly as a result they traditionally have lacked the strong social networks of local business people which provide impetus to growth coalitions in the USA (see examples in Fosler and Berger, 1982). Urban landownership in the USA also seems to be spread amongst a larger group of private owners who actively use land assets in accumulation strategies. In contrast, land ownership in the UK owes more to pre- or non-capitalist interests (landed aristocracy, the Crown, the Church, the universities, charitable trusts, local authorities, etc.) than to rentiers (Hudson and Williams, 1989; pp. 26–31). Finally, private-sector penetration of local party systems and other forms of urban political activity by businesses are less marked in the UK than in the USA.

Notwithstanding the above, it is possible to conceive of changes in the wider political and economic environment which could move the UK experience closer to that of the USA. The next section examines such changes, and identifies how in the early 1980s development of an equitable growth movement within UK local government become displaced by a general move toward forming informal and institutionalized partnerships with the private sector – a UK variant of growth coalitions – by the end of the decade.

13.2   THE MOVE TO A GROWTH COALITION MODEL IN THE UK

The early 1980s saw the displacement of the pre-existing model of local authority economic policy, based on area promotion and support for small businesses, by alternatives which rejected inter-urban competition for development and emphasized indigenous growth, quality of employment and social equity, i.e. that the fruits of such policies should reflect the needs of deprived sections of urban communities. Within this municipally led movement for equitable growth, property development was less important than people-based programmes. The pioneers of this approach were the more radical Labour councils whose political complexion had changed as a result of recent intra-party power shifts (Gyford, 1985). But their basic redistributive agenda and the sorts of policies and instruments which went with it, if not the most overt ideas about worker participation and control, spread quickly through the local authority system to become the new orthodoxy in the Labour-dominated urban authorities.

What Labour authorities lacked in this period were adequate municipal powers and resources, or the support of a wider coalition of interests who could help them to implement plans in anything but the most experimental and demonstrative form. Locally based public-sector attempts to strengthen urban economic prospects were relatively new in the early 1980s and local authorities had only just won, in the moderate form of the reshaped Urban Programme, a share in policy responsibilities. To the extent that forces within and allied to local government considered the notion of coalitions for the pursuit of economic policy objectives in the early 1980s, it entailed the election of a more sympathetic central government, a greater voice for consumers and workers (particularly local authority unions), and the use of municipal levers of power to influence the decision-making patterns of a weakened private sector.

The wider political and economic context of the early 1980s prevented the formation of coalitions between urban authorities and central government and/or private-sector interests. There was no common ground with a central government determined to scale down municipal functions and staff levels, and hostile to forms of economic intervention which did not only aim only to create private markets where none existed previously. Conservative governments of the 1980s were purveyors of the notion, common amongst US growth machine activists, of **value-free development** – the notion that all sections of urban communities benefit from the trickle-down effect resulting from increased economic activity. Differences between the central and local agendas revolved around attitudes to growth, not its desirability. Urban authorities serving impoverished communities with high levels of unemployment could not countenance an anti-growth stance if they were to provide the most prized products of economic policyjobs. The effects of the wider breakdown in central–local relations in the 1980s eroded the basis for intergovernmental partnerships whilst weakening enormously the local authorities' ability and willingness to develop equitable growth agendas.

The idea that national or local private-property interests, or the private sector more generally, could contribute to urban regeneration efforts was hardly sustainable in this period either. The recession which coincided with the first two years of Conservative government had a disastrous effect on traditional sectors clustered disproportionately in older urban areas, and urban property markets suffered badly. Private-sector interests lacked the cohesion, the organizational capacity and the will to become a significant contributor to regeneration efforts.

The transformation of urban economic policy-making and its organizational landscape in the 1980s resulted from the interplay between central government actions, changing perceptions and practices in the corporate sector, changes in local governments' performance of their functions, and the wider economic climate. At national level, central government waged an ideological financial and legislative campaign with a three-fold purpose: to change the basis of local authority economic intervention such that it was compatible with a Conservative vision of the urban economic order, to mobilize the private sector into participation in urban regeneration, and to extend central government influence over public programmes to further these aims (Harding, 1989b, 1990a,b). This strategy had numerous property implications.

A series of measures variously bribed, cajoled and forced urban local authorities to waive or minimize their regulatory (planning) functions and to operate an automatic presumption in favour of development. Local authorities found their ability to resist development which was considered to be at variance with local interests reduced. Indeed, their ability to mount independent programmes at all was undercut massively by factors like the abolition of the influential metropolitan and Greater London councils, increased Government direction over economic development programmes, the outlawing of contract compliance procedures, and reductions in their capacity to establish independent companies with which to implement economic policies outside statutory restrictions. Whitehall-led implementation of property initiatives became common through the work of agencies like the Urban Development Corporations (UDCs), Task Forces and City Action Teams. Public expenditure cuts also had their effect. Local authorities' construction role diminished rapidly as a result of capital cutbacks and restrictions on borrowing. They were thereby forced to be much more entrepreneurial with property assets than previously as a way of generating vital capital and revenue. A further, little-noticed effect, exacerbated by rising wages in the private professions, was the loss of key staff in areas such as valuation, estates and architecture, especially to the burgeoning consultancy sector which has played a significant role in UK-style growth coalitions.

Only in the mid-1980s, with the pick-up in the national economy and the shrinkage of global construction markets, did private property interests – primarily national ones – show signs of anything more than a piecemeal interest in urban regeneration efforts: this despite early government urban programmes favourable to the industry. Corporate umbrella organizations like Phoenix and British Urban Development (BUD) were formed by leading construction and development companies with a view to lobbying central government for further subsidies which would enable the corporate sector to realize profitable urban investments, and to identifying urban investment opportunities. The CBI, Phoenix and Business in the Community (BiC) also supported the formation of local business-led agencies to promote, co-ordinate and help execute local development strategies.

As a result, the organizational environment of the late 1980s contained more central government and business players, operating to a more straight-forward economic growth agenda in which redistributive elements tend to be marginal. The local authorities' reaction was a rearguard and prag-matic preservation of their economic development role and moves to support initiatives which could have positive effects on local economies even if the means to control the process had been much reduced. The changes thus pushed a variety of interests in the direction of a UK form of growth coalition.

13.3 PROPERTY INTERESTS AND GROWTH COALITIONS

Eleven organizations exhibiting some of the characteristics of US growth coalitions are examined here for evidence of property membership and the weight they attach to property development. (for further detail, see Harding, 1989a). Table 13.1 summarizes the findings. The 11 show significant varia-tion in form but it is not possible, in Logan and Molotch style, to read off involvement from a checklist of local organizations. The mix of public- and private-sector representatives varies between two outliers – TNI, which is wholly dominated by the private sector but within which senior public-sector executives serve in an ex-officio capacity, and SERC, whose diverse public-sector members are in a modest majority. The degree to which the 11 encompass different interests varies with the scale and complexity of the aims which they set themselves. Where these are circumscribed, as in the limited development brief of the VDC, so is the spread of members. At the

Table 13.1 Property and UK growth coalitions

Agency	Public–private membership split (approx.)	Private property interests as a proportion of private membership (large, moderate, small)	Importance of known rentiers within private-property interests (large, moderate, small)	Primary local authority role (ownership, regulation, information)	Importance of property within partnership strategy (primary, secondary, marginal)
Aberdeen Beyond 2000 (AB2)	1:4	S	S	–	S
Birmingham Heartlands Ltd (BHL)	3:5	L	S	O/R	P
Blackburn Partnership (BPp)	1:2	S	S	I	M
Calderdale Partnership (CPp)	4:5	M	M	I	M
Glasgow Action (GA)	1:4	S	S	O/R/I	S
Victoria Dock Co. (Hull) (VDC)	1:1	L	S	O/I	P
Leeds City Development Co. (LCDC)	1:1	S	S	O/I	P
The Newcastle Initiative (TNI)	1:2*	M	M	O/R/I	S
Ravenhead Renaissance (St Helens) (RR)	1:8	M	L	O/R	P
Sheffield Economic Regeneration Committee (SERC)	1:1	S	S	R/I	M
The Wearside Opportunity (TWO)	1:10	S	S	I	S

*Includes public-sector ex-officio.
Note: All data based on the position in Autumn 1989.

other extreme, GA, SERC and TNI draw on wider membership bases more reminiscent of US growth coalitions, and are characterized by more complex and wide-ranging strategies.

Within the 11, private rentiers, indeed place-specific capital of any kind, are not as significant as in US coalitions. This is clear from the non-local triggers which lay behind many of them. The CBI led on two (TNI and TWO); BiC on a further two – the Calderdale and Blackburn Partnerships. Others were reactions (not necessarily successful) to the Government's threatened imposition of UDCs – a strong factor in the development of BHL, LCDC, SERC and RR. The Scottish examples were led by the Scottish Development Agency (SDA), not rentiers (Chapter 11). Whilst in Glasgow the district council arguably kicked off, and continues to participate in the process of city centre property development (Boyle, 1990), in Aberdeen the local authority is more uneasy and plays a more limited role. Arguably, only in the case of the VDC was no external trigger necessary: the city council led the formation of a joint development company. Even here though inter-governmental policy relations in housing played a critical role in pointing the council in the direction of partnership, rather than the municipal building programme for which the relevant site was originally earmarked. None of this argues that local authorities are unwilling coalition partners. It is more true to say that external pressures and/or encouragement have been critical in drawing local private-sector figures together.

It is local authorities, contrary to growth coalition literature, which prove to be the key rentiers. This is consistent with (a) the historically more significant role of municipal property ownership in the UK, (b) the pressure to speculate with such assets that the 1980s has brought, (c) the fragmented, incoherent, often absentee (or simply unfathomable) urban private ownership patterns, particularly of land, and 4. the failure of government policy to provide the incentives to private owners that they have, albeit in negative forms, in the public sector. In only one of the organizations considered here (RR) did private landowners – initially British Gas and Pilkingtons, for whom property assets were incidental to production functions – take leading roles in property-based growth strategy. Support in this case comes from the local planning authority and central government (via the local Task Force, City Grant monies and roadbuilding approvals).

In other cases local authorities, UDCs or Development Agencies have used either their ownership positions or their capacity to assemble property for private development, as tools with which to develop coalitions. Examples included VDC (Hull City Council with Bellway Urban Renewals), GA (which rested on property development by Glasgow District Council and the SDA) and LCDC whose strength lies in its access to Leeds City Council's substantial land-holdings. Similarly, councils in Aberdeen, Birmingham and Newcastle have made municipal land-holdings and/or the threatened or actual use of Compulsory Purchase Orders a part of their contribution to growth coalitions in their respective cities. In most cases the *quid pro quo* of the developments has been the passing of ownership, either ultimately, or immediately – through the back-to-back acquisition procedure – from the public authority to developers or end users.

The *raison d'être* of many of the coalitions examined here, then, is the tackling of log-jams caused by lack of private rentier entrepreneurship; i.e. they mobilize *against* existing owners *for* development. Some aim to change the nature of ownership patterns, others (e.g. BHL and TNI) to provoke positive reactions from reluctant rentiers. In both cases progress has been slowed by rentiers hanging on to the hope values of their assets and by property speculation from institutions outside the immediate coalition. Private-sector representation on UK coalitions tends to come not from rentiers but from those interests involved in the intensification process (financial institutions, developers, consultancies and professional practices). However Table 13.1 illustrates that the latter are not dominant either. Allowing for the fact that formal membership alone does not necessarily signify direct in-volvement in the organization's property projects, the contrast with the USA becomes clear. The strongest role played by non-rentier property interests is in the contractor-dominated BHL where five major regional and inter-national construction contractors occupy half the board places, own 64% of the company shares and dominate the various consortia involved in BHL developments. Such dominance is rare. At the other extreme, SERC's 33 member board numbers only one private-sector representative who could unambiguously be said to be in the property field.

However, property interests can, in principle, be influential without formally being represented on partnership bodies. Both LCDC and TNI have wider networks of property interests on various development proposals, and consultants or other development-facilitators feature, in one way or another, in seven of the other organizations (the municipally led VDC and LCDC, and the BiC initiatives are the exceptions). Indeed the 11 suggest that a low level of formal property interest representation does not always mean low strategic salience being accorded to property development.

Property development in fact plays an important, though widely varying role within the programmes promoted by the 11 (see Table 13.1). At one extreme, the strategies of VDC, LCDC, RR and BHL are almost exclusively concerned with property development despite the fact that only in RR and BHL is membership slanted toward property interests. By contrast, the BiC-inspired CPp and BPp, to mid-1989, had done little more than market sites to national BiC companies and lobby for national infrastructural support. In between are a number of strategies in which property development is a component of wider purposes (e.g. city centre service-sector development in Aberdeen and Glasgow and the promotion of advanced manufacturing in Wearside). No clear pattern is evident either in the timescales adopted for property development or the location and type of sites involved.

It is altogether easier to identify public-sector roles in the 11. Other than public property ownership and land assembly powers, local authority contributions include the provision and dissemination of information and the production of planning frameworks. The latter, central to RR, VDC, TNI and BHL, and important to GA, SERC and TWO, suggests a growing desire for a form of local corporatism quite at odds with the neo-liberal government policies on land-use planning in the 1980s. Government influence is critical however, not just for manipulating a climate whereby coalitions were more likely. Government-appointed agencies are important. Task Forces and UDCs, for example, are intimately linked with the RR, TNI, SERC and TWO initiatives, as is the SDA in Glasgow and Aberdeen.

Whilst such involvement can facilitate greater central influence over partnership strategies, it also helps local actors gain access to crucial discretionary support programmes from Government. In contrast to the 1970s, pump-priming and infrastructural grants are more and more tied to the effectiveness with which local actors can present themselves as potential economic winners to Government, rather than relying on formulae-based indicators of social malaise and help for deserving communities. Central support through City Grants, UDC investment, SDA capital support and road-building approvals has been critical to profitability levels in the strategies of GA, BHL, VDC, TNI, RR and SERC, and will be so in future for others within the 11. A unified city voice is increasingly important in lobbying higher levels of government (national and European), thus favouring localities in which public–private coalitions are active.

13.4   THE IMPACT OF GROWTH COALITIONS

Logan and Molotch's work contributes to the longstanding 'who benefits?' debate in USA community-power literature by suggesting that growth coalitions favour exchange values in cities over use values in such a way that:

> In many cases, probably in most, additional local growth under current arrangements is a transfer of wealth and life chances from the general public to the rentier groups and their associates.
>
> (Logan and Molotch, 1987, p. 146)

Notwithstanding the USA–UK differences, will the pattern of benefits be so skewed on this side of the Atlantic? In a sense, any answer would be premature since most of the organizations examined here have been in existence for less than three years. Some general pointers are available, though. Certainly, the growing influence of an economically neo-Liberal government and the profit-seeking private sector has marginalized those voices advocating the specific targeting of benefits to the urban underprivileged since the mid-1980s. The agendas and strategies of the organizations examined here have, unsurprisingly, broadly followed this line, although the persistence of local authorities in stressing social equity has meant that coalition agendas are not entirely dominated by short- to medium-term profitability considerations.

There is some difference between those coalitions dominated by a property focus and those stressing enterprise development or corporate social responsibility. Thus the BiC-inspired initiatives have shown more interest in ethnic minority business support, youth training, priority recruitment campaigns, community schemes and so on. Such projects are of tiny importance compared to physical development programmes, however. The city visions promulgated by UK coalitions most often sidestep difficult social considerations in a desire not to deter inward investment through negative imagery. On occasion, as is the case for TNI, BHL and BPp, for example, issues like local housing conditions have been pushed on to coalition agendas by determined local authorities. In no case though has this resulted in much more than increased business awareness of the conditions suffered by some social groups, and of enhanced lobbying for public resources.

There is little evidence to suggest that UK coalitions will engender patterns of benefits dissimilar to those found in the USA, despite lower levels of private rentier activism. That is not to say that localized trickle-down benefits to underprivileged groups are imaginary. For example, there is a slow growth of awareness within the private sector about the wage inflationary effects of skill shortages and the problems posed by the sharp contraction in the youth labour supply in the 1990s. This has resulted in the 11 being associated with various COMPACTS, construction-sector training schemes and training audits as one way of dealing with potential recruitment problems which will have direct benefits for local workers. There is also, unsurprisingly, a significant measure of overlap between membership of the 11 and the prospective boards of the new Training and Enterprise Councils which are assuming responsibility for publicly funded training programmes. What is clear is that the social agenda of partnership, if it is to feature at all, must be pushed gently by local authorities in such a way that private-sector members see it as being in their own interests to act.

14

PROPERTY-LED PARTNERSHIP ARRANGEMENTS IN SCOTLAND: THE PRIVATE SECTOR DOMAIN

Greg Lloyd

14.1 INTRODUCTION

Local economic development is now conventionally organized and managed by means of partnerships between central government, local authorities, development agencies and the business community. The institutional arrangements employed to secure the partnerships have tended to vary according to local circumstances, the actual participants involved and the policy objectives of the individual initiative. In recent times, however, the structure of the partnerships has reflected the ideas manifest in the present Government's liberal market economic philosophy. This has resulted in greater emphasis on the role of the business sector in devising, financing and implementing local economic development policies – a process described as the 'quasi privatization of policy responsibility' (Moore and Pierre, 1988). The new private-sector led partnerships have also employed a wider range of policy instruments than was previously the case. In particular, land and property development has now become a principal mechanism used in conjunction with the more conventional financial and other incentives for securing local economic change.

This chapter reviews the nature of the public–private partnerships in Scotland and assesses the role played by land and property in the various initiatives being executed.

14.2 LOCAL ECONOMIC DEVELOPMENT, PARTNERSHIPS AND PROPERTY

There is now a growing literature documenting the origins and subsequent progress of public–private partnerships for the purposes of securing local economic development in the UK (Law, 1988a; Brindley and Stoker, 1988; Barnekov, Boyle and Rich, 1989; Harding, 1990a). The origins of the partnership approach to public policy implementation, however, may be clearly traced in the operation of the post-war land-use planning system. Whilst the dynamic for the development of land rested primarily with the private property development sector, the public sector was vested with the responsibility for ensuring that the development of land accorded with the wider community interest. The latter social interest was secured, in the main, through the preparation of development plans, the development control process and the provision of infrastructure and other supporting services. The balance between the public and private interests involved in the land-development process was not, however, an even one. Generally speaking, the private sector dictated the pace of development and the public planning authorities operated at the margins to secure the socially acceptable pattern of land use. This uneven balance of interests has endured to characterize the later public–private partnerships concerned with economic development (Haughton and Whitney, 1989).

In the 1970s, the notion of the partnership arrangement was extended to the field of economic development as a response to the continuing deterioration in the economic and physical circumstances of the inner cities. It was also a reaction to the perceived failure of earlier inner-city initiatives which had essentially failed to address the inherent structural weaknesses in the inner urban economies. The partnership idea was also mooted as a mechanism for enabling greater local authority participation in the regeneration schemes (Loughlin, 1986). The Inner Urban Areas Act 1978 explicitly introduced a number of interventionist measures to address the problems of the inner cities through different partnership arrangements between central government, local authorities and the private sector (Hasluck, 1987).

In the 1980s, there was a distinct break with the bipartisan view of the role of government intervention that had prevailed throughout the earlier post-war period. The partnership concept rested on an analytical perspective of the existence of market failures operating in the inner cities (and in other spheres of the economy). In the absence of a market-led solution to such problems, the conventional wisdom suggested government intervention was necessary to address the failures involved, but in a way which involved the private sector. Thus the public–private partnership arrangement was a perceived means of bringing together in a co-ordinated and managed way resources that would not have been allocated to the inner-city areas. The rejection of this approach clearly threatened the notion of the partnership approach. The emergent supply-side ideology was that of a liberal market economy where intervention by government was to be minimized in favour of private solutions to any failure or conflict. The Government's supply-side economic development strategy has endeavoured to remove the perceived disincentives of public-sector interventionism whilst embarking on the recapitalization of local economies (Martin, 1986). Within this general context, the partnership idea has been retained but recast so as to emphasize the role of the private sector (Brindley and Stoker, 1988). The role of local authorities has been diminished although they are still called upon to perform a supportive function in facilitating the private-sector led development initiatives (Leach and Stoker, 1988).

The changing relationship between the public and private sectors is a key issue. Harden (1987) has noted the specific corporatist approach of the present Government which he has argued:

> ... is at the sharp end of some of the economic changes which are presented ideologically in terms of the resurgence of the invisible hand of the market but which, in reality, mark a constitutionally important shift in the way the state conducts its business.
>
> (Harden, 1987, p. 37)

This has resulted in central government retaining for itself a key role of player in the market which may be contrasted with its more conventional stance as regulator, rule maker and monitor of economic processes and relationships. Thus, within the context of a liberal market economy, central government has established its position *vis-à-vis* the private sector. In the context of the partnerships designed to secure local economic development, this has resulted in a central government–business dialogue with local authorities effectively marginalized to the central decision-making processes. This redefinition of the relationship of the participants to a partnership has necessarily involved a realignment in central–local government relationships. Thus, centralism has involved the imposition of:

> ... specific duties on local authorities, curtailing administrative discretion by imposing detailed statutory procedures on local decision-making and by centralising discretionary decision-making by vesting broad powers of intervention in the Secretary of State.
>
> (Loughlin, 1986, p. 14)

This process applies to the specific activities of local authority economic development initiatives (Hayton, 1989).

The changing ideological context to public–private partnerships has also resulted in a change in the policy instruments employed to secure local economic development. Conventional economic development policy incentives were targeted primarily at capital and labour mobility (Armstrong and Taylor, 1985). As a consequence, the availability of land was considered a secondary matter: its provision to be secured by local authorities acting to facilitate the economic development process. The critical assumption that the land resource would materialize and integrate with the needs of capital was taken for granted. The new emphasis on supply-side economics, however, has highlighted the relatively neglected role played by land in the economic development process. There is now a much greater appreciation of the potential of land and property in securing local economic regeneration (Fothergill, Monk and Perry, 1987). Furthermore, there is greater attention paid to the possible inhibition on economic development that might arise from a restrictive public policy framework (Evans, 1983; White, 1986). This particular view of the likely effects of land-use planning controls is reflected in the Government's observation that planning:

> . . . imposes costs on the economy and constraints on enterprise that are not always justified by any real public benefit in the individual case. It can cause delay and uncertainty even where applications are eventually approved. Too often the very wide discretionary powers that the system affords are used to apply excessively detailed and onerous controls of a kind that would not be tolerated in general legislation. If the system is to remain effective it must be used in a way that does not impose an unnecessary degree of regulation on firms and individuals.
>
> (Department of Trade and Industry, 1985)

14.3 ECONOMIC DEVELOPMENT AND PARTNERSHIPS IN SCOTLAND

Economic development in Scotland is conducted increasingly along market-based and commercially opportunistic principles in which the private sector has been granted and has assumed an increasingly dominant role in the implementation of public policy. Local economic development in Scotland is now organized largely by the Scottish Development Agency (SDA). The use of such a body which occupies a place between central government departments (such as the Industry Department for Scotland) and the local authorities enables government to operate as a key player. It has been argued in this context that the existing

> . . . regional development agencies are the creatures of central government, reflecting its reluctance to put resources directly in the hands of local authorities. Through their semblance of devolved initiative, the agencies allow the centre to influence spatial policy priorities at arm's

length. This mode of intervention has been deployed and sustained in Scotland and Wales essentially because of its advantages, from central government's viewpoint, as a way of responding to well articulated regional interests there, rather than because it is intrinsically superior to alternative arrangements.

(Damesick and Wood, 1987, p. 262)

The emphasis on the SDA as the main conduit of governmental local economic development policy in Scotland has emphasized the objective of securing indigenous economic growth and enhancing the competitive performance of firms already established in regional and local economies (Morgan, 1986). Thus the SDA has been identified as a mechanism for providing 'the longer term potential of an administrative framework which enables better co-ordination of urban and regional policies in the promotion of economic change' (Randall, 1987, p. 235). This has involved the SDA establishing a considerable portfolio of public–private partnership arrangements for local economic regeneration.

The SDA was established in 1975 with the remit: to further economic development; to provide, maintain and safeguard employment; to promote industrial efficiency and international competitiveness; and to further the improvement of the environment. It was also subsequently given joint responsibility, with the Scottish Office, for the attraction of inward investment to Scotland. In its initial period the SDA concentrated on its industrial role, operating primarily as an investment bank with an emphasis on the acquisition and provision of land and property for the purposes of industrial development (Danson, 1980).

In the early 1980s, however, the SDA began to take an active interest in area-based economic development initiatives. This was a consequence of the Government's revision of its objectives and investment guidelines. The SDA's operating objectives were made more commercial and selective, with a particular emphasis on identifying and facilitating opportunities for economic development in Scotland. The revised investment guidelines stressed the development of entrepreneurship, support for particular growth sectors such as high technology, the improvement of industrial efficiency and competitiveness and the regeneration of local economies. The SDA's obligations to maintain and safeguard employment and promote industrial democracy were removed. As a consequence of these revisions, the SDA developed a **modified market** approach to local economic regeneration in Scotland. This approach is characterized as one which stresses the development of competitive and efficient enterprise and the leveraging of private investment (Moore and Booth, 1986a). The emphasis on industrial and company restructuring was overshadowed subsequently by increased investment on the physical renewal of selected areas in urban Scotland. The change of emphasis in the SDA's development strategy is reflected in part in the diminishing proportion of expenditure devoted to direct intervention in Scottish industry. By 1987–8, this allocation of resources had fallen from 25% to 6% (SDA, 1988).

The partnership arrangement was a natural consequence of these shifts in the emphasis and ideological targeting of the SDA and is fundamental to its area-specific schemes. These are a pragmatic attempt to secure the improvement of the performance of the defined local economy. The SDA (1981, p. 62) has stated that:

> . . . emphasis will be placed on economic and industrial regeneration and the crucial criterion in the selection of areas will be their potential for improved performance. Thus while the programme will focus on areas where current performance is poor, it will not exclude initiatives in relatively prosperous areas where substantial development opportunities are identified.

There are four types of SDA area-specific initiative (Gulliver, 1984). An important characteristic is the extent to which they have evolved over time. Thus, Moore and Booth (1986b, p. 386) have stated that the

> . . . fourth generation of area projects reveals a further move away from comprehensive urban regeneration towards more specific concerns with economic development and the explicit participation of the private sector in formulating and implementing programmes.

The first involves comprehensive urban renewal, of which GEAR is the classic example. The second type of initiative is the Task Force, which has been described as:

> . . . an instrument of direct public sector intervention in the provision of economic infrastructure. The objective is essentially to promote the conditions (through factory building, environmental improvements, financial packages) whereby the market and private sector investment become self-generating, enabling the Agency to progressively withdraw from its 'fire-brigade' role (Moore and Booth, 1986b, p. 367). The third type of initiative is the Integrated Area project which embodies

> . . . two general concepts which have subsequently guided the use of Agency resources for any activity: first, dependence – no activity is undertaken by the Agency which is likely to lead to any area or enterprise being dependent on the Agency for its future existence; and secondly, selectivity – resources are concentrated on areas and issues where potential has been identified for positive growth and development, i.e. selective intervention.
>
> (Gulliver, 1984, p. 325)

The final category of area-specific initiative consists of self-help projects which are facilitated through the promotion of a local enterprise trust.

Since the early 1980s, the SDA has embarked on an aggressive strategy of establishing a wide range of public–private partnerships in Scotland. The primary aim of this strategy was to increase the business component in public policy implementation and replace the public resource element with private-sector funds (Boyle, 1988a). In terms of the physical regeneration of inner-city areas, for example, the SDA has itself stated that it

> . . . pursues urban renewal in partnership with other organizations in both the public and private sectors to unlock the commitment and contribution of all parties. At the core of the approach, the Agency plays a vital pro-active brokerage role, identifying, packaging and promoting opportunities to the private sector and negotiating the support of local authorities.
>
> (SDA, 1989)

14.4   PUBLIC–PRIVATE PARTNERSHIPS IN SCOTLAND

There are a diversity of public–private partnerships now well established in Scotland, particularly in terms of their institutional arrangements and relationships. The majority of partnerships in Scotland are based on a traditional relationship between the public and private sectors and rest on what may be considered a conventional balance of interests between the public and private sectors. It is important to note, however, that the partnerships encompass a diverse range of institutional arrangements. In general, the public sector plays an important role often initiating and managing the scheme and providing the broad developmental context within which the private sector makes its contribution. Following Brindley and Stoker (1988), this approach would suggest that the partnerships are directed at areas of some risk when viewed from the perspective of the business sector (property developer). Accordingly, for the private sector to get involved the public sector must assume some of that (up-front) risk. This often takes the form of land assembly and preparation, the provision of infrastructure and the provision of resources to attract in the private-sector participants. In short, in these partnership arrangements the private sector relies quite extensively on the public sector.

It is possible to illustrate this type of public–private partnership where the public sector assumes the dominant role in the early (relatively high-risk) stages of the initiative with the Inverclyde Enterprise Zone and the Ferguslie Park Peripheral Estate Initiative.

In Scotland, three enterprise zones were designated up to the mid-1980s in response to a set of localized crises associated with industrial restructuring and collapse. The enterprise zones were established in Clydebank, Invergordon and Dundee–Arbroath (Tayside) (Lloyd, 1986). The Inverclyde enterprise zone was, subsequently, and to some extent, unexpectedly, designated in March 1988. Enterprise Zones were introduced in the Local Government, Planning and Land Act 1980

> ... to test, as an experiment, and on a few sites, how far industrial and commercial activity can be encouraged by the removal or streamlined administration of certain administrative or statutory controls.
>
> (Department of the Environment, 1980)

The Zones comprise the precise geographical designation of areas within which a range of fiscal and planning incentives are provided. The primary target of the measures is the regeneration of the property base of the Enterprise Zones.

Inverclyde is located some 20 miles west of Glasgow, on the south bank of the Clyde and forms part of the Port Glasgow–Greenock–Gourock segment of the regional economy. As Lever (1986) has pointed out, despite its proximity to Glasgow and the upper Clyde shipbuilding industry, Inverclyde forms a distinct labour market in terms of its local economic history and the processes of industrial change. In the 1980s, the local economy experienced a sharp contraction in its traditional industrial base. This was reflected in the local unemployment rate which increased from 12.8% in 1980, to 18.7% in 1984 to 21.4% in 1987. Despite this marked economic deterioration the public policy response was remarkably sluggish (Lever, 1986). In 1985, however, the SDA, in conjunction with Strathclyde Regional Council and Inverclyde District Council established the Inverclyde Initiative. This was a public-sector led partnership intended to diversify the local industrial base, set in place training schemes and encourage the establishment of new enterprises in the locality. The subsequent Enterprise Zone designation formed a logical extension to the established Inverclyde Initiative (Lloyd and Danson, 1990).

Urban policy in Scotland is laid down in *New Life for Urban Scotland* which established the framework for the planned redevelopment of inner-city areas and selected peripheral public sector housing estates in Scotland. The SDA was given the primary responsibility for managing the individual urban development initiatives through partnership schemes with the private sector. In the context of the peripheral housing estates the SDA-led partnerships are designed to involve the private sector in local regeneration schemes with the stated intention of 'making additional resources available, and in helping people to escape from dependency on the state and the isolation from markets which is such a characteristic feature of these estates' (Scottish Office, 1988, p. 14). Four peripheral-estate public–private partnerships were established, one of which was in Ferguslie Park (Lloyd and Newlands, 1989a).

Ferguslie Park is a public-sector housing estate located on the periphery of Paisley, to the west of Glasgow. The social and economic problems of the estate centre on the concentration of long-term unemployed and the lack of local employment and training opportunities (Community

Development Project, 1978). The estate is also characterized by poorly maintained open space and wasteland which is a consequence of property demolition. Following *New Life for Urban Scotland*, the Ferguslie Park Partnership was established in June 1988 with the intention of setting out a development strategy for securing the regeneration of the estate. The Partnership is comprised of the Scottish Office, SDA, local authorities, the private sector and the local community. The coordination of the available public-sector resources is intended to attract greater private-sector investment into the area and the private sector is to be granted greater involvement in the various schemes being implemented. The development strategy has involved the setting up of a Training, Employment and Enterprise Development Company to address the issues of unemployment and business development.

14.5 PRIVATE SECTOR INITIATIVES

There are also private-sector led economic development schemes being initiated in Scotland where the private sector effectively proposes, finances and subsequently controls the local arrangements. There are two principal examples of this type of business-led initiative: Glasgow Action and Aberdeen Beyond 2000. In these individual cases the business community has assumed the central role in initiating, controlling and managing the schemes and, furthermore, has adopted land and property schemes as their main development policy instrument. It is important, however, not to overlook the extent to which the private sector is asserting its role within the more conventional public–private partnerships. The enterprise trusts are a case in point. In 1988, there were 40 enterprise trusts established in Scotland, most involving local business, local authorities and the Agency. Although predominantly funded by the public bodies and designed as local partnerships, the boards of the enterprise trusts are generally dominated by the private sector (Keating and Boyle, 1986).

Glasgow Action was formed in 1985 with the support of the SDA and has subsequently come to occupy a key position in the promotion of the local economy. It has also acted as a catalyst for city-wide property-development schemes in Glasgow (Boyle, 1989a). Glasgow Action is essentially a private-sector organization concerned with the longer-term economic and physical viability of the city and has been described as a quintessential public–private partnership (Boyle, 1989b, p. 21). It has described itself as

> . . . a group of leading business people and politicians – and of the visionary plan they have for Glasgow's future . . . the thinking behind the plan is that the development of a strong business and consumer service industry base will stimulate the regeneration of the city as a whole . . . it aims to recreate Glasgow's entrepreneurial spirit.
>
> (Glasgow Action, 1985)

Although there are representatives from local authorities involved in the organization the leadership, control and direction remain firmly located in the private sector. Glasgow Action operates primarily as 'a catalyst, stimulating ideas, projects and schemes, building the appropriate connections between different actors in the process of urban development and promotion' (Boyle, 1989b, p. 22). The development of land and property is seen as central to this business-led approach to urban regeneration.

Aberdeen Beyond 2000 was established by a self-appointed *ad hoc* committee of business representatives drawn primarily from the private sector. Executive support and administration is provided by the SDA. Membership of the group is drawn from local city-based firms, including building contractors, multinational oil companies, the Chamber of Commerce and the local financial services sector. There are also representatives from Grampian Regional Council, Aberdeen District Council, the local academic institutions and the media. These organizations are also the principal sponsors of Aberdeen Beyond 2000.

Aberdeen Beyond 2000 was primarily a response to the rapidly changed circumstances of the local economy in 1985–6 as a consequence of the fall in oil prices which had a dramatic recessionary effect on economic and property sectors in the city (Lloyd and Newlands, 1989b). In June 1987, the Aberdeen Beyond 2000 group published its report of the same name. The stated aim was 'to stimulate action in partnership by political leaders, business, trade unions and the community itself towards the goal of realising the full potential of the people of Aberdeen in creating that prosperity'. Aberdeen Beyond 2000 stressed the need, however, that in putting forward its (business-led) vision of the future of the Aberdeen economy it was desirable and possible to build upon a local consensus. The report acknowledged the dependence of the local economy on the offshore oil servicing sector and argued the case for a 'sensible development' strategy . . . [based on] . . . a more diversified portfolio of growth assets (Aberdeen Beyond 2000, 1987). This was to be achieved by encouraging the development of indigenous economic activity by the greater utilization of local resources, skills, entrepreneurship, technology and environmental quality.

Aberdeen Beyond 2000 identified a number of more specific targets: a more diversified technological base to industry in Aberdeen, with expansion out of the oil-related sector; a more internationally oriented oil supply sector; a modernized food-processing sector; a substantially expanded tourism industry; and developed centres of excellence in education and research. The economic development strategy identified four key action areas and a planning and property development strategy was devised in support. This set out 'action to strengthen those elements of the local economic and physical infrastructure which support economic development' (Aberdeen Beyond 2000, 1987). The latter places greater emphasis on the role of the private sector in bringing these property-related schemes to fruition and attention was drawn to a number of controversial areas in Aberdeen, such as the green belt and the city-centre, where public policies appeared to inhibit the attraction or commitment of private-sector investment.

14.6 AN EMERGING PRIVATE-SECTOR DOMAIN?

The emergence of the private-sector led development initiatives represents a departure from the conventional arrangements associated with local economic development initiatives in Scotland. Both Glasgow Action and Aberdeen Beyond 2000 are indicative of assertive action on the part of the business community to influence the public policy agenda for economic development in their respective localities. This behaviour would appear to be longer term in character as private-sector interests seek to establish the perceived prerequisites for growth. It may be contrasted with the more short-term involvement of the private sector in the more conventional partnerships where the extent of their involvement (and reliance on public-sector resources) is a reflection of the risk involved. This type of business behaviour in seeking to assert its interests over a locality may be explained partially by reference to the concept of a growth coalition (Molotch, 1976 and see Chapter 10). This described the formation of business consortia in US cities keen to create and maintain the local preconditions for economic growth. Attention has been drawn to the behaviour of the growth coalition in relation to public policy formulation in the UK (Pickvance, 1985; Lloyd and Newlands, 1988; Cooke, 1988b). The growth coalition concept would appear to offer an insight into the ways in which the business community can confront and challenge public policies in order to win over the local development agenda to serve their specific interests. An understanding of this type of behaviour will prove to be crucial in Scotland as it is likely that economic development will be organized increasingly through local business consortia. This is illustrated by the Government's Scottish Enterprise proposal.

In December 1988, the government published its White Paper Scottish Enterprise: A New Approach to Training and Enterprise Creation (Industry Department for Scotland, 1988). This proposed the creation of a new body – Scottish Enterprise – to be formed from the effective merger of the SDA and Training Agency. The ultimate objective of Scottish Enterprise is 'the creation of a dynamic self-sustaining Scottish economy in which investment and training are private-sector led and financed.' This is to be achieved by a centralized administration charged with strategic policy issues and a network of employer-led Local Enterprise Companies (LECs) which are to be responsible for

. . . assessing the local labour market, arranging the delivery of national training programmes, developing training for specific local needs, designing business development services, raising private sector funds, organizing tenders for training contracts, publicizing opportunities and other such promotional activities as may be appropriate.

(Industry Department for Scotland, 1988, p. 11)

This parallels the introduction of the Training and Enterprise Councils in England and Wales. The creation of Scottish Enterprise will involve the business sector in the design and delivery of training, economic development and environmental improvement services in Scotland (Danson, Lloyd and Newlands, 1989; Danson *et al.*, 1990). In terms of behaviour the LECs may conform in very broad terms to the activities of the growth coalition model. This will be very evident where the business-led consortia seek to establish their private-sector perspective over, or in direct opposition to, the established public policy agenda for local economic development in Scotland. Furthermore, the LECs may in time mature to employ property development schemes within their overall local economic strategies, as evidenced by a recent debate over the planning powers to be made available to the Scottish Enterprise initiative (Lloyd, 1990). The changes would suggest, therefore, that the private sector is to assume an increasingly important role in local economic development in Scotland.

14.7   CONCLUSIONS

Public–private partnerships to secure local economic development in Scotland generally rest on a conventional balance of interests between public-sector agencies and the business community. These arrangements conform broadly to the concept of 'leverage planning' described by Brindley, Rydin and Stoker (1989), whereby public-sector finance is used to stimulate a relatively weak property development market and thereby facilitate a release of private-sector investment.

Given the relatively depressed economic and physical conditions within which many of the Scottish partnerships are located this form of institutional arrangement is perhaps to be expected. In addition, the evidence would suggest that the nature of these partnerships is to change with the private sector assuming a clearly dominant role with respect to policy formulation and its execution.

ACKNOWLEDGEMENT

I am grateful to the Carnegie Trust for the Universities of Scotland for providing the financial support for me to undertake the research on which this chapter is based.

15

FLAGSHIP PROJECTS IN URBAN REGENERATION

Franco Bianchini, John Dawson and
Richard Evans

15.1 INTRODUCTION

The term 'flagship' is one of the more recent additions to the urban vocabulary. Although used in a variety of contexts, it is most commonly applied to pioneering, large-scale urban renewal projects. The publication by the Confederation of British Industry *Initiatives Beyond Charity* (CBI, 1988) suggests that every city should have one or more flagship projects in order to break into the cycle of inner-city decline.

This chapter is a critique of the development of flagship projects in the UK. It presents a definition of the concept in its urban development context, examines its US origins and introduction into the UK and discusses the institutional arrangements which characterize flagship schemes. The chapter highlights the primary functions of flagships in the 1980s UK, particularly their role as catalysts and symbols of regeneration.

In assessing the impact and significance of 1980s flagships, the paper appraises their ability to fulfil their primary objectives but also asks searching questions about their capacity to engender widespread and balanced regeneration. Our evaluation draws out the thorny issues of the limitations of a predominantly city-centre based and trickle-down approach to economic development, and also raises questions of accountability and ideological issues.

To provide a working framework, we have confined our analysis to physical developments. We define flagship projects, therefore, as significant, high-profile and prestigious land and property developments which play an influential and catalytic role in urban regeneration. In the final analysis such projects will only justify their flagship status if they succeed in attracting a 'flotilla' of other developments in their wake.

15.2 ORIGINS

In establishing the origin of the term 'flagship', a clear distinction must be made between the word itself and its underlying rationale. While the word may have only recently been coined by the CBI, the underlying concept is hardly new. To understand its lineage, it is necessary to appreciate the CBI's and indeed the Government's broader strategy for the inner cities. Both espouse a property-led approach to regeneration which is intended to induce private-sector investment. This approach to urban regeneration has borrowed heavily from the experience of US cities.

15.2.1 The US experience

Baltimore was one of the first US cities to achieve major physical regeneration. The Charles Center in the heart of Baltimore was fundamental to this process and can be regarded as the prototype flagship project.

In 1956, the Greater Baltimore Committee, a group of progressive business leaders worried about the decline of the central business district (CBD) and the city's fiscal position, combined forces with the Downtown Committee of the Retail Merchants Association to produce a revitalization plan for the whole of the CBD. Its key component was the Charles Centre proposal – a mixed-use development proposal consisting of offices, retailing and apartments – which would effectively demonstrate that downtown development was a viable proposition. The city approved the project in 1958 and agreed to play a facilitating role by undertaking land acquisition and clearance. The private sector, however, provided most of the capital costs of $180 million. A non-profit, quasi-public development corporation, the Charles Center Management Office (CCMO) was set up to supervise the scheme's implementation.

The success of this scheme paved the way for a second and more ambitious urban renewal project in the dilapidated Inner Harbor Area. This entailed greater public investment in infrastructure such as parks, promenade and a marina and public subsidies for the construction of a series of 'anchor' developments including the World Trade Centre, a convention centre, a science centre and an aquarium. The project was implemented by the Charles Center-Inner Harbor Management Corporation (incorporating the former CCMO) which also marketed the scheme by emphasizing its tourism appeal.

The dynamic leadership of Mayor Schaefer, a powerful advocate of the

Baltimore Renewal Programme, who was instrumental in launching complementary public events programmes in the Inner Harbor Area, also proved
crucial. In its own terms the Inner Harbor Project has been a success and
has spawned further development both in the vicinity, such as the
Harborplace leisure retailing complex, the Hyatt Hotel, an amusement park,
and elsewhere downtown, for example, the Market Center Area Project.
These two projects demonstrated effectively the flagship principle and its
novel implementation mechanisms which have since been widely copied.

15.2.2 The UK context

Despite a growing awareness of inner-city problems the flagship approach
was not adopted in the UK until the 1980s. The explanation lies in a combination of factors including government policies, economic trends, shifts in
the attitudes of local institutions, local employers and local authorities and
in changing perceptions of the role and function of cities. More specifically,
the Government's predilection for physical regeneration, evidenced by the
UDC model, and an increasingly competitive international climate have
encouraged local authorities and business interests to combine forces in
promoting development opportunities within their locality.

The remarkable consensus about the usefulness of flagships among public and private actors involved in the process of urban regeneration could
be interpreted as the coming together of different interests. The commercial
logic of the developers meets the single-minded, property-led regeneration
logic of the development corporations, and the need for relatively quick
and visible results of the predominantly Labour-controlled, increasingly
powerless, fiscally strapped, urban local authorities. In short, Labour-
controlled local authorities often support flagship schemes because there
seems little else they can do to attract private- and public-sector resources
for physical renewal projects and to prove that they still have a role to play
in urban regeneration.

The revival of private-sector investment in property in the latter part of
the 1980s has given further impetus to cities' attempts to make the most of
their marketable assets such as waterfront real estate, heritage, tourism and
leisure facilities, and attractive environments. Naturally, flagship projects
which demonstrate such potential and perform a catalytic role sit well with
this approach. There is, however, no single development format driving
these projects and a myriad of institutional arrangements exist.

15.3 INSTITUTIONAL ARRANGEMENTS

In the late 1980s, public–private partnerships have emerged as a major facet
of urban regeneration. Although partnerships have diverse structures, remits

and impacts, all have tried to realize their cities' potential, which varies widely between places.

Bringing together the public and private sectors on an *ad hoc* basis has been instrumental in many flagship developments. However, the exact formation, balance and style of these informal partnerships vary between cities and projects. For instance, in Cardiff, Liverpool and London, UDCs have been the major public players, whilst in other cities local authorities have been the main driving force behind many flagship developments. North of the border, Glasgow's experience has a different complexion. There the Scottish Development Agency (SDA) has proved to be a vital catalyst for many of the city's high-profile initiatives.

However, formally institutionalized public–private partnerships have been less succesful. They have made, so far, only a modest impact on flagship development. Urban regeneration strategies adopted by partnerships have varied widely. Where property development has been the key objective, the strategy often adopted has used environmental and other image improvements to coax others into development. Even where strategies engage in more or less direct provision, there was little emphasis, prior to the CBI's Initiatives Beyond Charity agenda, on flagship schemes. Notable exceptions are Glasgow Action's indirect influence and, significantly, The Newcastle Initiative (TNI) which emerged from the CBI's blueprint with its emphasis on major flagship schemes. Whilst The Newcastle Initiative has encountered difficulties in realizing its flagship projects, it gives substance to central government wishes to involve key local business leaders in playing a more active role in civic affairs. John Hall, who was responsible for developing the Metro Centre in Gateshead, is viewed as the archetypal business leader and the CBI approach is being tested in Newcastle with his involvement.

Conversely, successful flagship developments have been, in some cases, catalysts for constructing a formal public–private partnership. For instance, the conversion of a huge 19th-century textile mill in Halifax into the Dean Clough Industrial Park, entirely a private sector development, contributed to the establishment of the Calderdale Partnership – the first of the 'one-town partnerships' established by Business in the Community (See Chapter 13). Also, co-operation between the public and private sector in planning Birmingham's International Convention Centre (ICC) helped pave the way for further joint ventures such as the Heartlands initiative.

Flagship projects may be entirely public-sector concerns. Birmingham's International Convention Centre, for instance, notwithstanding the public–private co-operation in its formative stages, is essentially a public-sector project. Likewise, Glasgow's new £37 million concert hall is predominantly a District Council initiative with grant assistance from European coffers.

Identifying exclusively private-sector funded flagships is less easy. Commercial flagships are commonly pioneering projects and are intrinsically, therefore, high-risk ventures which will mitigate against private-sector investment rationale. One exception is the Dean Clough Industrial Park in Halifax. In other cases, the question arises of whether privately funded schemes, such as the Princes Square retail centre in the heart of Glasgow, can be considered to be flagships. Although it has not played a significant pioneering role – its site lies within an established and thriving city centre retail zone – it is an innovative and high-quality project and has enjoyed a high profile in Glasgow's promotional literature.

15.4 FUNCTIONS OF FLAGSHIP PROJECTS

Throughout the decade most UK cities have initiated projects which have been conferred with flagship status. These developments have diverse backgrounds, characteristics and forms. The 1980s have witnessed the proliferation of orthodox property development flagships alongside innovative events – temporary flagships attracting intense media attention to a city for a limited period. Despite their apparent diversity, a common thread runs through all of them. They are all striving to recreate the image of the city. The negative perceptions of declining, dirty and inhospitable urban environments are being replaced by the city advertisers' marketing icons – gleaming office blocks, cultural centres and chic retail venues. Conviviality, quality and entertainment are the post-industrial city Utopia. Cities are no longer portrayed primarily as centres of production but of consumption. In changing perceptions of urbanism, the flagship project plays a central and crucial role.

We can identify several distinct functional themes applicable to flagships in the 1980s. First of all flagships have signalled intentions to regenerate derelict urban areas and to act as magnets for further developments. Such flagships may be substantial and prestigious property developments or temporary but equally high-profile events such as Garden Festivals. They concentrate scarce resources and are a means of attracting private finance by creating a physical environment and, via rising land values, a financial environment conducive to private-sector investment. Typically, such flagships focus on areas with the most development potential – for instance, areas imbued with heritage value or waterfront locations.

Flagships have also spearheaded economic development or tourism strategies. Flagships can provide a new strategy with a tangible asset that may act as both a symbol and magnet. They can demonstrate that a city, or an area of a city, is physically, economically and culturally restructuring with the grain of prevailing economic and societal trends. Cities strive to exploit the high-profile symbolism of flagships by using them as magnets to attract further investment, tourists and consumer expenditure. For instance, the Merchant City in Glasgow and Little Germany in Bradford herald the transformation of obsolete warehouses, which caused widespread blight, into upmarket mixed-use developments which are breathing fresh life into run-down urban districts. In other cases, flagship projects have underpinned regeneration themes or strengths identified by a city. Newcastle, for example, identified the themes of fashion and design, Japanese links, leisure and services, and higher education.

Prime property developments have also been exploited as flagships to promote new land uses in spatially specific, but not necessarily derelict, areas. For instance, the Westergate office development in Glasgow is taking place at the corner of Hope Street and Argyle Street, outside the traditional commercial core, as the city is encouraging the proliferation of office use in this locality.

Flagships are also central to promotional strategies that seek to transform the image of declining industrial cities and commonly form the cornerstones of a city's place-marketing strategy. At a broad level, flagships provide advertisers with the substance to back their images – they are a vital place-marketing device to enhance a city's attractiveness. Arguably, this has been achieved most comprehensively and most successfully in Glasgow. Cultural and tourist attractions such as the Burrell Collection, the 1988 Garden Festival and the 1990 European City of Culture celebrations, together with more direct investment magnets such as the Scottish Exhibition and Conference Centre (SECC), Princes Square and the St Enoch Centre, all form part of an overall package of attractions that help give Glasgow a dynamic, modern and cosmopolitan image.

More specifically, flagships have been employed as hooks upon which to hang other indigenous attractions. Promoting a flagship is an effective method for more fully exploiting and enhancing those cities' assets that are not well-known beyond their boundaries. The Burrell clearly achieved this for Glasgow. Not only did it provide the city with an additional and prestigious attraction but it enabled the city more effectively to market the city's existing cultural and heritage attractions.

Equally, more overtly commercial facilities can play a catalytic role in endorsing and focusing attention on a city's existing, minor facilities. For instance, both the SECC and ICC are high-profile conference and convention centres that place Glasgow and Birmingham on the international agenda. At the same time, the initiatives inevitably raise the status of their cities generally as major conference and convention locations. In turn, therefore, smaller venues should also share in the benefits of their city's improved standing.

As the impact and influence of flagship projects on economic development have evolved through the 1980s, so new techniques are emerging. Whilst concentration of resources is perceived as preferable to dispersal – maximizing impact on the national and international stage – there is growing awareness of the need to initiate a series of developments over time. These pacing devices, to borrow the SDA's language, are intended to maintain interest, attention and investment focused on a city. Moreover, artificially creating ambitious development horizons in this way is perceived as an effective means of inspiring, and consolidating progress towards, urban renewal.

15.5 DO FLAGSHIPS WORK?

15.5.1 Positive impact: an evaluation

In terms of their primary functions and objectives flagships have demonstrated consistent achievements. The experience of Bradford's National Museum of Photography, Film and Television illustrates many of the aspects of the potential contribution of flagship projects to urban regeneration outlined above. In its first five years of existence the Museum attracted over three million visitors, 824 000 in 1988 alone, thus becoming the sixth most visited museum in the whole country (Hunter, 1988). The success of the National Museum highlighted the potential of tourism, leisure and culture for the future development of the Bradford economy, and inspired a whole series of public and private regeneration initiatives in these fields. Bradford's new credibility as a centre for museum activities was certainly a factor in the decision by London's Victoria and Albert museum to transfer to the city's Lister's Mill its important Asian collections – an appropriate choice given also the large percentage of local residents of Asian origins.

More generally, the National Museum was crucial in increasing the annual number of recorded visitors to Bradford from virtually none (1980) to around six million (1988) (Donkin, 1989; Hunter, 1988). One of the consequences of such expansion was that Bradford was recognized as an important tourist destination by the English Tourist Board. Moreover, the National Museum has been able to utilize European monies which have in turn strengthened the case for a range of other projects and infrastructural improvements to receive EC funding.

The presence of the National Museum promoted the association in popular consciousness of the name of Bradford with the media industries. It certainly strengthened, for instance, the credibility of Bradford's bid for Channel 5, a new television channel to be created under the Government's Broadcasting Bill.

Lastly, the potentially beneficial impact of flagships on local economies should not be underestimated. Flagships acting as catalysts for the tourism and convention industries, in particular, can have positive spin-offs on retailing, hotel, catering and other local consumer service industries.

Similar observations could be made about the role of flagships like the Burrell Collection in spearheading Glasgow's transformation to a 'city of culture', or of the National Exhibition Centre and the International Convention Centre in supporting Birmingham's audacious claim to be the 'communications capital of Europe' (Birmingham ICC, no date).

15.5.2 Problematic implications of flagship projects

It would be wrong, however, to conclude from this account that flagship projects are an infallible and non-controversial formula for urban regeneration. Flagships, by definition, are more than self-contained property investments. Their origins in the revitalizing of declining industrial cities means that they have to be judged against wider criteria. What has been their impact on unemployment and economic investment and how have their benefits been distributed? In these terms their achievements have been mixed.

Issues of redistribution and access

One of the potentially controversial areas is the difference between the definition of 'community' adopted by the initiators of flagship projects and that adopted by grassroots groups. There is little evidence that the economic benefits flowing from investment in property-led regeneration strategies focused around flagships will automatically trickle down to local communities. For instance, forecasts show that only 1800 of the 47 000 jobs which it is estimated may be created by the LDDC Canary Wharf development on the Isle of Dogs are likely to go to local residents, and that over 70% of these jobs could be low-skill, part-time and low-paid (Parkinson and Evans, 1990). The LDDC experience suggests that far from producing a trickle down of economic benefits to local communities, property-led regeneration strategies based on flagship schemes can make life even more difficult for small local businesses and low-income residents. Such strategies push up rents and land values, thus making, for instance, the construction of affordable housing a less economically viable proposition. They contribute, in some cases, to displacement and spatial segregation by social class.

The fact that flagship schemes are often city-centre based can also be controversial. For instance, in Glasgow the establishment of prestigious projects in the city centre (St Enoch, Princes Square, the refurbishment of the Merchant City, the planned construction of a new concert hall and associated shopping development at the top of Buchanan Street) has been accompanied by growing deprivation in the increasingly peripheral housing estates of Pollok, Drumchapel, Castlemilk and Easterhouse. Male unemployment in Easterhouse, for example, still exceeds 40%. It is open to question whether local residents will be able not only to benefit from the creation of new city-centre based employment, but also to enjoy as consumers the new attractions the city centre has to offer. The new city centre conviviality may well be too difficult for many Easterhouse residents to access. It may well be too expensive, too awkward to reach by public transport and even characterized by a slightly alien, unwelcoming social atmosphere. In other cases, even flagship projects based in city centres are not properly physically and functionally integrated into the rest of the urban fabric and of the city's life – a problem experienced by the Albert Dock development in Liverpool.

Impact on public spending priorities

Flagship projects can absorb human and financial resources which could be used for much-needed improvements in public services and infrastructure. For instance, after a radical Thatcherite administration gained control of the City of Bradford Metropolitan Council (through a by-election in September 1988) the development of flagships in the city centre was accompanied by drastic cuts in the social services and education budgets, by the privatization of various leisure centres and the discontinuation of grants to neighbourhood-based voluntary organizations (Dunn, 1989). It is also clear that the cost of maintaining and servicing flagships can constitute a long-term drain on public finances.

Problems of accountability

All these problems are related to the larger issue of the accountability to local citizens of the agencies initiating flagship schemes. The problems of secrecy and of the lack of genuine consultation and of channels through which ordinary citizens and community groups can influence the conception and the development of flagships apply not only to the UDCs (Dawson and Parkinson, 1990), but also to Labour-controlled local authorities. This is the case in Birmingham, where the City Council's redevelopment plans for the city centre were vigorously opposed by a local residents' pressure group formed in 1988, Birmingham for People. Its objective was 'to open up the issues for public debate. . . . Glossing over the choices and disagreements, in pursuit of a phoney "positive image", will not help the right policies to be hammered out' (Birmingham for People, 1989, p. 3). It fears, for instance, that the ICC development will result in a city catering solely for business people, tourists and wealthy consumers instead of for local residents.

A zero-sum game?

Accountability is important also in terms of access to information on the performance of flagships. There is a need for independent assessments of the extent to which such schemes have attained their stated objectives. Such dispassionate evaluations are necessary in order to inform the planning of future flagship projects. It is clear that in some cases **imitation effects** prevail over rational planning, resulting in the proliferation of standardized models of flagships which do not take the characteristics of the locality where they are built into adequate consideration and which may, in the long term, turn out not to be economically viable. Possible dangers are pre-figured by the US experience – for example by the crisis of the 1980s waterfront 'festival marketplaces' of Norfolk, Virginia, of Flint, Michigan, and even of Manhattan's South Street Seaport (*Newsweek*, 1989). In the UK context, excessive provision of regional facilities such as concert halls and theatres could lead to problems as venues compete for finite numbers of both patrons and new cultural productions. Hendon and Shaw (1987, p. 215) have demonstrated that in the USA 'almost everywhere arts facilities have expanded faster than repertoire' thus creating difficulties for cities trying to market themselves as regional cultural centres. 'Put simply, how many successful convention centers, sports stadia, Disney-worlds and harbor places can there be?' asks David Harvey (1987, p. 278). It is a pertinent question. The growing competition between cities using flagship projects to sell themselves as tourist, convention, shopping and cultural centres, and trying to attract mobile international capital, may well result in a zero-sum game, and may dangerously increase reliance on variables – such as changes in the international financial markets and in the level of the consumers' dis-posable income – over which cities have virtually no control.

The risk of cultural standardization

Another potentially damaging consequence of the imitation effect high-lighted above is that even flagships avowedly carried out in the name of diversity and in observance of local traditions and identities can degenerate into the easy option of adopting serial design solutions and of fabricating fake heritage themes, thus contributing to the standardization of the physi-cal fabric and of the aesthetics of the city.

A social and political diversion?

There are, lastly, ideological implications of the role of flagships in urban regeneration which are worth considering. David Harvey, for instance, considers flagships to be a key ingredient of regeneration strategies, one of the aims of which, he claims, is to divert attention away from growing social problems and conflicts within the city, fuelled by the emergence of spa-tially segregated urban underclasses and by intensifying ethnic, racial and class polarization (Harvey, 1989c). Some local authorities share the view that by concentrating resources on image building through prestigious, high-visibility projects there is a danger that – although flagships were not intentionally conceived as instruments for social and political diversion – 'successful' schemes may obscure the deterioration in the quality of life for considerable but increasingly less-visible minorities of urban dwellers.

15.6   CONCLUSION

In conclusion, the use of flagship projects can offer cities considerable opportunities and benefits. But it also has controversial implications and there are serious limits to what they can achieve. Some of the claims by civic boosters about the ability of flagships to tackle deep-seated economic problems and to distribute benefits fairly among different social groups are grossly exaggerated. Flagship projects can have a significant role in breaking the spiral of urban economic decline by helping cities to improve their internal and external images, to find niches in the new international division of labour, and to pursue consumption revenues of various kinds through tourism, retailing and other consumer service industries. They are useful, and maybe even necessary, elements of an urban economic regeneration strategy, but they are by no means sufficient. It would be wrong, therefore, to use the establishment of prestigious buildings, well suited though they might be to function as political statements and to meet the needs of the electoral cycle, as an alternative to less immediately visible and longer-term strategies aimed at stimulating indigenous growth through investment in education, training, enterprise development, communications, research and technology.

16

STRUCTURES FOR DEVELOPMENT PARTNERSHIPS IN THE 1990s: PRACTICE IN WEST YORKSHIRE*

*David Whitney and
Graham Haughton*

It is a commonplace observation that the Government has placed the notion of partnership close to the centre of its urban policies. Action for Cities (Cabinet Office, 1987: and 1988), Progress on Cities (Cabinet Office, 1989) and People in Cities (Cabinet Office, 1990) have all underlined this. In early March 1990 the publicized relaunch of the inner cities initiative by the Prime Minister and others reaffirmed its political currency. The word 'reaffirmed' is used advisedly, for in a sense interdependence between the public and private sectors in urban development is far from being new. What does represent a shift in policy however is the *extent* to which the private sector in the 1980s and 1990s has been asked to assume responsibilities for and take leadership in urban policy and project development.

At present, partnership initiatives are extremely fragmented, patchy in sectoral and geographical coverage, and diverse in approach. Overall, compared to say North America and many Western European countries, the coming together in Britain of the public and private sectors through formal partnerships has often at heart simply represented weak coalitions of mutual short-term benefit. This picture though is changing rapidly, albeit in a piecemeal fashion.

* This paper has been reprinted from *The Planner*, 1st June 1990, with kind permission of the authors and editor.

In this paper we examine the recent growth of structures and working arrangements for public–private partnerships in the five West Yorkshire local authority areas. The diversity encountered in just this one sub-region offers some fascinating insights into the processes of entering into and falling out of public-private partnerships. A rich range of issues is thrown up by the various forms of local collaboration between sectors, including the motivations of the partners; the market share of urban economic development activity which a partnership can claim as its concern; the local over-crowding of the partnership arena; the 'half-life' of a partnership, given that most claim a long term understanding; and the ways in which the interests of partners coincide and how they can be reconciled where they do not. Our main intention here is to uncover some of the diversity of partnership practice by concentrating on the outcome of the main initiatives which have recently emerged in West Yorkshire.

16.1   FAIRSHARES PROJECT AND CALDERDALE COMMUNITY PROJECTS COMPANY

Fresh partnership working arrangements in Calderdale (Halifax) between the public and private sectors have derived from two external 'top down' initiatives in the mid-1980s which have progressed largely separately, but which now have potential for useful interaction. The first to become operational was the Inheritance Project (now renamed Fairshares – Inheritance and Community Development – Project), established within the department of the District Council Chief Executive. This 'task force' unit was a key recommendation of the regeneration strategy provided for the district by the national Civic Trust (1984 and 1986). The strategy was premised on a partnership approach: building a collaborative relationship with sectors and agencies sharing objectives for regeneration. It was seen from the outset that the unit to lead implementation would itself be a combination of local authority employees and private sector secondees, and that wherever possible it would seek joint funding for action and operate closely with private sector partners. This it has assiduously pursued since its inception in 1985, and Fairshares is now progressing a broad range of projects across the district.

Fairshares has the potential to become a valuable form of collaborative economic development, given continuing political support, drawing deeply on indigenous community and commercial resources. It needs to be distinguished clearly from the more officially structured arrangements for joint action between sectors encountered elsewhere in West Yorkshire.

This Civic Trust-inspired initiative attracted Business in the Community (BIC) in 1987 to establish the 'Calderdale Partnership'. This focused on local business initiatives with commercial environmental or community objectives across the borough, and was set up for two years from the end of 1987, being supported managerially by BIC. An executive group of key public–private 'leaders' (The Focus Group) was devised to steer the partnership, and more recently a Calderdale Community Projects Company (CCPC) was formed, funded by local business leaders.

The CCPC, supported by the Focus Group, therefore represents the second of the two active partnership structures in Calderdale. It is a company limited by guarantee, whose directors are drawn from the private sector, with the sole exception of the District Council Chief Executive. Its objectives are 'to support the Calderdale Partnership by undertaking on a commercial basis, projects which benefit the community, and which would not otherwise have been undertaken without the intervention of the company' (Atkinson, 1989). A particularly interesting potential for the future is the use to which CPCC can be put as an implementation vehicle supporting the work of the Fairshares Project.

What does appear suprising, given the economic development needs of Calderdale, is the very limited role which the CCPC has thus far discovered for itself. It clearly wishes to avoid duplicating the work of other actors in the local economy, but the potential for innovative action conceived collaboratively through the executive Focus Group would, on the face of it, seem enormous.

Calderdale provides an intriguing insight into the evolution of partnership thinking in one locality over recent years. From one initial local authority-led approach, new business-led partnerships have emerged. What has also emerged is a fairly chronic over-crowding on the partnership platform, with the various organizations all struggling to gain credibility and to avoid stepping on each others' toes. This tip-toe dance looks set to continue for some time yet, until one or other initiative is elbowed off the crowded platform. An attempt to rationalize activities in recent times by a local business leader fell on barren ground, as each set of actors jealously continued to guard their own patch. Interestingly, where in some other localities it is business-led partnerships which have emerged to replace former local authority-led initiatives, in Calderdale the top-down business-led initiative has been insufficiently locally rooted to oust earlier partnership ventures more deeply rooted within Halifax and Calderdale. In this respect, one of the early acts of Calderdale Inheritance, to attempt to establish strong roots into the community through a series of widely-based Town Forums, has added to its legitimacy and longevity.

16.2   BRADFORD BREAKTHROUGH LIMITED

Bradford in the 19th century was a place with a strong tradition of civic responsibility amongst major employers. Through much of the present century this fell into abeyance, for all manner of reasons. Key amongst these was that employers were happy to leave the Chamber of Commerce to represent their business interests and the local authority to represent both business and area interests. The prevailing perception of the council was that it was competent and fair, so the best thing was to 'sit back and leave them to it'.

In the late 1980s this virtual 'consensus politics' was rapidly turned on its head, creating new opportunities and drives for business-led partnership activity. The election of a radical Conservative administration in Bradford in 1988 is the key local factor of note. The council became committed to pursuing central government policies, in particular in the sense of 'rolling back the frontiers of the state'. Business leaders were increasingly encouraged to take on far greater civic responsibilities.

In 1989 a report to a senior officer in the local authority identified over 200 local representative, umbrella and partnership organizations, reflecting in some part the rich cultural, religious and ethnic diversity of Bradford. The experience of bodies representing labour market issues is illustrative of events. The Chamber of Commerce is the longest standing organization, but not the most influential. In addition there are various sector bodies (engineering, wool and textiles, etc.), the Careers Association (chaired by a businessman) and Bradford Council for Voluntary Services (recently experiencing major local authority funding cuts). This list is far from exclusive of longer standing bodies, but provides the major actors and some idea of their scope. More recent initiatives to emerge have been: Bradford Breakthrough Ltd, Bradford Partnership (industry: education links), Bradford Manpower Forum, Bradford Enterprise Forum, Bradford Local Employer Network (LEN) and Bradford Training and Enterprise Council (TEC).

Before focusing on one particular agency, Bradford Breakthrough Ltd, we want to make two points about this level of partnership and related interest group activity in Bradford. Firstly, there is a tremendous level of duplication of activity.

This is not least because all these organizations lack significant funding, so they tend all to fall back on a mixture of providing strategic vision, exhortation and local boosterism. The crowded platform effect (add one new player to a static/inadequately expanding crowded platform and someone somewhere else eventually has to fall off) is already at work – the LEN has now ceased activities in anticipation of the TEC. The TEC moreover has experienced some difficulty in attracting business leaders, not least because of the many other local organizations calling upon the time and resources of the few active participants. Another inhibiting feature in TEC development interestingly enough is that in Bradford's tense (and volatile) political atmosphere few want to be involved in a new politically divisive organization, particularly one which seeks to marginalize the well-respected local authority.

Relatedly, the second issue is that of exclusion. Ethnic minority representatives are scarce, where present at all, in all the organizations mentioned. Women too are severely under-represented. The new TEC is in fact proving better in this respect than its forebears, with a chairwoman and a prominent Asian businessman on its board already.

A recent Business in the Community partnership initiative in 1989 fell on fertile ground in Bradford, following the previous high-profile Chamber of Commerce-led 'Bradford Bouncing Back' campaign in the city in the early 1980s. The newly radicalized Conservative administration in the area lent enthusiastic support to the proposal, and together with the City Action Team, private sector supporters and others, it funded and acted as technical adviser to the establishment in December 1989 of a company limited by guarantee: Bradford Breakthrough Ltd. This seeks to galvanize the interest and commitment of the business sector to economic regeneration. It comprises twelve local leading businessmen as directors together with the local authority Chief Executive. Somewhat unsurprisingly it reflects in structure the CBI model advocated strongly in *Initiatives Beyond Charity* (1988).

The company aims 'to encourage private and public sector co-operation and to act as a focus for others in the economic and social improvement and development of the Bradford area'. It intends to 'identify and promote a clear 'vision' for tomorrow's Bradford area, capitalizing on existing strengths, promoting confidence and emphasizing the 'quality of life' and to build on that 'vision' through identification of new economic, cultural and promotional opportunities'. The emphasis in its style of working will be opportunistic action, the private sector directors bringing ideas, access to central government channels, the devotion of time and networking into the local business community. The local authority will be looked to, to contribute intelligence, goodwill and conceivably in the future seconded staff. Discussions have already started on a broad range of projects and 'Project Champions' identified.

It is too early to make a meaningful evaluation of this particular initiative, which appears set to try to impose a 'business vision' of how Bradford should develop without the legitimacy of broader public involvement and without any financial resources of its own of any significance. In a sense then, by adding its 'vision' to all the others available locally, Bradford Breakthrough Ltd may simply add a further element of local confusion rather than clarity and direction.

16.3   KIRKLEES JOINT VENTURE COMPANY (1989)

Partnership in a number of forms between public and private sectors and other agencies has characterised Kirklees' recent approach to economic and social regeneration. Huddersfield 2000 and Enterprise Dewsbury were established in the late 1980s as collaborative groups representing very widely based interests in the area concerned to identify and promote economic regeneration. These two bodies joined with Kirklees District Council subsequently to form a private company limited by guarantee to act as a partnership vehicle, through which regeneration initiatives could be implemented, namely 'Kirklees: An Engine for Growth'. This initial local partnership was conceived as a demonstration of the Kirklees partnership approach, to facilitate dialogue with national companies and generally to promote confidence in its potential investment partners. Within the forum of Huddersfield 2000 a regeneration strategy was produced and the idea of a balanced rolling programme of property development conceived. Subsequently, in February 1989 Kirklees decided to set up a formal Joint Venture Company with a chosen private sector partner to implement the rolling programme concept. Henry Boot plc was chosen as partner, and projects are now being actively progressed across the district through joint working groups.

The objectives of the company will be to promote and assist 'the economic and social regeneration of Kirklees by undertaking a rolling programme of profitable and unprofitable projects in Kirklees' (1989). The Joint Venture Company ('JVC') aims to operate very much more on an equal partnership basis than the private-sector led and dominated Calderdale or Bradford models. There is explicit recognition in the Memorandum of Understanding that each partner is committed to bring resources to the partnership out of which a valuable synergy should emerge. From Henry Boot: accessing finance and other resources from companies in the group, access to City Grant or other grants, loans or tax reliefs, and widely-based project management skills. From Kirklees: land and property resources, statutory powers, intelligence and political support.

There are three features worthy of note concerning this public–private partnership. The first is the rolling programme approach which Kirklees can lay claim to have pioneered. The private sector will forgo an element of returns to capital employed in construction contracts. Projects with major development gains will be used in a well-orchestrated, sequential manner to subsidize unprofitable schemes, introducing the advantages of cross-subsidy. The private sector will act as a development agency, packaging schemes and accessing grants. Finally, to fulfil the construction work programme, the developer will also be expected to establish new training opportunities for disadvantaged groups, ensuring community and increasingly commercial benefit through upgrading the local skills base.

The second feature is the resource equality with which the partnership is to be operated. Equal equity investment will be made through loan or share capital, entitling each partner to an equitable return on investment. In addition, there is a commitment to joint working in the use of respective non-financial resources for the support of the objectives of the partnership. The third feature is the determination to continue with the JVC, ensuring equal control by each of the parties for the future. This is despite the difficulties now thrown up by the Local Government and Housing (LG&H) Act 1989 concerning 'controlled' or 'influenced' categories of companies and the 'business association' tests referred to in the Act. Kirklees has engaged in long and protracted negotiation with central government to avoid the ensnarement of its partnership in penal capital allocation controls, and the future is not entirely clear even now.

In West Yorkshire, the Kirklees experience has been very influential. However, it remains to be seen how enduring the experiment will prove to be, particularly if economic conditions take a significant downturn. One possible danger is that these locally co-ordinated land and property deals could, to an undesirable extent, come to replace rather than integrate into a more rigorous overall local planning framework.

16.4 LEEDS CITY DEVELOPMENT COMPANY

Whilst in the recent past Leeds has generally been successful in attracting a high level of investment in both jobs and property as a regional centre, development has traditionally been on a 'scheme by scheme' basis. More recently however Leeds has concluded that there can be considerable benefits in forging a longer term partnership between the public and private sectors. In November 1987 it formed the LCDC as a key vehicle for itself initiating and developing partnerships with the private sector. Just what motivational factors were at work in this decision given the current uncertainty over the possible imposition of a mini-UDC by central government, is inevitably open to conjecture. The company is itself a partnership grouping between the city council and a range of private sector business interests. Its objectives are to: 'achieve a comprehensive and co-ordinated programme of social, economic and environmental regeneration' by promoting land, property and infrastructure development (LCDC, 1987).

Very shortly after its formation, the company signed separate agreements with P. and O. and Mountleigh as the first of what was intended to be a number of joint ventures with development and construction partners in the private sector. Councillor Mudie, then Council Leader commented at the time: 'It is an ideal arrangement. The council has the land which needs developing and these two firms have the cash as well as the development and building know-how. Nothing will be too big or too small. The main advantage of our deal is that once suitable sites have been found we know we have the builders, developers and cash' (*Leeds Post*, March 12, 1988).

In fact, the original private sector partners have not been as prominent as originally envisaged. Instead, the 30 or so existing and planned projects have incorporated a much wider range of developers. Indeed, the original commitment to a small number of developers can be seen as counter-productive in that it initially alienated some local developers, a situation to a considerable extent now resolved. Currently, a suitable private partner for a particular scheme is selected and worked with. The LCDC buys city council land and brings this into the partnership along with its own expertise, and the developers bring financial and project management resources. With the uncertainty of the Local Government and Housing Act 1989, LCDC looks set to move closer towards the city council rather than opting to go further at 'arms length'. LCDC is run through a board drawn equally from the council, on a cross-party basis, and the private sector. The technical resources of the city council have been orchestrated into separate project teams as 'special resources' which liaise with the private sector in guiding development proposals from feasibility studies through to implementation.

Although it can, and does, claim to be a public-private sector partnership, in truth LCDC bears little resemblance to the types of partnership which the Government is attempting to promote. Instead, it is largely a jointly controlled vehicle for involving the private sector in developing local authority land holdings. Interestingly, attempts to forge a broader-based public-private partnership, the 'Leeds Initiative', have been in the pipeline for some time now, but have yet to emerge.

16.5 'WAKEFIELD WORKS'

In recognition of the growing restrictions over its ability to devote capital resources to economic regeneration objectives, Wakefield Council has very recently entered into a long term partnership with AMEC Regeneration to secure a rolling programme of development projects across the authority area.

There are close parallels with the Kirklees approach, as well as some fundamental differences. Similarities include: the philosophy of cross-subsidy between commercially viable and less viable schemes (mixes of 'plums' and 'lemons' as it has become known locally); the intended long-term relationship; the drawing upon the respective strengths of both sectors to undertake schemes comprising development, training and promotion; and, the joint participation of partners in the identification and the implementation of a rolling programme, managed through a slimline and joint Development Steering Group.

The key Wakefield departure – reflecting lessons from the Kirklees experience – has been its determination to retain a loose and informal partnership structure. In recognition of the then impending legislation, it was deliberate policy to avoid a company model which could be entrapped by 'business association' tests. The Memorandum of Understanding consequently emphasizes that the partnership is not expressed 'as being legally binding'.

It merely 'records the intentions of the Council and AMEC regarding their joint participation' and 'provides a framework for the Council and AMEC to work together on key areas directed at securing the regeneration of the area' (Wakefield Works, 1989). Both parties can readily withdraw, but thus far they recognize the advantages of a long-term collaboration, namely the secure financial returns to the company and the targeted mix of community-related benefit.

16.5.1   Partnership issues

A moment's pause for reflection about the motivations of the partners in formal development partnerships found in this review of West Yorkshire suggests that partnerships are far from cosy or easy sorts of relationships. More than one party referred to the 'learning curve' of the initiatives for most of the partners. Devising agendas for mixes of projects where both sets of partners will bring their own priorities and predilections, has tested forbearance and trust. This is a particularly important dimension where rolling programmes involve extensive forward funding for private sector partners and possibly the exclusion or postponement of favoured schemes by the local authority.

Parties to these arrangements have clearly found their resources to be complementary, to a considerable degree. Whilst it is too early to evaluate fully the results of these initiatives, in principle the benefits seem clear. The private sector often is seeking to secure a form of 'base loading' for its operations, in contrast to the normal troughs and peaks of the development cycle. It is finding access to the local exercise of statutory powers, local intelligence and, not least, local political support. The local authority on the other hand has access to project management skills, company or group expertise, business acumen, channels to financial institutions, grant sources (particularly City Grant in Urban Programme areas) and additional networks to central government. It is frankly unclear how equal the partnerships are, and many participants dismiss such considerations as academic. To them the essence lies in the coming together of new energies, and new possibilities deriving from a wide-ranging resource exchange.

Who is leading the collaboration, and how wider involvement is managed if one sector is dominant, emerges as a significant issue. For planners, the key dimension of this is to what extent partnerships, though attempting to provide a coherent strategy and vision for an area, in practice instead tend to implant a fragmented, partial and short-term vision. The main causes for concern here are the selective nature of many partnership agreements and also the extent to which their strategies and vision clash with, rather than complement, those of other organisations.

The evidence from this review underlines the truism that different partnership models will be needed to fit different local operational circumstances. One can go on to say that 'top-down' initiated partnerships such as the Calderdale Partnership may be less likely to endure without 'bottom-up' arrangements to carry them on. The West Yorkshire experience also highlights that the 'correct' model will not automatically suggest itself for an area, and moreover that as local circumstances change, not least because of earlier partnerships, so new working arrangements will need to be established.

Fecundity for local partnership activity would appear to be in considerable measure contingent upon political factors, rather than say the relative strength of local economic restructuring imperatives. In West Yorkshire political volatility seemed to be especially relevant, with (until the recent elections) hung or marginal councils (Bradford, Calderdale) getting much more involved, and much earlier in partnership activities than more stable (in this case Labour-controlled) authorities (Wakefield, Leeds).

Finally, even within the past three to four years the concept and practice of partnership have been rapidly evolving. In the process some older initiatives have fallen off the edge of the 'crowded platform' or had to change their style of operation. In an atmosphere of heady experimentation we can be certain that partnership will continue to evolve in new ways through the 1990s, as partners learn from each other, learn how to deal with each other, and also learn from other partnerships.

PART FIVE ─────────

CITIES AND PROPERTY DEVELOPMENT

─────────────────

17

CITY LIMITS

___ *Kevin Robins and James Cornford*

17.1 AN URBAN RENAISSANCE?

According to a recent Arts Council publication, the UK is experiencing an 'urban renaissance' with culture and the arts coming to play a new role in revitalizing and re-enchanting city life. The arts 'create a climate of optimism – the "can do" attitude essential to developing the "enterprise culture" Government hopes to bring to deprived areas; they 'provide focal points for community pride and identity' (ACGB, 1987). The positive significance of the arts in the 1980s and 1990s is defined against the negative reference point of the 1960s. For the Arts Council, the 1960s have come to symbolize the alienating force of modernism: at that time, urban renewal 'resulted in concrete tower blocks on a vast, inhuman scale, destroying established communities in the process'. Now, in the 1990s, we must learn the lessons of the past and 'get it right this time': 'To succeed, redevelopment must consist of more than bricks and mortar. It must rebuild communities' (*ibid.*) *An Urban Renaissance* is an opportunist document, one reflecting the 'can do' attitude of the Arts Council in the face of the new enterprise logic. Its very conformism, however, also makes it a good statement of what is now turning out to be a broad consensus on the nature and course of urban regeneration. In its key terms – enterprise, renaissance, culture, image, community – is reflected a new optimism for our times.

It is the same optimism and vision that characterizes Prince Charles' recent pronouncements on architecture and urban planning. In the Prince's discourse, there is the same emphasis on restoring the spirit of enterprise and rebuilding community, and the same belief that this might be the basis of a 'new renaissance for Britain'. And, again, there is the same starting point, based on the critique of modernism and particularly of its post-war manifestations. As Patrick Wright has argued, the Prince of Wales' ideas are centred around 'a highly schematic interpretation of the British nation and its history since the Second World War' (Wright, 1989, p. 27). After the high point of UK history in 1945, the country entered a bleak 40-year decline, a period of bureaucratic planning and of 'destructive modernization'. The present period offers a potential way beyond this inhumanity and alienation; it could be 'the miraculous moment of reawakening when the return to true values can begin' (*ibid.*). This might be the historical moment to move beyond modernization and beyond modernism. For the Prince, the way forward is through both the revival of traditional forms of building and the stimulation of neo-vernacular and community architecture (Jencks, 1988). A new era of post-modernism will be about a return to human scale and the re-creation of community. As the Prince argued in his Pittsburgh speech, in 1988, 'man seems to function best in small, recognisable units – hence the village – where he is part of a community of people to which he can relate.' The future beyond modernism is rooted in the ruralism, particularism and organicism that have long characterized UK architecture and planning (Rustin, 1989). After 40 years of devastation and devaluation, this is now presented as the key to reviving and re-enchanting cities and communities.

Prince Charles' account of post-war disenchantment and his hopes for a revitalization of urban sensibilities have come in for a great deal of criticism. What is striking, however, is the popular resonance and appeal of his vision. What is also striking is the convergence of the Prince's analysis with that of many of his critics. There is, we want to argue, a more radical and critical account of the past and future of cities, that, in its fundamental structures, bears some resemblance to the royal scenario. This account, too, tells the story of a post-war phase of urban development that is now coming to an end; it, too, is concerned with the possibilities of renaissance and re-enchantment. In this approach, too, the cities of the world are considered to be at a turning point. And this turning point is also about moving beyond 'the faceless abstraction of modernist urban development' (Lash, 1988).

Within this discourse, the key issue is about the shift from the Fordist to the post-Fordist city (Cooke, 1988a). It is in the recent work of David Harvey, particularly, that this has been most fully developed (Harvey, 1987, 1989a, 1989b). Harvey argues that we have seen the shift from a managerial approach to urban governance in the 1960s to contemporary forms of entrepreneurial governance. This shift in urban politics is associated with 'a transition from locationally rather rigid Fordist production systems backed by Keynesian state welfarism to a much more geographically open and market-based form of [post-Fordist] flexible accumulation' (Harvey, 1989a, p. 12). It also involves the shift from modernist to postmodernist forms of design, cultural forms and lifestyle. For Harvey, postmodernism signifies:

> . . . a break with the idea that planning and development should focus on large scale, technologically rational, austere and functionally efficient 'international style' design and that vernacular traditions, local history, and specialised spatial designs ranging from functions of

intimacy to grand spectacle should be approached with a much greater eclecticism of style.

(Harvey, 1987, p. 262)

Postmodernity, he argues, 'is nothing more than the cultural clothing of flexible accumulation' (*ibid.*, p. 279). There is, then, a clear logic of development: from managerialism/Fordism/modernism to entrepreneurialism/post-Fordism/post-modernism. The trajectory of change remains indeterminate and, ultimately, uncertain, though Harvey does suggest that there is a potential for a progressive outcome. For Harvey, too, the re-enchantment of cities is on the agenda.

In the writings of Harvey, and of other critical commentators, we have an account of postwar urban development that, surprisingly, echoes that of Prince Charles. And, if the ideas for ways beyond modernist abstraction and faceless bureaucratic managerialism are often very different, it is nonetheless the case that the underlying concerns are again remarkably similar. The critique of modernism is at the heart of these shared concerns. The logic of modernism was centred around efficiency, functionalism and impersonality; as it eroded the sense of place so it undermined the sense of identity. Against this uniformity of the modern movement, David Ley has argued, we are now seeing a renewed interest in regional and historical styles of architecture and in the diversity of local cultures.

In contrast to the isotropic space of modernism, post-modern space aims to be historically specific, rooted in cultural, often vernacular, style conventions, and often unpredictable in the relation of parts to the whole. In reaction to the large scale of the modern movement, it attempts to create smaller units, seeks to break down a corporate society of urban villages, and maintain historical associations through renovation and recycling.

(Ley, 1989, p. 53)

'The post-modern project;', Ley emphasizes, 'is the re-enchantment of the built environment' (*ibid.*).

Post-modernism is about the struggle for place in the face of modernist 'rationality' and abstraction. In one strand of thinking, the return to the particular is about revalorizing locality, community and the vernacular. For Ley, it is about the 'attempt to restore meaning, rootedness and human proportions to place in an era dominated by depersonalising bulk and standardisation' (*ibid.*, p. 53). For Michael Rustin, we must confront the limitations of abstract universalism and again acknowledge the boundedness of human lives in time and space: 'Even though mobility and choice of place has grown, territorial locations remain nodes of association of continuity, bounding cultures and communities' (Rustin, 1987, p. 33).

According to Geoff Mulgan, there is renewed interest in the soft architecture of the city, that is 'its feel and atmosphere, its social networks and its sense of community and citizenship' (Mulgan, 1989, p. 19). From this perspective, reclaiming the city is about re-establishing personal and collective roots. The re-enchantment of the city is about the re-enchantment of identity and community.

An alternative post-modern response to the abstraction and rationalism of modernism has been a renewed concern with urban spectacle and imagery. This development is rooted in the new consumerism of post-Fordist times, with its culture of fashion, advertising, design and display. 'The relatively stable aesthetic of Fordist modernism', writes David Harvey, 'has given way to all the ferment, instability, and fleeting qualities of a postmodernist aesthetic that celebrates difference, ephemerality, spectacle, fashion and the commodification of cultural forms' (Harvey, 1989b, p. 156). This is the theatrical side of postmodernism. This is about identities in a 'no-place space' in which 'traditional senses of culture are decontextualised, stimulated, re-duplicated and continually renewed and restyled' (Featherstone, 1989, p. 9). This is the city of malls, museums, theme parks, shopping centres and tourist sites, the city 'in which cultural disorder and stylistic eclecticism become common features of spaces in which consumption and leisure are meant to be constructed as "experiences"' (ibid., p. 17). In this city, 'the concern with fashion, presentation of self, "the look" on the part of the new wave of urban *flaneurs* points to the process of cultural differentiation which in many ways is the obverse of the stereotypical images of mass societies in which serried ranks of similarly dressed people are massed together' (ibid., pp. 4–5). For Featherstone, this mobilization of spectacle and display could be a positive force in urban life, pointing to the deconstruction of existing symbolic hierarchies and the opening up of a playful, popular democratic impulse. Spectacle and theatricality might even be used for positive political ends to reconstruct civic identity and transform urban relations (Bianchini, 1989). It may, however, also be the case that this is a form of social control: 'The orchestrated production of an urban image can, if successful, create a sense of social solidarity, civic pride and loyalty to place and even allow the urban image to provide a mental refuge in a world that capital treats as more and more place-less' (Harvey, 1989a, p. 14). Through spectacle and image, it may be possible to create a spurious sense of to-getherness and participation in urban life.

17.2   THE CRISIS OF URBAN MODERNITY?

There are some important observations here, and in different ways, these various accounts contribute something to our understanding of contemporary urban change. Nonetheless, some real objections can be levelled at what are rather limited and partial projections of urban futures. If cities are in crisis, we suggest, their very real problems are not being addressed adequately by these new urban regeneration agendas. And if urbanity is in crisis, then we doubt that fashionable projects for urban renaissance are meaningful responses. The new urban postmodernism is simply too partial and limited, and fails to confront – and often to even recognize – some of the more profound developments affecting urban futures.

What is at issue is the significance of the modern city. There is the question of what it now is; there is the question of what its consequences have been; and there is the question of whether it is being supplanted by something called the post-modern city. For most of those we have been discussing, the answers are straightforward. The urban post-modernists are moved by a sense of having been betrayed by post-war architects and planners. In one respect, this might be seen, as the more sensitive modernists themselves recognize, as a reflection of 'modernism's inability both to adapt itself to changing needs and more specifically to learn from its mistakes' (Rogers, 1989, p. 27). Invariably, however, it tends to be seen in more dramatic terms, as a crisis of modernism and of modernity itself. The uniformity and inhumanity of contemporary planning are seen as manifestations of modernist abstraction and universalism. The hope is then that the present might perhaps be a turning point. If there is a crisis of the modern (or Fordist, or managerial) city, then there may, perhaps, be the prospect of creating the post-modern (post-Fordist, post-managerial) city.

It is difficult not to see this kind of historical scheme as simplistic and reductionist. The binary opposition of modernism to post-modernism, or of universalism to particularism, may have a certain heuristic value, but there is the real danger that it will flatten the complexity and contradictoriness of social transformation. There is the danger that we will see change in terms of abrupt and decisive stages separated by historical divides. Such historical binarism invokes a teleological development in which modernism will (necessarily) give way to post-modernism, Fordism to post-Fordism, managerialism to entrepreneurialism. In this way, the 'dysfunctions' of the modernist city can be safely consigned to the historical dustbin. Disenchantment is buried in the past, while the future can be unproblematically given over to the project of re-enchantment.

What this fails to address are the real complexities and contradictions thrown up by urban modernization. If there is now a revival of interest in community and sense of place, this can only be seen in the context of what is in fact the increasing fragmentation and segmentation of urban life. According to Castells, the dual city is 'the urban expression of the process of increasing differentiation of labour in two equally dynamic sectors within the growing economy: the information-based formal economy, and the downgraded labour-based informal economy'. The fundamental meaning of the dual city, he continues, 'refers to the process of spatial restructuring through which distinct segments of labour are included in and excluded from the making of new history' (Castells, 1989, pp. 225, 228). In the contemporary metropolis, territories of the new post-modern *flaneurs* and consumers coexist with the ghettos of ethnic minorities and the socially marginalized. Against the post-modernists, Margit Mayer argues that 'it is not a "pluralism" of lifestyles and consumption patterns which reigns, but rather that the high income consumers' ideas and definitions of the "good life" have become the influential ones' (Mayer, 1989, pp. 10–11). We are seeing the consolidation of the divided city, in which 'urban space, while it is functionally and economically shared, is socially segregated and culturally differentiated' (*ibid.*, p. 12; *c.f.* Esser and Hirsch, 1989). And, if there is a renewed concern with public space and public life, this is in contradictory relation to an increased privatism. New communications and media technologies, particularly, encourage further privatism and isolation: 'households are plugged into the world, but not open to it' and 'in this sense, the city exists no more' (Häussermann and Siebel, 1987, p. 227).

Changing urban governance is not about engineering the transition from the bad old times to the benign new times, but, rather, it is about trying to find new ways to hold these contradictions in tension. If there is an urban crisis, it will not be resolved in the straightforward way the post-modernists suggest. We should not, then, think of the present as a point of (evolutionary) transition from the modern to the post-modern city. It is not about settling accounts with modernity in order to make way for an urban renaissance; it is not about the shift beyond modernist disenchantment to the re-enchantment of cities. As Zygmunt Bauman reminds us, postmodernism is not an achieved state: it is, rather, about 'modernity taking a long and attentive look at itself, not liking what it sees and sensing the urge to change' (Bauman, 1990a, p. 23). What has been called the 'new urbanity' is not about resolving the crisis of cities – not yet at least. It is, rather, about a rupture that is now 'forcing us to re-think our understanding of cities and of good uses of the city' (Häussermann and Siebel, 1987, p. 7). Just because we feel the need to rethink and the urge to change, we should not assume that history has obligingly come up with the answers. The new urban sensibility that is emerging may be more about not liking what it sees in the modern city than about really imagining an alternative vision.

This historical teleology of the post-modern perspective encourages soft optimism and voluntarism in the policy and political arenas. It seems but a short step from imagining the user-friendly city to its felicitous realization: it is simply a matter of soft social engineering, centred around refashioned cultural and consumption districts, and of cosmetic design and facades, whether they be hi-tech glitz or neo-historicist classicism. The burden of our argument is that the crisis of urban modernization is a good deal more intractable. We must consider what is, in fact, a profound and long-term crisis of the city and of urbanity. At one level, this is a question of the very scale of physical and social problems in the modern city. Inequality, segmentation and alienation are inscribed in the physical and social landscape of cities (and this is a matter for urban politics, not urban cultural regeneration). But, at another level, there is a very real crisis of urbanity itself. What do we think cities are for? What are the values that should regulate urban life? What does civic identity mean (or not mean) now?

Thirty years ago, Lewis Mumford began *The City in History* with some thoughts on this question of urbanity, and on the imperative 'to find a new form for the city.' 'Can the needs and desires', he asks, 'that have impelled men to live in cities recover, at a still higher level, all that Jerusalem, Athens, or Florence once seemed to promise?' Or, alternatively, might 'post-historic man' no longer have any need for the city? Might 'what was once a city . . . shrink to the dimensions of an underground control centre . . . and all other attributes of life be forfeited'? (Mumford, 1961, pp. 3–4). Since then, other writers have highlighted the devaluation of older forms of urbanity and the crisis of the city as an imaginative focus. Michael Walzer, for example, has described the erosion of what he calls 'open-minded spaces' – ones that have in the past been the 'breeding ground for mutual respect, political respect, civil discourse' – and their replacement by intimate spaces and 'single-minded', that is instrumental and functional, spaces (Walzer, 1986). Richard Sennett has written of the growth of 'purified communities' which devalue the complexity, difference and otherness that have been so much at the heart of classic urban culture (Sennett, 1973). Arguing that our relation to the city is marked by a 'crisis of language', by a 'loss of semiotic apprehensibility', William Sharpe and Leonard Wallock suggest that the 'waning sense of city as place is intimately linked to the inability to say what the city might mean' (Sharpe and Wallock, 1987, pp. 29, 15, 26). Johannes Birringer points to 'the end of the city as an imaginative or emotional focus even of cultural alienation' (Birringer, 1989, p. 122).

The very idea of the city itself is now thrown into doubt. 'The question that is brought to mind', Jurgen Habermas writes, 'is whether the actual *notion* of the city has not itself been superseded' (Habermas, 1985, p. 326). The problems of town planning, he argues, 'are not primarily problems of design, but problems of controlling and dealing with the anonymous system-imperatives that influence the spheres of city life and threaten to devastate the urban fabric' (*ibid.*). The new urban agglomerations and systems seem remote from traditional conceptions of city life and culture. Is it then possible to reconcile older notions of urbanity with the system-functional imperatives of contemporary society? Can we sustain 'mediating institutions that can nurture direct relationships in a world increasingly characterised by indirect ones?' (Calhoun, 1986, p. 341).

In spite of the rhetoric of renewal and renaissance, we have argued, contemporary urban regeneration schemes are not the harbingers of a new urbanity. They are, rather, the response of a particular group to the crisis of the modern city. It is about what urban culture and sensibility might continue to mean for that particular group. This post-modern vision is about the pleasures of consumption, about the enjoyment of public spaces, about sustaining elements of culture and tradition, and about stimulating a certain level of diversity and difference. Because of its partiality, however, it is only about revitalizing fragments of the city. It is about insulating the consumption and living spaces of the post-modern *flaneur* from the 'have nots' in the abandoned zones of the city. It is about a particular group learning to live with, and adapt to, urban crisis through the cultivation of exclusive and sequestered 'post-modern' enclaves. The question is whether the crisis of urban modernity can be confronted otherwise.

18

PROPERTY-LED URBAN REGENERATION: AN ASSESSMENT

Patsy Healey,
Simin Davoudi,
Mo O'Toole,
Solmaz Tavsanoglu
and David Usher

18.1 INTRODUCTION

This book has examined, primarily through empirical research on development activity and the relations of the development process, the experience of urban policy in the 1980s. The primary thrust of this policy was to achieve urban regeneration through attracting and assisting investment by the private sector in property development.

The rationale for this policy contained many ambiguities (see Chapter 3). Its main objective was to reverse the flight of private capital out of investment in the built fabric of cities and to create active markets where these had become stagnant or collapsed altogether. This was to be achieved by removing a variety of supply-side blockages. The most significant of these were assumed to be public-sector land-ownership and development activity, and the inefficiency and lack of market awareness with which local government exercised its role in regulating land use and development activity via the planning system.

The market-directed revitalized built fabric was in turn to contribute to economic and social regeneration through providing appropriate buildings and locales for the new rising sectors of economic activity. A refurbished fabric also symbolized a new imagery of vital urbanity. Flagship development projects (Chapter 5) and promotional imagery were used vigorously to supplant the imagery of rustbelt cities and clothcap citizens which, it was assumed, would inhibit inward investment by the private sector, with the lifestyle imagery of a globalized 'yuppiefied' middle-class, and production practices modelled on Japanese ideal types (Chapter 11).

This strategy clearly implied a major role for the property development industry. The dynamics of this industry have never been well understood (Healey and Barrett, 1985). One aim of this book has been to contribute to a better understanding of the industry, and how it may be affected by public policy. The primary focus of the book has been upon development activity, the actors in the development process and the institutional relationships through which development activity has taken place. How realistic was the strategy of urban regeneration through private-sector property development? What are the limits of such a policy? What could it contribute? What adverse effects might result?

The 1980s was a particularly interesting period within which to study the development industry. Not only was it given a major role in urban policy. It also lived through a roller-coaster property cycle, from stagnation in most sectors in the early part of the decade, to boom conditions in the second half of the decade, levelling off to stagnation and slump by 1990 (see Chapter 4). Urban policy coincided with and actively promoted the boom, encouraging inward investors to take up previously neglected development opportunities. It is thus possible to observe both the impact of major boom-slump property cycles on the property markets and economic relations of cities with fragile local economies, and the consequences of opening up development opportunities in such cities to firms with more national and international orientations.

The 1980s also coincided with a renewal of interest in the quality of urban life, but in parallel with acute questioning about the validity of the notion of the 'urban' and the 'city' (Chapter 17). Was the 'rediscovery of the urban' merely about ensuring that every urban region was equipped with the types of locale expected by the affluent and mobile professional and managerial classes? Or did it prefigure an attempt to reassert and reconstitute some key relationships of individual cities, to renew the sense of the distinctive qualities and relationships of individual places?

This concluding chapter attempts to draw together the findings of the research on development activity in older industrial conurbations in the 1980s as reported in this book in relation to the main themes highlighted in Chapter 1. These were: the dynamics of the development industry in fragile local economies; the institutional relationships of development activity; and the impact of urban policy on development activity. Comment is then made on two major issues for future urban policy, namely: who has benefited from the policies pursued and who has not; and the image of the future city embodied in urban policy and development activity in the 1980s and its relevance to the 1990s. Finally, some ideas are offered for a new agenda for urban policy for the 1990s and beyond.

18.2 THE DEVELOPMENT INDUSTRY IN FRAGILE LOCAL ECONOMIES

There can be no doubt that the older industrial conurbations witnessed a significant increase in the amount of development activity in the mid-to late 1980s (see Chapters 5 and 6). This refurbished existing stock provided new stock in new designs and new locations. Much land left derelict from former industrial production was reclaimed and built on, and the built fabric generally was spruced up. Several local builders, developers, agents and landowners were active in the rebuilding process, and a number of firms from outside particular urban regions became involved in development projects. Some reorganized themselves specifically to exploit the opportunities created by urban renewal and Enterprise Zone opportunities. Everywhere, the public sector was engaged actively in the development process, encouraging and facilitating development activity.

The processes, agencies and relationships of development have been very diverse, as the contributions to this book illustrate. It is nevertheless possible to identify some key driving forces affecting development activity generally. In Chapter 3, it was suggested these might be consumer demand, landowner strategies, competition between local and **extra-local** property interests, and the movement of finance capital. Landowners, both public and private, emerge in several chapters as key agents. Among the private landowners, some were firms based in specific regions or cities (Chapters 9 and 13), others were large national production firms (Chapters 8 and 10). Such firms were typical rentiers, as described by Logan and Molotch (1987), marooned by the consequences of economic restructuring, seeking to salvage some site value, and, if very fortunate, to see the fortunes of their properties transformed by the reconstitution of their locale into one of the buoyant nodes of new property opportunities. In this rentier game, local authorities and other public agencies played a key role. As Harding observes (Chapter 10), they dominated most local property markets as landowners, seeking rentier returns themselves. Along with production companies, public agencies in the 1980s used development activity as a way to raise capital. In addition, local authorities signed up to the urban policy strategy, seeking to generate jobs and other local assets through property development.

Landowners in older industrial conurbations were actively encouraged in this behaviour by the property boom and by urban policy. The boom only partly related to a real demand for new property. It was fuelled vigorously by the flow of national and international banking capital into development (Chapter 4). Landowners thus exploited opportunities created by the movements of finance capital and by consumer demand. The ready availability of capital in turn encouraged the expansion of property companies in various ways. While some were locally based, many operated regionally or nationally. However, these latter tended to take up local opportunities only when these were reasonably secure, either because of public support or because local firms had already shown them to be viable (Chapter 9). Although information about locally based companies is limited, it seems likely that they had less access to easy credit, took more risks, and were accustomed to support from local authorities. The boom presented local rentiers and property developers in effect with the opportunity to speculate, in the hope of attracting some of the benefits of the new demands and the easy capital available. Urban policy in turn actively encouraged speculation by talking up property opportunities in urban areas (see Chapters 11 and 15), and by redirecting the funding for urban policy initiatives so that it flowed directly into development projects. However, the funds available were disbursed increasingly through institutional arrangements which were more accessible to sophisticated and non-local property interests. Thus, in the competition to capture speculative gain, urban policy tended to be less helpful to local entrepreneurs than the rhetoric of 'encouraging enterprise' locally suggested.

Its effect was to fuel rentier speculation. However, as Harding points out (Chapter 13), close analysis of the various projects and partnerships of the 1980s does not show evidence of the kind of local private-sector dominated 'rentier' growth machines described in the United States by Logan and Molotch (1987). The major economic activities in UK cities have long been based outside the region, with much less interest in the fortunes of the cities in which they are located than their US counterparts. The main driving force behind the projects and the partnerships in older industrial cities in the UK was typically the public sector (see Chapter 9 and Part 5).

As the speculative bandwagon got underway, consumer demand as a constraint was constantly downplayed. Yet throughout the 1980s, supply-side speculation bumped up against the real constraints on demand for new property. Liverpool experienced this throughout the decade according to Couch and Fowles (Chapter 7); and Newcastle had problems in any industrial and commercial projects not associated with urban policy incentives (Chapter 6). Even in the buoyant conditions of Greater Manchester, demand asserted itself as a constraint as the boom ran out by 1989 (Chapter 5). With a full-blown property recession by mid-1990, property companies, local authorities who promoted development and, particularly the Urban Development Corporations, were

> ... increasingly stuck with projects they cannot complete, offices they cannot fill and land they cannot sell.
>
> (*Economist* 1990b, p. 35)

Urban policy, macro-economic credit policy and rentier interests in the public and private sectors thus drove the UK's rustbelt cities into a vigorous boom-bust cycle. What have the effects been? On the positive side, a substantial amount of property has been revitalized. A lot of this revitalization has been undertaken by local investors of one kind or another (see Chapters 6 and 9). Some local entrepreneurial activity has been fostered, with the experience of partnerships growing into attempts to build more substantial local growth coalitions between public and private sector agents. As a result, the physical fabric of many cities looks more sprightly and varied, and the institutional fabric is certainly alive with activity, if often fragmented. The publicity of regeneration has had the effect of changing the image of industrial cities held by investors, and by those seeking to escape congestion in the South East. There has been a significant movement of firms and households from the South into industrial and business premises created by the development activity.

However, the strategy, with its focus on a few locales (the city centre, waterfronts), has concentrated development and investment activity on a few places only. With little investment to go round, other areas have been blighted (Chapters 6 and 7). Some of the larger and more complex projects, especially if uncompleted by 1989, are now affected by the recession. Unfulfilled schemes then come to symbolize depressed property conditions, exaggerating the slump in the same way that the hype about projects in the 1980s exaggerated the boom. Meanwhile, rather than strengthening local entrepreneurial capacity, national urban policy, with its focus on the inward-investor property company, has in effect led to competition with local development capacity. It is possible that the main consequence has been to shift local development activity from a former dependence on national production companies and the various agencies of the public sector to dependence on national development companies and the public sector.

Within this general picture, however, the different cities have had a variety of experiences. In each, there has been considerable effort by local interests in the public and private sectors to make constructive use of the opportunities available while avoiding the pressures of 'global takeover', of excessive boom and bust, of an exaggerated service-led path to revival, and an ideologically driven urban policy. These pressures, all of which threatened the long term economic health of cities with 'fragile' local economies, were confronted and negotiated at the level of projects, within companies, and in promotional initiatives. They were not addressed through a general urban development strategy for the city.

18.3   THE INSTITUTIONAL RELATIONSHIPS OF DEVELOPMENT ACTIVITY

While the public sector remained a major force in shaping development activity in older industrial cities, the rules governing the relationships between state and market in the development process changed significantly in the 1980s. In the 1960s, it was assumed that the public sector provided a framework for development activity and property markets through comprehensive development plans, while at the same time providing physical infrastructure in advance of development. In the 1980s, the initiative in development activity was firmly shifted by national policy to the private sector. Plan frameworks were allowed to fall into disuse, and infrastructure investment depended on private sector contributions in buoyant property markets, or public urban regeneration projects and subsidies elsewhere. Development was thus encouraged to be negotiated project by project on an ad hoc basis, in a situation of uncertainty about what development would take place in an area and how it would be provided. According to the ideology of urban policy, market entrepreneurs were to determine where development should happen, how much should be provided, and in what form. Public sector facilitation was to follow the market lead, through partnership with the private sector where necessary. How far did this happen in the older industrial areas? Through what kinds of relationships did it happen?

At the level of development projects, if the assumption of urban policy was correct, private sector developers should come forward, opening up new locations and property types. The research reported here suggests a different practice. In most of the instances discussed (Chapters 9, 10, 13), the public sector took the initative, trying out ideas (Chapter 7), coordinating and managing development (Chapter 10), and handing over opportunities to the private sector once the early investments had been made and the risks minimized. The public sector subsidized development, undertook land assembly, provided sites with infrastructure and became the risk taker. In many ways, this continued traditional relationships in older industrial areas where weak local economies have for long been sustained by public investment and strategy. The tools and the rhetoric may have been new, but the relationships illustrate 'business as usual'. Frieden (1990) comes to a similar conclusion with respect to the role of the public sector in defining development opportunities in US cities. Ironically, it was the apparently successful experience of these cities which, in the UK in the 1990s, was used to symbolize a new approach of private-sector property regeneration (Barnekov et al., 1989). What was different, however, was the shift from planning frameworks to *ad hoc* projects, and to short-term preoccupations with flagship schemes and leverage ratios, rather than providing a stable framework within which markets could again become active. The case of the Merchant City in Glasgow shows what could be achieved when the public sector was able to wait several years for results.

At the level of the relations of local economies, the UK's older industrial cities were dominated in the post-war period by big manufacturing production interests typically headquartered outside the area, and by central government's regional policy, i.e. by the relationships of Fordist production.

Many of these relationships had by the 1980s been rationalized away, with regional policy being downgraded. Nevertheless, the big production companies are still present as landowners (Chapters 10 and 13), and the old production relationships have been substituted with new (if much smaller) flows of finance from central government, and by other big production interests, particularly the construction companies. As a result, the relations of local economies remained dependent on big outside firms, or on central government resources. However, neither the institutions of urban policy nor the new extra-local companies necessarily have a tradition of local contacts with which to assist in the negotiation of the many highly localized aspects of development projects. As a result, new networks and relationships have had to be constructed. The effort in partnership-building is an expression of this activity. But these new relationships challenge old relations, particularly those built up between local development interests and local authorities.

At the level of urban governance, the institutional relationships of the 1980s with respect to property development were very different to those of the 1970s. Local authorities were downgraded, their resources were limited and some responsibilities and some parts of their territories were taken away from them (see Chapters 5 and 10). The Metropolitan Counties, which had taken an overview of development and infrastructure needs and provided a valuable base of information, were abolished in 1986. A plethora of new agencies and initiatives was established. Each new initiative altered the way resources were made available for development activity. In theory, the objective was to make urban governance more efficient and entrepeneurial: to shift from a managerial to an entrepreneurial form (Harvey, 1989b). In practice, the public sector's ability to deliver its role in the development process was fragmented and unclear. Behind the hype of development opportunities lurked a potential and often a reality of institutional confusion. Talk of the need for leadership and image (Chapters 11 and 13) often masked a vacuum as regards regional consensus around realistic strategic directions.

In this context, one function for the new partnerships and relationships so actively constructed in the 1980s was to re-establish some mechanism for collaboration between parties who were fragmented and often ideologically divided by these changes. Some of these partnerships begin to look like new forms of urban governance in the making. This raises important questions not only in relation to the membership and constituencies of the partners, but about the interests and ideas they propagate. To some extent, close examination of the personnel involved in partnerships suggests once again 'business as usual'. Only a few of the personnel of the new agencies and networks are new actors to the local scene. Many have left earlier positions in the city, often in the public sector. They typically carried with them good local knowledge, which helped to avoid some of the pitfalls the new initiatives and schemes could head towards. This continuity of personnel limited the loss of information inevitable with institutional fragmentation.

But such personnel were not necessarily cautious of the new ideas. There has been no survey of the key personnel of urban regeneration policies in the 1980s, but it is not unlikely that those who left secure positions in public agencies did so to try out new ideas and new ways of doing things. The sceptical Jeremiahs perhaps remained in their old positions. There is no research from which to generalize, but cities had a number of policy analysts and locally sensitive property consultants urging caution. Most went unheard and were marginalized, for the project of urban policy through private sector property development not only involved channelling resources in new ways according to new rules, it was also vigorously promoted through ideas about appropriate strategies and processes. The rhetoric of urban regeneration provided a language with which to coordinate disparate activities, and smooth the path of private-sector developers. It has arguably been as important as changes in the resources and rules through which urban policy has been pursued in changing what development opportunities have been identified and promoted. But local awareness of real constraints on demand helped to moderate some of the inflation in development possibilities that the ideology of entrepreneurial initiative promoted.

Just as there were changes in the development and investment opportunities in local land and property markets, so there was some change in the organization and relationships of the development industry. There are still few accounts of how building firms, property development companies and consultancy firms reorganized during the 1980s. There is evidence to suggest that the 1980s witnessed the formation of a considerable number of new companies. Some of these benefited from opportunities in London Docklands and the Enterprise Zones. Others entered into new partnerships to allow expansion, while several big construction companies set up property development units (Chapters 9 and 10). How far these initiatives significantly changed the organization and relationships of the development industry needs further study.

The most visible changes, however, have been in the relationships of urban governance and in the agency arrangements through which the facilitating role of the public sector was delivered. While some of these arrangements have helped particular companies and partnerships to succeed, achieving a successful development in the 1980s has more usually involved battling against very considerable institutional odds, as Chapter 10 illustrates. During boom conditions, such transaction costs could be borne. Under current conditions, it is no wonder that many in the development industry are calling for better public-sector coordination (NAO, 1990) and/or a 'one-stop shop'.

18.4   THE IMPACT OF URBAN POLICY ON DEVELOPMENT ACTIVITY

There can be no doubt that urban policy in the 1980s had a major impact on development activity and land property markets in older industrial cities in the 1980s. The policy changed the flows and institutional relationships through which development took place. It brought in new firms and re-sources, if at the cost of considerable subsidy, both overt and hidden. It changed some of the rules of the development game. And it promoted the strategy of regeneration for these cities through a speculative rentier strat-egy, linked to transforming production economies into primarily service nodes. But urban policy also held potential dangers for locally based ele-ments of the development industry and for local economies. Avoiding these dangers and maximizing the local benefits of urban policy required great care and sensitivity to local circumstances by the various agencies of urban governance. However, the institutional fragmentation of governance made this a difficult project, requiring the construction of complex alliances in a volatile situation.

Urban policy was thus one of the key driving forces of development activity in older industrial cities. It had a powerful influence on **where** development took place (Chapters 5 and 6). It influenced **what** was built (for example, high-density waterfront housing schemes, big flagship mixed-use projects). It affected **who** was involved in the development process (notably encouraging outsiders, and sustaining close relationships between national government and the big construction companies, for example, the BUD consortium (Chapter 13)). It influenced the **institutional relations** of development both by creating new agencies itself, and indirectly through the way companies organized themselves to take advantage of new oppor-tunities in urban regeneration projects.

This impact was achieved primarily by the traditional tasks of the public sector in urban redevelopment, namely: the coordination of development activity; land assembly; testing out new ideas; providing subsidy; and risk minimization. To this extent, as already noted, UK experience parallels that described in the United States (Frieden, 1990), although with a much stronger top-down emphasis and a more short-term orientation. The public sector played the role of opening and making markets, with the private sector fol-lowing up the opportunities created (Chapters 9 and 10). The difference was that subsidies were targeted at particular projects and zones, rather than being available as of right throughout the older industrial cities. Nor was there any effort in 'planning' market opportunities at the level of the urban region. Firms seeking to benefit from urban policy had to be pre-pared to invest time and effort in identifying and testing project possibilities and building up relationships with a range of different government agencies which were themselves required to work to new criteria in new ways. The firms which learnt the new games quickly won out in obtaining the benefits of the policy, but in turn ran the risk of developing a dangerous dependency on the public sector. In effect, the development industry had to be prepared to live with the highly politicized management of the urban policy 'gravy train'. For the vigorous rhetoric of the policy was only partly aimed at revaluing the investment opportunities in the older industrial cities. It was also a strongly ideological project (Parkinson, 1989).

However, urban policy as such did not significantly influence the amount of development which has taken place (Chapter 5). It was the combination of urban policy incentives and a property boom which pushed at the boundaries of realistic local economic demand, creating overprovision in some sectors, particularly the office market (Chapters 4 and 6). Urban policy was targeted at supply-side factors, not at demand. For a while, the cities benefited from the economic upturn in both the industrial and service sectors, and were able to capture firms and households seeking to escape congestion costs in the South. But once the recession hit both sectors by the second half of 1990, the constraint of demand once again became obvious. Finally, the policy did not influence the overall quality of urban areas, merely affecting a few locales in the city.

The policy has also had a number of adverse effects, although the significance of these is as yet not easy to establish. Combined with boom-slump conditions, it has perturbed local development capacity. It is not clear that opening up local economies to vigorous external pressure necessarily strengthens a local economy. Nor has the policy ensured an appropriate supply of building stock available for the demands and needs of the local economy. Particular problems are already evident with respect to industrial buildings and low-cost housing. The lack of both may inhibit the development of the industrial and commercial dimensions of the economy. Nor is it obvious that urban policy has filtered benefits into the local economy on any scale. There is some evidence of localized impacts from investment in projects and zones, and some firms which managed to make use of the benefits have expanded. But there is also evidence that the concentration of development activity in particular zones, notably the Enterprise Zones and Urban Development Corporations, blighted development activity elsewhere (Chapters 5 and 6). Similarly, the disadvantaged in older industrial cities received little benefit, apart from the provision of some training deals and some environmental improvements.

So 1980s urban policy could be interpreted as an attempt to play an old role in city rebuilding in a new way. Rather than providing a market-orientated development framework for city land and property markets, or realizing government rhetoric of 'rolling back the state' and letting the private sector move in, the public sector was reorganized and cajoled into mimicking the private sector. The specific role-model for the public sector was the entrepreneurial deal-maker, innovating, investing speculatively and

taking risks at the level of projects. Ignorant or contemptuous of the historical role of the public sector in protecting land and property markets from
the collective damage caused by unskilled speculators (Weiss, 1987; Stach,
1987), urban policy fostered such speculation. The costs to the public purse
of underwriting the risks the speculators took became clear as the slump
found them out.

18.5   COSTS AND BENEFITS

What then were the benefits of the policy? Robinson (1989a, p. 41) argues
that the principal beneficiaries were property interests, middle-class com-
muters, visitors to the cities and those interested in gentrifying stock around
the areas being revitalized. The contributions in this book suggest a more
diverse picture. 'Yuppies' moved into the Merchant City in Glasgow (Chapter 9), but local people took up the new housing in Hebburn (Chapter 8).
Landowners have benefited everywhere where property values have sustained an increase. Some local development firms have done well, as have
some regional and national companies, but their ability to do so in the long
term depends on their ability to manage the boom-slump cycle to their
advantage. Firms in need of modern premises in the cities have found more
of it available. People able to contemplate house purchase have a wider
choice of stock available to them than in the early 1980s. Those who use
city centres can enjoy the more lively modernized atmosphere which is
perhaps the most obvious product of 1980s urban policy. Some people
have found a wider range of jobs available to them, though many of the
jobs created in the new buildings are low-paid service jobs.

Some people have actually lost as a result of the policy. A number of
development firms, particularly locally based ones, have suffered from the
competition from extra-local firms and from the boom-slump cycle. Firms in
search of cheap industrial sites have found opportunities closed off as former
industrial sites have been cleared (see Chapter 9 and Thomas and Imrie,
1989). Those who enjoyed the wastelands as a leisure and ecological resource
have also lost several assets. Others have been adversely affected by rising
property values, closing off the possibilities of finding housing or business
premises in some revaluing areas. Others again have suffered as funds for
the social and environmental objectives of the Urban Programme component of urban policy have been squeezed to make space for the property
development initiatives. More widely, it could be argued that rate and tax
payers have suffered the opportunity cost of speculating with public money
in the built stock of local economies rather than in, for example, training,
community development or low-cost housing.

The key issue here is whether the target of urban policy as such should
be to promote private-sector property development. It could be argued that

stimulating the property sector is more appropriately a matter for national economic strategy. The appropriate focus for urban policy might rather be on specifically urban dimensions, for example the quality of life of people locked into particular places, or the opportunities for locally based firms, or the nexus of supports needed to sustain and expand the economic potential of the urban region. This would lead urban policy away from a preoccupation with the project and locale, and with the mechanics of specific promotional partnerships, to the nature of the urban, the city, and of the relationships which are important to sustain the economy, culture and environment of urban regions. It could help to drive development activity primarily by effective demand, rather than landowner strategies, the international/national movement of finance capital, or the competitive struggle of extra-local development companies to capture local development opportunities.

18.6 THE FUTURE CITY

The project of urban regeneration was to reconstruct the economic, socio-cultural, political-institutional and physical-environmental fabric of cities blighted by the collapse of Fordist manufacturing industrial complexes. This was to be done in a way which reflected and helped to implant in cities the principles of a market-led approach to urban management.

The rhetoric may have been of a development industry harnessed to the policy objective of demolishing the physical heritage of the Fordist past, to replace it with a thrusting post-modern landscape in the key locales of the new service economy: the city centre, the waterfront housing and leisure complexes, and the office/business parks. The reality shows much more continuity with past traditions of a close relationship between public and private sectors in the development process. This partly reflects the economic conditions of older industrial cities, which suffered chronically from the downside of uneven economic development. What was lost from this tradition in the 1980s was any discussion of the strategic relationships of an urban region and where property development fitted into this. Public and private agencies were in effect caught up in a competitive struggle between different interpretations of 'what the market wants'. The Urban Development Corporations have been forced to argue that the market likes waterfronts, wherever they are, despite the obvious competition from well-serviced sites on urban peripheries (Chapter 6).

But what kind of city is emerging from all this? Is it, as Robins argues (Chapter 17), a city of 'universalized' locales co-existing within urbanized territories? Is it a physical city at all in any traditional sense? Or does the city exist merely in our imagination, hovering above the various locales as a mental construct, and varying according to the interests and perceptions of those inhabiting locales?

Harvey has argued (1985, Chapter 10) that the structured coherence of the city of one regime of production is likely to be replaced by the structured coherence required by its successor. If so, the problems of perceiving city structure are merely transitional, as we work out what the new order should be like. Or it may be that the future for the older industrial cities is a permanent dependency on national and supra-national transfer payments. In which case, the effort of city rebuilding to foster economic regeneration is largely a wasted one. Alternatively, it may be argued that the future city, the city of the post-modern era, is in fact structureless, an amalgam of disjunctive locales (Soja, 1989), a territorial net within which diverse bits and pieces of activity and value co-exist, each separately tied into different economic, cultural and physical relationships across regional, national and international space. If this is so, then the focus on projects and locales, and on particular relations, such as the inward investing national property company, may be an appropriate expression of the requirements of the future non-city.

The issue of what kind of city is urban policy for remains a major challenge for future urban policy. There is currently much policy discussion of the need for a more coherent approach to the management of the economy and environment of cities. The development industry is itself in the forefront of this demand, seeking protection from its own excesses. But what are the key qualities, the key relationships, the key locales and the key actions of this enterprise? Urban policy in the 1980s could ignore this issue, assuming that the market would build, through a diversity of projects, what would turn out to be the future city. Those active in markets are now reminding the public sector that markets work best with clear ground rules and governing ideas. Among these, as far as land and property markets are concerned, is some conception of the spatial structure of the city, which in turn requires attention by political communities to what kind of city they want to help the market to make. But what capacity for urban governance does this imply?

18.7   RETHINKING URBAN POLICY AND URBAN GOVERNANCE

If rebuilding the city was the major contribution of urban policy to regenerating local economies, the key project for the 1990s may well be to rebuild the capacity for urban governance. The agenda of urban policy was shifting rapidly by 1990:

> By the end of the decade, many were arguing that urban regeneration required a wider vision and a broader package of programmes for finance, education, training, enterprise development and social provision than an agency single-mindedly devoted to physical regeneration of a narrowly defined area could achieve.
>
> (Parkinson, 1989, p. 437)

Does this mean that property development activity and the development industry should be sidelined by urban policy in the 1990s? Should the special instruments of property-led urban policy – the Enterprise Zones, the Urban Development Corporations and the City Grant Regimes – now be abandoned?

It is clear that the rentier/speculator conception of property development needs to be abandoned, but this does not mean that the role of the private sector in property development should be ignored. The cities will continue to need new and refurbished stock, but the key task is to link property development investment to the real demands and needs of the developing local economy, and the cultural-environmental concerns of local citizens. However, if private-sector development capacity is to be capable of under-taking this task in a situation where another boom is neither expected nor desired, a continuing proactive role from the public sector will be needed. Given the difficult market conditions which are normal in fragile local economies, the development industry will only be able to respond to de-mand if the public sector maintains its traditional role of assembling and servicing sites, and providing subsidy where demand generated as a result of local economic initiatives cannot be met by the land and property market on its own. This particularly applies to industrial land. More generally, the development industry in cities should benefit from strategies aimed at stabilizing market conditions and reducing uncertainty. Effective policies linking strategic infrastructure investment to land allocation and development nodes are likely to be helpful. This will require some form of strategic framework or development plan at the level of the urban region. Develop-ment incentives and infrastructure spending should be focused on the nodes and relations identified in such plans, which would thus link land allocation with public expenditure. It might also be helpful to detach Enterprise Zone benefits from zones, and make them available for specified firms developing in predefined conditions. It could be that Urban Development Corporations could take on a new role in facilitating development at the key locations identified in development plans, administering development initiative benefits and other subsidies currently deployed via central government's regional offices.

There is also a strong case for linking development activity much more closely to other areas of local economic development. The development sector, along with the building industry, should be analysed as an element within the local economy, in terms of its networks for material supply and sub-contracting, training and capital supply needs. This might have the advantage of helping shape a local development capability more responsive to the needs of the local economy than the investment-driven speculation encouraged in the 1980s. Another suggested direction for UDCs parallels this development, proposing a role as an urban economic development agency, closely linked to local authorities, the new Training and Enterprise

Councils and other economic development initiatives in urban areas, thus by taking on a broader economic development agenda for a city (*Economist*, 1990b, p. 36).

But such specific actions will need to be part of an approach to urban governance which moves beyond the fragmentation of the 1980s. If the development industry wants a more stable framework for its operations, it will need some assurance that those responsible for providing the framework have the political legitimacy to do this. While a diversity of task-related agencies may continue to be appropriate, the only way to overcome fragmentation, with its inefficiencies of duplication and competition, is to have some clear focus for urban governance. This has to be able to represent a broad spectrum of local interests, including the various economic interests in an urban region. The case for strengthening city government, and/or regional government looks increasingly compelling.

The Conservative administrations of the 1980s arrived at their policy of urban regeneration through private-sector property development almost by accident. They sought to change the rules of the relations between the public and private sectors, but in doing this were informed by little clear conception of how general principles might work out in the property development relations of different cities. The government appeared to operate with a simple notion of the entrepreneurial developer, and of a city as a collection of projects. Thanks to the boom, considerable resources flowed into development promoted in this way.

It is now time to think more clearly about the role of city rebuilding within the overall development of the city's economy, environment and culture. The quality of the urban environment by 1990 had a higher profile than it did 10 years before. This is reinforced by the initiatives in urban policy at EC level (EC, 1990). The experience of property-led urban regeneration in the 1980s illustrates three important principles about the role of property development in the local economy and quality of life in older industrial regions. First, the key problem is to reduce the instability in property markets which a weak local economy produces. The public sector must contribute to providing as much certainty in development horizons as is possible to encourage and sustain a local development industry. Second, partnerships in various forms are inevitable in such regions. A key question is the terms and accountability of such partnerships. Third, long-term horizons, a strategic orientation and some degree of consensus among local agencies, both public and private, are critical if a region is to avoid being merely a victim of spatial investment trends in the global economy. The challenge for older industrial regions is thus not to shift from a managerial to an entrepreneurial form of urban governance, but from a Fordist form of territorial management dominated by the public sector as provider and regulator, to a form where local agents in the public, private and voluntary sectors collaborate to manage their opportunities effectively within a global economic context.

REFERENCES

Aberdeen Beyond 2000 (1987) *Aberdeen Beyond 2000*, SDA, Aberdeen.

ACGB (1987) *An Urban Renaissance: The Role of the Arts in Urban Regeneration – The Case for Increased Public and Private Sector Co-operation*, Arts Council of Great Britain, London.

Adams, C.D., Baum, A.E. and McGregor, B.D. (1989) The availability of land for inner city development: a case study of inner Manchester, *Urban Studies*, **25**(1), 62–76.

Adams, D. (1990) Meeting the needs of industry: the performance of industrial land and property markets in inner Manchester and Salford, in *Land and Property Development in a Changing Context* (eds. P. Healey and R. Nabarro), Gower, Aldershot.

Ambrose, P. (1986) *Whatever Happened to Planning*, Methuen, London.

Ambrose, P.J. and Colenutt, B. (1975) *The Property Machine*, Penguin, Harmondsworth.

Amin, A. and Robins, K. (1990) The re-emergence of regional economies? The mythical geography of flexible accumulation. *Environment and Planning D: Society and Space*, **8**, 7–34.

Amin, A. (1990) From hierarchy to hierarchy: the dynamics of corporate restructuring in Europe. Paper for the *European Association of Evolutionary Political Economy*, Florence (November).

Armstrong, H. and Taylor, J. (1985) *Regional Economics and Policy*, Philip Alan, London.

Atkinson, G. (1989) *Calderdale Projects Company.*

Audit Commission for Local Authorities in England and Wales (1989) *Urban Regeneration and Local Economic Development – the Local Government Dimension*, HMSO, London.

Ball, M. (1988) *Rebuilding Construction*, Routledge, London.

Barnekov, T. and Rich D. (1989) Privatism and the limits of local economic development, *Urban Affairs Quarterly*, December.

Barnekov, T., Boyle, R. and Rich, D. (1989) *Privatism and Urban Policy in Britain and the United States*, Oxford University Press, Oxford.

Barras, R. (1979) *The Returns from Office Development and Investment*, CES Research Series, No. 35, Centre for Environmental Studies, London.

Barras, R. (1985) Development of profit and development control: the case of office development in London, in *Land Policy: Problems and Alternatives* (eds. S.M. Barrett and P. Healey), Gower, Aldershot.

Barrett, S.M., Stewart, M. and Underwood, J. (1978) *The Land Market and the Development Process*, SAUS Occ. Paper No. 2, SAUS, Bristol.

Barrett, S.M. and Whitting G.M. (1983) *Local Authorities and Land Supply*, SAUS Occ. Paper No. 10, SAUS, Bristol.

Bauman, Z. (1990a) From Pillars to Post. *Marxism Today*, March, 26–31.

Berkowitz, B.L. (1984) Economic development really works: Baltimore, Maryland, in *Urban Economic Development* (eds. R.D. Bingham and J.P. Blair), Sage, London.

Berry B. (1985) Islands of renewal in seas of decay, in *The New Urban Reality*, (ed. P. Peterson) Brookings Institution, Washington, pp. 69–96.

Bianchini, F. (1989) Cultural policy and urban social movements: the response of the 'new left' in Rome (1976–1985) and London (1981–1986), in *Leisure and Urban Process*, (eds. P. Bramham, I. Henry, H. Mommaas and H. van der Poel), Routledge, London.

Birmingham for People (1989) *What kind of Birmingham? Issues in the redevelopment of the city centre*, Birmingham.

Birmingham International Convention Centre (no date) *The Brochure*.

Birringer, J. (1989) Invisible cities/transcultural images. *Performing Arts Journal*, No. 33/34, 120–36.

Blakeley, E. (1989) *Planning Local Economic Development*, Sage, London.

Boddy, M. (1982) *Local Government and Industrial Development*, SAUS Occ. Paper No. 7, SAUS, Bristol.

Borrell, R. (1988) The sun must go on rising. *Evening Chronicle*, TNI Supplement, 15 June, Newcastle.

Boyle, R. (1988a) The price of private planning: a review of urban planning policy in Scotland, in *The Scottish Government Yearbook 1988* (eds. D. McCrone and A. Brown), University of Edinburgh, Edinburgh, pp. 193–9.

Boyle, R. (1988b) Glasgow's growth pains. *New Society*, 8.1.88.

Boyle, R. (1989a) Private sector urban regeneration: the Scottish Experience, in *Regenerating the Cities: the UK Crisis and the US Experience* (eds. M. Parkinson, B. Foley and D. Judd), Manchester University Press, Manchester, pp. 63–78.

Boyle, R. (1989b) Partnership in practice: an assessment of public–private collaboration in urban regeneration – a case study of Glasgow action. *Local Government Studies*, March/April, 17–28.

Boyle, R. (1990) Glasgow: urban leadership and regeneration, in *Leadership and Urban Regeneration – Cities in North America and Europe* (eds. M. Parkinson and D. Judd), Sage, London.

Bradford Breakthrough Limited *Article of Association*.

Bradford, M.G. and Steward, A. (1988) *Inner city refurbishment: an evaluation of private–public partnership schemes*, CUPS Working Paper No. 3, School of Geography, University of Manchester, Manchester.

Brindley, T. and Stoker, G. (1988) Partnership in inner city urban renewal – a critical analysis. *Local Government Policy Making*, **15**(2), 3–12.

Brindley, T., Rydin, Y. and Stoker, G. (1989) *Remaking Planning: the Politics of Urban Change in the Thatcher Years*, Unwin Hyman, London.

Bruton, M. and Gore, A. (1980) *Vacant Urban Land in South Wales*, Department of Town and Country Planning, UWIST, Cardiff.

Bryant, C.R., Russworm, L.H. and McLellan, E.G. (1982) *The City's Countryside*, Longman, London.

Bryson, B. (1989) Glasgow Isn't Paris, But. *New York Times Magazine*, 9.7.89, 34–65.

Burns, W. (1967) *Newcastle – A Study in Replanning at Newcastle upon Tyne*, Leonard Hill, London.

Cabinet Office (1987) *Action for Cities*, HMSO, London.

Cabinet Office (1988) *Action for Cities*, HMSO, London.

Cabinet Office (1989) *Progress on Cities*, HMSO, London.

Cabinet Office (1990) *People in Cities*, HMSO, London.

Calderdale Partnership (1989) *Vision in Calderdale*.

Calhoun, C. (1986) Computer technology, large-scale social integration and the local community. *Urban Affairs Quarterly*, **22**(2), 239–349.

Cameron, G., Monk, S. and Pearce, B. (1988) *Vacant Urban Land: A Literature Review 1976–1986*, DoE, London.

Cameron, G.C. (1990) First steps in urban policy evaluation in the United Kingdom. *Urban Studies*, **27**(4), 475–95.

Cameron S.J. (1987) *Recent Approaches to Problem Council Housing in Tyneside*, Working Paper No. 3, Department of Town and Country Planning, University of Newcastle, Newcastle.

Castells, M. (1989) *The Informational City*, Basil Blackwell, Oxford.

Catalano, A. and Barras, R. (1980) *Office Development in Central Manchester*, CES Research Series, 37.

Cawson, A. (1985) Corporatism and local politics, in *The Political Economy of Corporatism* (ed. W. Grant), Macmillan, London.

Cheshire, P. (1990) Explaining the recent performance of the European Community's major urban regions. *Urban Studies*, **27**(3), 311–33.

Civic Trust (1984) *Halifax in Calderdale: a Strategy for Prosperity*.

Civic Trust (1986) *Calderdale the Challenge*.

Community Development Project (1978) *Concentrated Unemployment and a Local Initiative*, CDP, Paisley.

Confederation of British Industries (CBI) (1988) *Initiatives Beyond Charity*, CBI, London.

Cooke, P. (1983) *Theories of Planning and Spatial Development*, Hutchinson, London.

Cooke, P. (1988a) Modernity, postmodernity and the city. *Theory, Culture and Society*, **5**(2–3), 475–92.

Cooke, P. (1988b) Municipal enterprise, growth coalitions and social justice. *Local Economy*, **3**(3), 191–200.

Cooke, P., ed. (1989) *Localities*, Unwin Hyman, London.

Cooke, P. (1990) Modern urban theory in question. *Transactions of the Institute of British Geographers*, **15**(3), 331–43.

Coster, G. (1989) Breadmaking. *The Guardian*, 16.12.89, 4–5.

Couch, C., Basnett, M., Doward, L. and Holmes, T. (1989) Urban vacancy in Liverpool, in *Land and Property Development: New Directions* (ed. R. Grover), E and FN Spon, London.

Cox, A. (1984) *Adversary Politics and Land: The Conflict Over Land and Property Policy in Post-war Britain*, Cambridge University Press, Cambridge.

Damesick, P. and Wood, P. (1987) Public policy for regional development: restoration or reformation? in *Regional Problems, Problem Regions and Public Policy in the UK* (eds. P. Damesick and P. Wood) Clarendon Press, Oxford, pp. 260–26.

Danson, M. (1980) The Scottish Development Agency. *Public Enterprise*, **19**, 12–14.

Danson, M., Lloyd, M.G. and Newlands, D. (1989) Scottish enterprise: towards a model agency or a flawed initiative? *Regional Studies*, **23**(6), 557–64.

Danson, M., Fairley, J., Lloyd, M.G. and Newlands, D. (1990) Scottish enterprise: an evolving approach to integrated economic development in Scotland, in *The Scottish Government Yearbook 1990* (eds. A. Brown and R. Parry), University of Edinburgh, pp. 164–94.

Darley, G. (1989) History as bank. *Financial Times*.

Davenport, P. (1990) Bridging the past with pride. *The Times* (London), 31 October.

Davoudi, S. and Healey, P. (1990) *Using Planning Consultants: the Experience of Tyne and Wear Development Corporation* Urban Regeneration and the Development Process: Project Paper No.2, Department of Town and Country Planning, University of Newcastle upon Tyne, Newcastle.

Davoudi, S. and Usher, D. (1990) *Who is Developing What in Tyne and Wear?* Project Paper Series No. 1, Department of Town and Country Planning, University of Newcastle upon Tyne, Newcastle.

Dawson, J. and Parkinson, M. (1990) Merseyside Development Corporation 1981–89: physical regeneration, accountability and economic challenge, in *Hollow Promises? Policy, Theory and Practice in the Inner City* (eds. M. Keith and A. Rogers), Mansell.

Dear, M. (1986) Postmodernism and planning. *Environment and Planning D: Society and Space*, **4**, 369–84.

Department of the Environment (1980) *Enterprise Zones – a Consultation Document*, HMSO, London.

Department of the Environment (1988) *DoE Inner City Programmes 1987–88: a report on achievements and developments*, DoE, London.

Department of the Environment (1989a) *Strategic Planning Guidance for Greater Manchester*, HMSO, London.

Department of the Environment (1989b) *Review of Derelict Land Policy*, DoE, London.

Department of the Environment (1990) *Renewing the Cities: a Report on the DoE Inner City Programmes in 1988–89*, HMSO, London.

Department of Trade and Industry (1985) *Burdens on Business*, HMSO, London.

Donkin, R. (1989) *Financial Times*, 8.4.89.

Donnison, D. and Middleton, A., ed. (1987) *Regenerating the Inner City: Glasgow's experience*, Routledge and Kegan Paul, London.

Drewett, R. (1973) The developers: decision processes, in *The Containment of Urban England* (eds. P. Hall *et al.*), George Allen and Unwin, London.

Dunleavy, P. (1981) *The Politics of Mass Housing: 1945–75*, Clarendon Press, Oxford.

Dunn, P. (1989) The hungry poor fail to bounce back. *The Independent* 2.12.89.

Economist, The (1990a) The construction industry: all fall down. 22.9.90, 39–43.

Economist, The (1990b) A chilly climate for catalysts. 3.11.90, 35–6.

Esher, L.G.B. (1971) *Conservation in Glasgow: a preliminary report*, Glasgow Corporation, Glasgow.

Esser, J. and Hirsch, J. (1989) The crisis of Fordism and the dimensions of a (postFordist) regional and urban structure. *International Journal of Urban and Regional Research*, **13**(3), 417–37.

Estates Gazette (1990) *Focus on Newcastle – Recovery Under Way*, 24th March.

European Commission (EC) (1990) Green Paper on the Urban Environment, Commission of the European Communities, Brussels.

Evans, A.W. (1983) The determination of the price of land. *Urban Studies* **20**, 119–29.

Fainstein, S., Fainstein, N., Hill, R.C., Judd, D. and Smith, M.P. (1986) *Restructuring the City*, Longmans, New York.

Featherstone, M. (1989) City cultures and postmodern lifestyles. Paper presented at the 7th European Leisure Congress *Cities for the Future*, Rotterdam, June.

Fosler, R.S. and Berger, R.A. (eds) (1982) *Public–Private Partnership in American Cities: Seven Case Studies*, Lexington Books, Lexington, Mass.

Fothergill, S. and Gudgin, G. (1982) *Unequal Growth*, Heinemann, London.

Fothergill, S., Monk, S. and Perry, M. (1987) *Property and Industrial Development*, Hutchinson, London.

Frieden, B. (1990) City centres transformed: planners as developers. *Journal of American Planning Association* (JAPA), **56**(4), 423–8.

Gamble, A. (1988) *The Free Economy and the Strong State*, Macmillan, London.

Gibson, M.S. and Langstaff, M.J. (1982) *An Introduction to Urban Renewal*, Hutchinson, London.

Gibson (1986) Housing renewal; privatisation and beyond, in *The Housing Crisis* (ed. P. Malpass), Routledge and Kegan Paul, London.

Giloth, R. (1990) Beyond common sense: the Baltimore renaissance. *Local Economy*, **4**(4), 190–297.

Glasgow Action (1985) *Glasgow – the Need for Action*, Glasgow.

Glasgow District Council (1987) *Ingram Square Development – Merchant City*, A Report of Surveys carried out in August–November 1986, Housing Department, Glasgow District Council, Glasgow.

Glasgow University (1986) *The Merchant City and the Market for New Private Housing in Central Glasgow*, Centre for Housing Research, Glasgow University, Glasgow.

Goodchild, R. and Munton, R. (1985) *Development and the Landowner*, George Allen and Unwin, London.

Greater Glasgow Tourist Board (No date) *Renaissance*.

Gulliver, S. (1984) The area projects of the Scottish Development Agency. *Town Planning Review*, **55**(3), 32–334.

Gyford, J. (1985) *The Politics of Local Socialism*, London.

Habermas, J. (1985) Modern and postmodern architecture, in *Critical Theory and Public Life* (ed. J. Forester), MIT Press, Cambridge.

Haider, D. (1989a) Marketing places: the state of the art. *Commentary*, Spring, 10–16.

Haider, D. (1989b) Making marketing choices. *Commentary*, Summer, 12–22.

Hannay, P. (1988) Till wealth do us part. *Architect's Journal*, Jan., 26–31.

Harden, I. (1987) Corporatism without labour: the British version, in *Waiving the Rules. The Constitution under Thatcher* (ed. C. Graham and T. Prosser), The Open University Press, Milton Keynes, pp. 36–55.

Harding, A. (1989a) *Partnership Experience in UK Cities*, Paper for Liverpool City Council, Public–Private Partnership Study (unpublished).

Harding, A. (1989b) Central control in British urban economic development programmes, in *The New Centralism – Britain Out of Step in Europe?* (ed. C. Couch and D. Marquand), Basil Blackwell, Oxford.

Harding, A. (1990a) Public–Private partnerships in urban regeneration, in *Local Economic Policy* (ed. M. Campbell), Cassell, London.

Harding, A. (1990b) Local automony and urban economic policies, in *Challenges to Local Government* (ed. D.S. King, and J. Pierre), Sage, London.

Harvey, D. (1982) *The Limits to Capital*, Blackwells, London.

Harvey, D. (1985) *The Urbanisation of Capital*, Blackwells, London.

Harvey, D. (1987) Flexible accumulation through urbanisation: reflections on 'postmodernism' in the American city. *Antipode*, **19**, 260–86.

Harvey, D. (1988) Voodoo cities. *New Statesman and Society*, 30.9.88, 33–5.

Harvey, D. (1989a) *The Condition of Postmodernity*, Blackwells, Oxford.

Harvey, D. (1989b) From managerialism to entrepeneurialism: the transformation of urban governance in late capitalism. *Geografissker Annaler*, **71B**, 3–17.

Harvey, D. (1989c) Down towns. *Marxism Today*, **33**(1), 21 January.

Harvey, R. and Williams, A.M. (1979) *Divided Britain*, Bellhaven, London.

Hasluck, C. (1987) *Urban Unemployment. Local Labour Markets and Employment Initiatives*, Longman, London.

Haughton, G. and Whitney, M. (1989) Unequal urban partners. *The Planner*, December 9–11.

Haussermann, H. and Siebel, W. (1987) *Neue Urbanitat*, Suhrkamp, Frankfurt.

Hay, B. (1989) The cranes have arrived!. *North East Times*, February.

Hayton, K. (1989) The future of local economic development. *Regional Studies*, **23**(6), 549–56.

Healey, P. (1984) Manchester city council, in *Local Planning in Practice (3): Camden and Manchester* (eds. C. Fudge and P. Healey), SAUS Working Paper No. 32, SAUS, Bristol, pp. 86–141.

Healey, P. (1991) Urban regeneration and the development industry. *Regional Studies*, **25**(2).

Healey, P. (1991) *From Shipyard to Housing Estate*, Department of Town and Country Planning, Newcastle University and South Tyneside Metropolitan Borough Council, Newcastle.

Healey, P. and Barrett, S.M. (1985) Land policy: towards a research agenda, Chapter 1, in *Land Policy: Problems and Alternatives*, (eds. S.M. Barrett, and P. Healey), Gower, Aldershot.

Healey, P. and Barrett, S.M. (1990) Structure and agency in land and property development processes. *Urban Studies*, **27**(1), 89–104.

Healey, P. and Nabarro, R. (eds.) (1990) *Land and Property Development in a Changing Context*, Gower, Aldershot.

Healey, P., McNamara, P.F., Elson, M.J. and Doak, A.J. (1988) *Land Use Planning and the Mediation of Urban Change*, Cambridge University Press, Cambridge.

Hewison, R. (1987) *The Heritage Industry*, Metheun.

Hillman, S. (1983) Leveraging prosperity in Baltimore, in *The City as a Stage* (ed. K.W. Green), Partners for Liveable Places.

Hirsch, F. (1977) *Social Limits to Growth*, Routledge, London.

Home, R.K. (1982) *Inner City Regeneration*, Spon, London.

Hudson, R. and Williams, A.M. (1989) *Divided Britain*, Bellhaven, London.

Hula, R.C. The Baltimore renaissance, in *Urban Leadership and Regeneration* (eds. D. Judd and M. Parkinson), Urban Affairs Annual Review, Sage, California.

Hunter, J. (1988) A national museum in an inner city role, in *Birmingham Film and Television Festival Forum Cities and City Cultures*, p. 23.

Ibbott, M. (1984) *Public Land Registers: an assessment*, Working Papers in Land management and development, No. 4 Department of Land Management, University of Reading, Reading.

Independent, The (1988) 22nd June.

Industry Department for Scotland (1988) *Scottish Enterprise: a New Approach to Training and Enterprise Creation*, HMSO, Edinburgh.

Investment Property Databank (1990b) *Monthly Index*, IPD, London.

Jencks, C. (1988) *The Prince, the Architects and New Wave Monarchy*, Academy Editions, London.

Judd, D. and Parkinson, M. (1990) *Leadership and Urban Regeneration – Cities in North America and Europe*, Urban Affairs Annual Reviews, Vol. 37, Sage, London.

Keating, M. and Boyle, R. (1986) *Remaking Urban Scotland*, University of Edinburgh Press, Edinburgh.

Key, T., Espinet, M. and Wright, C. (1990) The distinctiveness of the late 1980s, in *Land and Property Development in a Changing Context* (eds. P. Healey and R. Nabarro), Gower, Aldershot.

King, R. (1985) Corporatism and the local economy, in *The Political Economy of Corporatism* (ed. W. Grant), Macmillan, London.

Kirklees Joint Venture (1989) Memorandum of Understanding.

Lash, S. (1988) Bright lights, big city. *Times Higher Education Supplement*, 16 February.

Law, C. (1988a) Public–private partnerships in urban revitalisation in Britain. *Regional Studies*, **22**(5), 446–51.

Law, C.M. (1988b) *The Redevelopment of Manchester Docks*, Discussion Papers No. 33, Department of Geography, University of Salford, Manchester.

Law, C.M. (1988c) From Manchester Docks to Salford Quays: a progress report on a redevelopment project. *Manchester Geographer*, No. 58.

Law, C.M. (1989) Inner city policy on the ground: the Manchester experience. *Cities*, **4**, 336–46.

Lawless, P. (1989a) From radical intervention to partnership: regeneration in Sheffield, 1979–1989, paper presented to *Political Leadership and Urban Regeneration Conference*, University of Liverpool, November.

Lawless, P. (1989b) *Britain's Inner Cities*, Paul Chapman, London.

Leach, S. and Stoker, G. (1988) The transformation of central-local government relationships, in *Waiving the Rules: the Constitution under Thatcher* (eds. C. Graham and T. Prosser), Open University Press, 95–115.

Leeds City Development Company (1987) *Publicity Information Pack*.

Lever, W. (1986) From ships to chips in Greenock – Port Glasgow, in *Global Restructuring. Industrial Change and Local Adjustment* (ed. P. Cooke), ESRC, London, pp. 195–200.

Ley, D. (1989) Modernism, postmodernism and the struggle for place, in *The Power of Place* (eds. J. Agnew and J. Duncan), Unwin Hyman, Boston.

Leyshon, A. and Thrift, N. (1990) The chartered surveying industry, in *Land and Property development in a Changing Context* (eds. P. Healey and R. Nabarro), Gower, Aldershot.

Liverpool City Council (1987) Past Trends and Future Prospects (February).

Lloyd, M.G. (1986) The Enterprise Zone experiment in Scotland. *Scottish Planning Law and Practice*, **18**, 43–5.

Lloyd, M.G. (1990) Planning for enterprise in Scotland. *Local Government Studies*, November/December.

Lloyd, M.G. and Danson, M. (1990) The Inverclyde Enterprise Zone. A continuing experiment in regeneration? *Scottish Geographical Magazine*.

Lloyd, M.G. and Newlands, D. (1988) The growth coalition and urban economic development. *Local Economy*, **3**(1), 31–40.

Lloyd, M.G. and Newlands, D. (1989a) Recent urban policy development in Scotland: the rediscovery of peripheral housing estates. *Scottish Geographical Magazine*, **105**(2), 116–19.

Lloyd, M.G. and Newlands, D. (1989b) Aberdeen: planning for economic change and uncertainty. *Scottish Geographical Magazine*, **105**(2), 94–100.

Logan, J. and Molotch, H. (1987) *Urban Fortunes: The Political Economy of Place*, University of California Press, London.

Loughlin, M. (1986) *Local Government in the Modern State*, Sweet and Maxwell, London.

MacGregor, B.D., Baum, A.E., Adams, C.D., Fleming, S.C. and Peterson, J. (1985) *Land Availability for Inner City Development*, Department of Land Management, University of Reading, Reading.

McLaren, D. (1989) *Action for People: A Critical Appraisal of Government Inner City Policy*, Friends of the Earth, London.

McNamara, P.F. (1983) Towards a classification of land developers. *Urban Law and Policy*, **6**, 87–94.

McNamara, P.F. (1984) The role of estate agents in the residential development process. *Land Development Studies*, **1**, 101–12.

McNamara, P. and Turner, G. (1987) *Chartered Surveyors and the Site Finding Process*, Occasional Paper Series No. 1, Department of Estate Management, Oxford Polytechnic, Oxford.

Markowski, S. (1978) *A Study of Vacant Land in Urban Areas*, Centre for Environmental Studies, London.

Marriott, O. (1967) *The Property Boom*, Pan, London.

Martin, R. (1986) Thatcherism and Britain's industrial landscape, in *The

Geography of Deindustrialisation (eds. R. Martin and B. Rowthorn), Macmillan, London, pp. 238–90.

Massey, D. (1984) *Spatial Divisions of Labour*, Macmillan, London.

Massey, D. and Catalano, A. (1978) *Capital and Land: Landownership by Capital in Great Britain*, Edward Arnold, London.

Massey, D. and Meegan, R. (1982) *The Anatomy of Job Loss*, Methuen, London.

Mayer, M. (1989) From administration to management. Paper presented to the Cardiff Symposium of *Regulation, Innovation and Spatial Development*, University of Wales, 13–15 September.

Middleton, M. (1987) *Man Made the Town*, Bodley Head.

Molotch, H. (1976) The city as a growth machine: towards a political economy of place. *American Journal of Sociology*, **82**(2), 309–32.

Moore, C. and Booth, S. (1986a) The Scottish development agency: market consensus, public planning and local enterprise. *Local Economy*, **1**(3), 7–19.

Moore, C. and Booth, S. (1986b) Urban policy contradictions: the market versus redistributive approaches. *Policy and Politics*, **14**, 361–87.

Moore, C. and Pierre, J. (1988) Partnership or privatisation? The political economy of local economic restructuring. *Policy and Politics*, **16**(3), 169–78.

Morgan, E. (1990) A shortage of factories: will the private sector respond? in *Land and Property development in a Changing Context* (eds. P. Healey and R. Nabarro), Gower, Aldershot.

Morgan, K. (1986) Re-industrialisation in peripheral Britain: state policy, the space economy and industrial innovation, in *The Geography of De-Industrialisation* (eds. R. Martin and B. Rowthorn), Macmillan, London, pp. 322–60.

Mumford, L. (1961) *The City in History*, Martin Secker and Warburg, London.

Mulgan, G. (1989) A tale of new cities. *Marxism Today*, March 18–25.

Nabarro, R. (1990) The investment market in commercial and industrial development: some recent trends, in *Land and Property Development in a Changing Context* (eds. P. Healey and R. Nabarro), Gower, Aldershot.

National Audit Office (1990) *Regenerating the Inner Cities*, HMSO, London.

Newsweek (1989) Rough sailing on the waterfront. *Newsweek*, 27.3.89.

Nicholls, D.C., Turner, D.M., Kirby Smith, R. and Cullen, J.D. (1980) *The Private-Sector Housing Development Process in Inner City Areas*, Department of Land Economy, The University of Cambridge, Cambridge.

Northern Development Company (1989) *Welcome to NDC*, NDC, Newcastle upon Tyne.

Northern Development Company (1990) *The Great North*, NDC, Newcastle upon Tyne.

Northumbrian Branch of the RIBA (1988) *The Newcastle Initiative Theatre Village Study*, Draft Report.

O'Donnell, J.D. (1989) The eclipse of the entrepreneurial developer. *Urban Land*, July.

Parkinson, M. (1989) The Thatcher Government's urban policy, 1979–1989. *Town Planning Review*, **69**(4), 421–40.

Parkinson, M. and Evans, R. (1990) Urban Development Corporations, in *Local Economic Policy* (ed. M. Campbell), Cassell.

Peterson, P. (1985) Technology, race and urban policy, in *The New Urban Reality* (ed. P. Peterson), Brookings Institution, Washington.

Peterson, P. (ed.) (1985) *The New Urban Reality*, The Brookings Institution, Washington.

Pickvance, C.G. (1985) Spatial policy as territorial politics: the role of spatial coalitions in the articulation of spatial interests and in the Demand for Spatial Policy, in *Political Action and Social Identity. Class, Locality and Ideology* (eds. G. Rees *et al.*), Macmillan, London, pp. 117–42.

Piore, M.J. and Sabel, C.F. (1984) *The second Industrial Divide*, Basic Books, New York.

Public Sector Management Research Unit (1988) *An Evaluation of the Urban Development Grant Programme*, Department of the Environment, Inner Cities Directorate, HMSO, London.

Punter, J. (1988) Postmodernism. *Planning Practice and Research*, **4**, 22–8.

Randall, J. (1987) Scotland, in *Regional Problems, Problem Regions and Public Policy in the United Kingdom* (eds. P. Damesick and P. Wood), Clarendon Press, Oxford, pp. 218–37.

Robinson, F. (1989a) *Urban 'Regeneration' Policies in Britain in the Late 1980s: Who Benefits?* CURDS Discussion Paper No. 94, University of Newcastle upon Tyne, Newcastle.

Robinson, F. (ed.) (1989b) *Post Industrial Tyneside*, City of Newcastle.

Robson, B. (1988) *Those Inner Cities*, Clarendon Press, Oxford.

Rogers, R. (1989) In praise of the modern. *Marxism Today*, March, 26–31.

Rule, S. (1990) Andy Capp flap stirs up turmoil on Tyneside. *Sunday Times*, 18 June.

Rustin, M. (1987) Place and time in socialist theory. *Radical Philosophy*, 47, 30–6.

Rustin, M. (1989) Postmodernism and antimodernism in contemporary British architecture. *Assemblage*, **8**, 89–103.

Saunders, P. (1985) Corporatism and urban service provision, in *The Political Economy of Corporatism* (ed. W. Grant), Macmillan, London.

Scottish Development Agency (1981) Annual Report 6, SDA, Glasgow.

Scottish Development Agency (1988) Annual Report 13, SDA, Glasgow.

Scottish Development Agency (1989) Partnership in economic and environmental renewal, SDA, Glasgow.

Scottish Office (1988) *New Life for Urban Scotland*, Scottish Office, Edinburgh.

Sennett, R. (1973) *The Uses of Disorder: Personal Identity and City Life*, Penguin, Harmondsworth.

Sharpe, W. and Wallock, L. (1987) From 'great town' to 'nonplace urban realm': reading the modern city, in *Visions of the Modern City* (eds. W. Sharpe and L. Wallock), John Hopkins University Press, Baltimore.

Sim, D. (1985) Local authority influence on the private house building industry. *Housing Review*, **34**, 92–5.

Simmie, J. (1981) *Power, Property and Corporatism: The Political Sociology of Planning*, Macmillan, London.

Simmie, J. (1985) Corporatism and planning, in *The Political Economy of Corporatism* (ed. W. Grant), Macmillan, London.

Smith, N. (1979) Towards a theory of gentrification. *Journal of the American Planning Association*, **45**(4).

Smith, T. Dan (1960) Development problems of a regional capital, Paper presented to the *Town Planning Institute's Annual Spring Meeting*, 26 May.

Smith, T. Dan (1970) *An Autobiography*, Oriel Press, Newcastle upon Tyne.

Soja, E. (1989) *Postmodern Geographies*, Verso, London.

Solesbury, W. (1990) Property development and urban regeneration, in *Land and Property Development in a Changing Context* (eds. P. Healey and R. Nabarro) Gower, Aldershot.

South Tyneside Metropolitan Borough Council (1989) File record on the Hebburn Project.

South Tyneside Metropolitan Borough Council (1986) File record on the Hebburn project.

Stach, P. (1987) Zoning – to plan or to protect. *Journal of Planning Literature*, **2**(4), 371–83.

Steller, J.D. (1982) An MXD takes off: Baltimore's Inner Harbor. *Urban Land*, March.

Strathclyde Regional Council (1981) *Strathclyde Structure Plan*, Strathclyde Regional Council, Glasgow.

Swanstrom, T. (1985) *The Crisis of Growth Politics: Cleveland, Kucinich, and the Challenge of Urban Populism*, Temple University Press, Philadelphia.

The Newcastle Initiative (1988) *The Newcastle Initiative*, TNI, Newcastle upon Tyne.

Thomas, H. and Imrie, R. (1989) Urban redevelopment, compulsory purchase and the regeneration of local economies. The case of Cardiff Docklands. *Planning Practice and Research*, **4**(3), 18–27.

Tym, Roger and Partners *et al.* (1986) *Trafford Park Investment Strategy: Final Report*, Manchester.

Tyne and Wear Development Corporation (1988) *Forward to 1991*, Tyne and Wear Corporation, Newcastle upon Tyne.

Tyne and Wear County Council (1981) Structure Plan Annual Reports.

Tyne and Wear County Council (1982) Structure Plan Annual Reports.

Tyne and Wear County Council (1983) Structure Plan Annual Reports.

Tyne and Wear County Council (1984) Structure Plan Annual Reports.

Tyne and Wear Development Corporation (1989a) *Draft Marketing Plan 1989/90*, Tyne and Wear Development Corporation, Newcastle upon Tyne.

Tyne and Wear Development Corporation (1989b) *A Vision for the Future*, Tyne and Wear Development Corporation, Newcastle upon Tyne.

Tyne and Wear Metropolitan Districts (1988a) (unpublished) Background Papers for Strategic Guidance.

Tyne and Wear Metropolitan Districts (1988b) *Strategic Guidance for Tyne and Wear*, Topic Papers, second update.

Tyne and Wear Metropolitan Districts (1989a) (unpublished) Background Papers for Strategic Guidance.

Tyne and Wear Metropolitan Districts (1989b) *Strategic Guidance for Tyne and Wear*, Topic Papers, second update.

Usher, D. (1989) Building solutions with public money: the experience of City Grant. *Northern Economic Review*, Autumn, No. 18.

Wakefield Works (1989) *Memorandum of Understanding*.

Walzer, M. (1986) Pleasures and costs of urbanity. *Dissent*, Summer, 470–5.

Wannop, U. (1984) The evolution and roles of the Scottish development agency. *Town Planning Review*, **55**(3), 313–21.

Watson, G. (ed.) (1986) *Recycling Derelict Industrial Land in the Black Country: an Initial Assessment and Conference Transcript*, Oxford Working Paper No. 97, Department of Town and Country Planning, Oxford Polytechnic, Oxford.

Weiss, M.A. (1987) *The Rise of the Community Builder*, Columbia University Press, New Brunswick.

White, P. (1986) Land availability, land banking and the price of land for housebuilding: a review of recent debates. *Land Development Studies*, **3**(2), 101–11.

Wright, P. (1989) Re-enchanting the nation: Prince Charles and architecture. *Modern Painters*, **2**(3), 26–35.

Yin, R. (1989) *Case Study Research*, 2nd edn, Sage, California.

INDEX